Let the Glory Out

MY SOUTH AND ITS POLITICS

★ ★ ★ ★

ALBERT GORE, SR.

HILL STREET PRESS **d** ATHENS, GEORGIA

A HILL STREET CLASSICS BOOK

Published in the United States of America by
Hill Street Press LLC
191 East Broad Street, Suite 209
Athens, Georgia 30601-2848 USA
706-613-7200
info@hillstreetpress.com
www.hillstreetpress.com

Hill Street Press is committed to preserving the written word. Every effort is made to print books on acid-free paper with a significant amount of post-consumer recycled content.

Printed in Canada.

Library of Congress Cataloging-in-Publication data available upon request.

ISBN# 1-58818-028-X

Other editions:
Microsoft Reader 1-58818-031-X
Rocket Book 1-58818-030-1
Glassbook 1-58818-029-8
Peanut Press 1-58818-032-8

10   9   8   7   6   5   4   3   2   1

First printing

Introduction

IN 1970, after thirty-two years of service in both the House and the Senate, my father lost his Senate seat in large measure because of his courageous stands for civil rights, economic and social justice, and his principled opposition to the war in Vietnam.

On election night of that year, my father spoke the words from which he drew both the title and one of the lessons of this book: "defeat may serve as well as victory to shake the soul and let the glory out."

My father deeply believed in a politics of principle. In many ways, he was unprepared for the unprecedented smear campaign that was run against him in 1970 orchestrated in part by the Nixon White House and financed in part by illegal contributions. In all his time in Congress, my dad had never even employed a press secretary because he thought that was an inappropriate use of taxpayer money.

He spoke with his whole heart, no matter the consequences. And even in defeat, his conscience won. Turning the old segregationist battle cry on its head, he declared that night, "The Truth Shall Rise Again." I learned from him at an early age that that was what mattered.

My father was the forerunner of a new generation of Southern politicians who strived to connect the South to the rest of America. This book was intended not only as a personal reflection, but also as a tribute to the South he served and loved—a South that was reaching beyond its past, toward a brighter and more inclusive future.

Many Tennesseans came to know my father through his live Sunday morning radio program, where he presented the news from Washington "as I see it." This was his accounting of things not just as he saw them, but as he dreamed they could be.

We lost my dad a year and a half ago and in the eulogy that follows, I tried to give some measure of the Albert Gore I knew: a loving father, a fighter for working people, a man who embraced and embodied the American ideal of courage.

In the foreword that accompanied the original printing of this book, my father wrote, "my fondest hope for this endeavor is that it may inspire some idealistic youths to worthy public service."

All my life, that is what my dad did for me. I hope that with this new edition of his second book, souls may be shaken anew, and the glory may be unleashed for a new generation of seekers, idealists, and servants of the people.

AL GORE

Carthage, Tennessee
August 2000

Remarks by the vice president at the funeral of his father,
former Senator Albert Gore, Sr.

War Memorial
Nashville, Tennessee

PRESIDENT AND Mrs. Clinton, so many honored guests from our nation and our state. The Lord gave and the Lord hath taken away. Blessed be the name of the Lord.

My father was the greatest man I ever knew in my life. Most of you know him for his public service and it could be said of him, in the words of Paul, that this man walked worthy of the vocation wherewith he was called.

There were those many, many who loved him—and there were a few who hated him. Hated him for the right reasons. It's better to be hated for what you are than to be loved for what you are not.

My father believed, in the words of the Scripture, "Woe unto you when all men shall speak well of you." He made decisions in politics that were such that he could come home and explain to his children what he had decided and why. He went into the world with peace; he held fast to that which was good. He rendered to no one evil for evil. He was of good courage. He strengthened the fainthearted. He supported the weak. He helped the afflicted. He loved and served all people who came his way.

None of this was a secret to the world. As most of you know, there was a time when some people thought my father should seek the highest office in the land. Here's what he said about that idea: "The lure of the presidency never really overwhelmed me, though, there were times when the vice presidency seemed extremely attractive." Now, that's humility. And he did love mercy and do justly. The last advice he gave me, two weeks ago, when he was almost too weak to speak, was this: Always do right.

He was born in an isolated, poor dirt farm on the banks of the Roaring River in Jackson County, Tennessee. His father was a friend of Cordell Hull who, of course, later made all the families in this part of the country proud by becoming a congressman and a senator, and then Secretary of State.

My grandfather and Cordell Hull floated logs down the Cumberland River to the point where it meets the Caney Fork at Carthage. My father's boyhood dreams were taken by the currents of both men's lives. He was always a farmer, and he became a statesman.

Soon after he was born, his whole family moved to Smith County, to a place just west of Carthage called Possum Hollow. He grew up in what he described as a self-giving, self-respecting household. And he said that, although the chores were heavy and the discipline absolute, there was love in our family and reverence for each other.

He went to work as a teacher, in a one-room schoolhouse in a mountain community in Overton County named Booze. He was eighteen years old and had three months of college. His students called him Professor Gore. He read voraciously and taught himself to use language with precision. The Leather-Stocking Tales were his favorites.

I always marveled at his vocabulary and, as I grew older, at his unusual pronunciation of certain words. For example, instead of "woond" he always said "wownd." I used to challenge him on the words I was certain he'd mispronounced. But invariably the dictionary also contained his preferred version, with the italic note: "archaic." As many have said since his passing, he was an original.

As he continued his education at Murfreesboro State Teachers College, and continued working in all his free hours, he learned the lessons of hard times, trucking livestock to market only to find that they had sold for less than the hauling fee. The Great Depression awakened his political conscience. He often told me of the deep emotions he felt watching grown men with wives and children they could neither feed nor clothe, on farms they could no longer pay for. Grown men who were so desperate that tears streamed down their cheeks when they received their meager checks for a whole season's work on their crops.

The kindling for his political philosophy piled up on Sunday afternoons among the whittlers, with whom he sat under the shade trees of the Carthage Square, and listened as Congressman Hull talked of important business in the Nation's Capital. When my father first heard Franklin Delano Roosevelt on the radio, the kindling caught fire.

He became the youth chairman in Tennessee for FDR in 1932. The following year, he became a candidate himself, for the first time, for Smith County's Superintendent of Schools. He lost the election, and then his teaching job—but he gained respect from those who heard him. Indeed, when the man who won the race unexpectedly turned gravely ill soon after the election, he surprised the County Court by recommending my father as his replacement before he died. This gift from his dying former rival made a deep and lifelong impression on my father. It was one of the reasons why he never said a harsh word about any of his opponents for the rest of his career.

He soon began YMCA night law school, even as he continued as Superintendent of Schools, and awoke well before dawn to also tend his crops. I don't think I ever saw him tired, but he must have been sleepy after such long days and nights, facing an hour's drive yet to return from Nashville to Carthage on old Highway 70. So he went looking for coffee.

And he found it at the old Andrew Jackson Coffee Shop, which stood not 100 yards from here. He loved to tell the story of how the coffee didn't taste good unless it was poured by a beautiful young waitress named Pauline LaFon. She was going to law school by day and working nights. They say opposites attract. They didn't marry right away; she left for Texarkana, put up her shingle, and practiced oil and gas law. But his coffee turned bitter, and eventually he persuaded her to come back as his wife.

Of all the lessons he taught me as a father, perhaps the most powerful was the way he loved my mother. He respected her as an equal, if not more. He was proud of her. But it went way beyond that. When I was growing up, it never once occurred to me that the foundation upon which my security depended would ever shake. As I grew older, I learned from them the value of a true, loving partnership that lasts for life.

After managing the successful campaign of Governor Gordon Browning, he became Tennessee's first Commissioner of Labor, and started unemployment compensation in the face of powerful opposition. He enforced mine inspection laws for the first time in our history. He administered our first minimum wage law; it was twenty-five cents an hour. He defended the right to organize. He was always, always for working men and women.

He loved practical jokes. His humor often had an edge. One Saturday night in the early 1930s, at a party he organized in a barn by the Cumberland River for a group of friends in Carthage, he planted the suggestion that quite a few rattlesnakes had been seen in the area the preceding day. Then, surreptitiously, in the shadows thrown by the fire, he attached a fishhook to the pant-leg of his friend, Walter Merriman. At the other end of the hook was tied a large black snake he had killed in the barn before the party guests arrived.

Rejoining the circle, he bided his time for a moment, and then suddenly pointed towards Merriman's leg and shouted, "Snake!" The more Merriman jumped and ran, the more determined the pursuing snake appeared. The prank worked a little too well when the fishhook dug into Merriman's calf. Certain that it was a rattlesnake's fang, he collapsed in fear.

It took several months for the friendship to be repaired — but the story became such a local legend that someone told me about it again last night at the wake.

It's difficult to follow the rhythm of his life without hearing the music that held him in its sway ever since the spring day a fiddler named Uncle Barry Agee played at the closing cere- monies of Miss Mary Litchburg's first-grade class. It was a mag- ical experience that ignited a passion for playing the fiddle, so powerful that, later in his life, he sometimes worried that, if he gave into it, it would somehow carry him away from the politi- cal purposes to which he was also powerfully drawn.

Before long, by the grace of his mother and with the help of his brother, he marshaled the impressive sum of five dollars to buy his own fiddle, and soon thereafter his classmates nick- named him Music Gore.

He always told lots of stories, but without a doubt the one he told most often was about a Possum Hollow hoedown held at his house, to which several musicians were invited, including a traveling mandolin player with one leg named, Old Peg, who spent the night in their home.

My father had just finished the eighth grade and his devo- tion to music had become, in his words, all-absorbing. The next morning he helped his father hitch up the harness for Old Peg's horse and buggy. Each time he told this story, the buggy grew more dilapidated. Before long, it had no top; the harness was mostly baling wire and binding twine. He counted that scrawny horse's ribs a thousand times for me and my sister, and then counted them many times again for his grandchildren.

As Old Peg left the sturdy Gore household, the buggy was practically falling apart. As the impoverished picker wobbled precariously down his less-traveled road, my grandfather waited until he was just out of hearing range, then put his hand on my father's shoulder and launched a sentence that made all the difference: "There goes your future, Albert." My grandfather's humor had an edge to it, too.

Don't ever doubt the impact that fathers have on their children. Children with strong fathers learn trust early on, that their needs will be met; that they're wanted; that they have value. They can afford to be secure and confident. They will get the encouragement they need to keep on going through any rough spots they encounter in life. I learned all those things from my father. He made all the difference.

Boys also learn from their fathers how to be fathers. I know I did. When my father first ran for Congress, at the age of twenty-nine, he worried that people would think he was too young, so he vowed to always wear his coat and he affected a formal demeanor. With Old Peg still wobbling through his unknown future, candidate Gore vowed also to never play the fiddle—in public.

Which brings me to what was, by our official family count, my father's second-most frequently told story. It's Saturday night in Fentris County, July 1938. The crowd had gathered in the hot, crowded courtroom for my father's speech on reciprocal free trade. There's a bustle through the door at the rear of the crowd. Three of my father's musician friends are working their way through the crowd toward the podium, and one of them holds a fiddle over his head. He, my father, speaks louder and more rapidly about the evils of tariffs, hoping, he claims, that the fiddle will go away.

By now, though, his alter ego is standing directly in front of him, holding the fiddle in outstretched arms and demanding loudly, "Play us a tune, Albert!" Trapped by this powerful drama, he seizes the fiddle and unleashes his music. And then the crowd goes wild. My father always chuckled when he delivered his favorite punchline, "They brought the house down."

Once he was reconciled to who he really was, there was no turning back, and the crowds did love it. He brought the house down wherever he went.

In August, he was elected in the Democratic primary. That was it, because back then no Republicans ever ran. In September he went to Washington with his wife and baby daughter, my sister Nancy, not one year old, and he was invited to play his fiddle in Constitution Hall with Eleanor Roosevelt in the audience.

Fourteen years later, when I was four, he moved to the Senate. The incumbent he defeated, Senator Kenneth D. McKellar, was a powerful chairman of the Appropriations Committee, and sought to remind the voters of his power to bring money to the state with his omnipresent slogan, "A thinking feller votes McKellar."

In keeping with my father's campaign philosophy, he never had a negative word about his opponent and always admonished his supporters never to remove a McKellar sign. Instead, acting on my mother's advice, we put up new signs directly underneath McKellar's—every time we found a sign that said, "The thinking feller votes McKellar," we put our new sign directly underneath it proclaiming, "Think some more and vote for Gore."

By defeating McKellar, and more broadly, the Crump machine, he helped to establish the terms of a new politics for Tennessee and the entire South—a progressive politics that rejected race baiting and connected our region to the rest of America. And he carried those values on to the national stage.

In 1956, my father hoped to be Adlai Stevenson's running mate. So did Estes Kefauver, who felt he had earned it. And so did my father's friend and Senate classmate, John F. Kennedy. It was quite a convention.

I'm particularly proud that my father was way ahead of his time in fighting for civil rights. Discrimination against blacks deeply offended his sense of justice. He talked about it to Nancy and me often.

When I was eight years old, we lived in a little house in Carthage on Fisher Avenue, halfway up a hill. At the top of the hill was a big, old mansion. One day as the property was changing hands, the neighbors were invited to an open house. My father said, "Come, son, I want to show you something." So we walked up the hill and through the front door. But instead of stopping in the parlor or the ornate dining room or the grand staircase with all the other guests, my father took me down to the basement, and pointed to the dark, dank, stone walls and the cold mettle rings lined up in a row—slave rings.

Long after he left the classroom, my father was a teacher. And I thank God that he taught me to love justice.

Not everyone was eager to learn. One unreconstructed constituent once said, in reference to African-Americans, though that was not the term he used, "I don't want to eat with them, I don't want to live with them, I don't want my kids to go to school with them." To which my father replied gently, "Do you want to go to heaven with them?" After a pause came the flustered response, "No, I want to go to hell with you and Estes Kefauver."

All that driving between Carthage and Nashville, and between Carthage and Washington, made him impatient for better roads. During World War II, he had been the first congressman to decline a commission as an officer and joined the Army as a private. FDR called all the congressmen back from service. He later went back in, and during his service in Germany, he was impressed by the autobahn. In 1956, he personally authored and passed into law the Interstate Highway Bill, the largest public works endeavor in the history of humankind.

We traveled down here this morning from Carthage on old Highway 70, the same road he first took to Nashville seventy-five years ago. It's a long way. He's taking his last trip home on I-40, part of the 44,000 miles of interstate that he created.

He wrote and passed the first Medicare proposal ever to pass on the Senate floor, in 1964. One year later, after the Democratic landslide, Medicare became law. For more than a decade he controlled all tax policy on the Senate floor, because the majority of his colleagues had absolute trust in his conscience, his commitment to fairness, and his keen understanding of the law.

He was the best speaker I ever heard. When he spoke on the Senate floor the cloakrooms emptied, the galleries began to fill, the pages sat in rapt attention. He had a clarity and force that was quite remarkable. People wanted to hear him speak and they wanted to know what he said, because they knew that whatever he said he believed with his heart.

Time and again, with the crispness of his logic and the power of his oratory, he moved his listeners to adopt his opinions and cheer. Indeed, in his very first speech on the floor of the House of Representatives in 1939, the next day *The New York Times* reported that his remarks—and I quote—"stopped the show, and received an ovation of proportions such as are usually reserved for elder statesmen." His speech changed enough votes to defeat the bill he opposed. That's what happens when you bring the house down.

Keeping alive the tradition of Hull, he fought tirelessly for reciprocal free trade—and he always emphasized that word, "reciprocal."

But he often quoted Hull, his mentor, as saying, "When goods do not cross borders armies do."

He was an early supporter of Israel. As chairman of the Foreign Assistance Appropriations Subcommittee, in 1948, he authored and passed the first American aid to the new Jewish state. He was the nation's leading expert on outer space law and authored the treaty banning weapons from space. He led the fight to negotiate and ratify the Anti-Ballistic Missile Treaty, an agreement which many believe was a turning point in the nuclear arms race.

And of course, he was an early, eloquent, and forceful opponent of the Vietnam War—and it cost him his seat in the Senate.

My father was brave. I mean really brave. He opposed the poll tax in the '40s, and supported civil rights in the '50s. By the time he was in his final Senate term, I was old enough to understand clearly the implications of the choices he made when he repeatedly rejected the advice of many fearful political allies who had urged him to trim his sails. He was proud to support the Voting Rights Act of 1965. He was damned if he was going to support Hainesworth or Carswell, Nixon's suspect nominees for the Supreme Court. And I was so proud of that courage.

And even then, he almost defied the odds and won. But a new ill wind was blowing across the land. And in many ways he was unprepared for the meaner politics that started in 1970. For example, he never, ever had a press secretary on his payroll, for thirty-two years. He was offended by the very thought of using taxpayer's money to pay the salary of someone whose principal job was to publicly flatter him.

He preferred to speak plainly for himself. Indeed, many older Tennesseans will tell you that what they remember most about my father was his Sunday radio broadcast on WSM, where he presented the news from Washington "as I see it."

The night he lost in 1970, he made me prouder still. He said, defeat may serve as well as victory to shake the soul and let the glory out. And then he turned the old Southern segregationist slogan on its head and declared, "The truth shall rise again."

I heard that. The next day was the first time I ever remember our roles being reversed, the first time I gave back to him what he taught me. We were in a canoe on the Caney Fork, just the two of us. Near to despair, he asked, "What would you do if you had thirty-two years of service to the people given to the highest of your ability, always doing what you thought was right, and had then been unceremoniously turned out of office? What would you do?" I responded, "I'd take the thirty-two years, Dad."

It's not correct to say that he went back to his farm; throughout his entire career in public service he never left his farm. He loved to raise Angus cattle. In the audience today are quite a few Angus breeders from around the country who were among his closest friends. It was his recreation. He always said, "I'd rather find a new black calf in the weeds than a golf ball in the grass."

Our farm was also an important school where he taught me every day. He must have told me a hundred times the importance of learning how to work. He taught me how to plow a steep hillside with a team of mules. He taught me how to clear three acres of heavily wooded forest with a double-bladed axe. He taught me how to take up hay all day in the sun and then take up the neighbor's hay after dinner, by moonlight, before the rain came.

He taught me how to deliver a newborn calf when its mother was having trouble. He taught me how to stop gullies before they got started. He taught me how to drive, how to shoot a rifle, how to fish, how to swim. We loved to swim together in the Caney Fork River, off a big flat rock on the backside of his farm.

Once my father was giving a magazine reporter from New York City a short tour of the farm when he came across a cow stuck in the river mud. The reporter had no idea what to make of it when he stripped naked and waded into the mud, emerging a half hour later with his cow.

After he left the Senate he went into business. For ten years he ran the second largest coal company in America, driving back and forth on the Interstate connecting Tennessee with Lexington, Kentucky. At the time of his death he was still serving as the senior director on the board of Occidental Petroleum.

But just as with farming, he had always been in business. He owned a feed mill, a hardware store, and sporting goods store, a towing and auto repair shop. He sold boats and motors. He had a gasoline station. He leased the space for three restaurants, a barber shop, a beauty shop, a natural gas distributor, a veterinarian's office, and a union hall. He ran a commercial egg production house with 10,000 chickens. He built and operated the first so-called pig parlors in this part of the country. He developed real estate and built houses and apartments for rent. He was always busy.

When I eventually left journalism and entered politics, he was also a source of invaluable advice in my races for the House and Senate, and later when I ran for President he personally campaigned in every single county in both Iowa and New Hampshire. I constantly run into people in both states who know him well, not from his days in the Senate, but from his days as a tireless octogenarian campaigner.

In 1992, when then Governor Clinton asked me to join his ticket, my father became an active campaigner once again. At the age of eighty-four, he and my mother took their own bus trip that year, and what a crew was on that bus—Albert and Pauline Gore, Tony Randall, Mitch Miller, and Dr. Ruth.

He convinced one young man from our campaign to come back to the farm with him. But the fellow soon left, and asked me, how do you tell a man who is working beside you and is eighty-four years old that you are quitting because it's too hot and the work is too hard? I could have told him I learned the answer to that one when I was still young—you don't.

At eighty-five, he embarked on a major new project—the antique mall and car museum in south Carthage. Two years ago, when he was eighty-nine, he was still driving his car. I had great difficulty persuading him to stop. When I asked my friends and neighbors in Carthage to help, one of them said, "Oh, don't worry, Al, we know his car—we just get off the road when we see him coming."

Once, though, he didn't know his own car. He left the store, got in somebody else's car and drove home. Carthage is the kind of place where people often leave the keys in the ignition. Luckily, the store owner drove my father's car up to his farm, left it in the driveway and then drove the other fellow's car back to the store before he knew it was missing.

There are so many people in Carthage who have bent over backwards to help my parents, especially over the last few years. My family is so grateful for the quality of kindness in Smith County, and we thank you. And during the months and weeks before my father's death, we've been blessed with the devotion of a wonderful collection of around-the-clock caregivers and doctors and nurses.

Reverend Billy Graham wrote recently, "We may not always be aware of the presence of angels. We cannot always predict how they will appear. But angels have been said to be our neighbors." All I know is that my family is mighty grateful to the people who have shown so much love to my father. And we found out that a lot of our neighbors in Smith County and the surrounding counties really are angels. A lot of them are here today, and on behalf of my family I want to say thank you.

He died bravely and well. As it was written of the patriarch, Abraham, "he breathed his last and died at a good old age, an old man and full of years, and he was gathered to his people. And we know that those who walk uprightly enter into peace, they find rest as they lie in death."

As many here know, it's hard to watch the sharpness of a parent's face, hard to watch, in the words of the poet, "how body from spirit does slowly unwind until we are pure spirit at the end."

We're a close family. But the time we had together over the last few weeks to say good-bye truly brought us closer still. We're grateful to all those who have reached out to us, many of whom understand the need because they, themselves, have suffered loss. As is our custom here, neighbors brought food and we tried to concentrate on making ready for today.

So here's what I decided I would like to say today—to that young boy with the fiddle in Possum Hollow, contemplating his future: I'm proud of the choices you made. I'm proud of the road you traveled. I'm proud of your courage, your righteousness, and your truth. I feel, in the words of the poet, because my father "lived his soul, love is the whole and more than all."

I'll miss your humor, the sound of your laughter, your wonderful stories and your sound advice, and all those times you were so happy that you brought the house down.

Dad, your whole life has been an inspiration. I'd take the ninety-one years—your life brought the house down.

Foreword

IN TRYING to describe and interpret the people and the politics of the South, I have drawn heavily from the experiences and observations of a long, happy, and fruitful career in public office—county, state, and national. The reader is warned that while the experience and understanding from which I write is, on one hand, intimate, it is at the same time academically limited. Moreover, I have imagined that most other political leaders, as well as the people whom they have served or disserved, have approached these episodes in much the same manner.

Far from attempting to write a history of either the South or of Southern politics, I have no further aim than to portray and interpret events and conditions from my perspective as they relate to the politics of the 1970s.

It has been my desire to avoid severe or uncharitable judgments, but a determination to be candid has constantly guided my pen in writing about the politics I have seen, felt, loved, and sometimes hated. The result will be, I hope, agreeable to some, but others will doubtlessly find my assessments harsh and disagreeable. That is the story of my life, in a way, and it has been wonderfully rewarding.

A number of friends and relations have generously contributed to this book. Without their assistance, it would not have been possible. I single out a few in special gratitude: my wife, Pauline; my daughter, Nancy, and her husband, Frank Hunger; my son, Albert, Jr., and his wife, Mary Elizabeth; Mrs. Christine Coe and Mr. and Mrs. Thomas Ragland; Pat Caddell; three distinguished professors—Dr. Hugh Graham, University of Maryland; Doctors Leiper Freeman and Dewey Grantham, Vanderbilt University; and former members of my Senate staff, William Allen, Jack Lynch, and Mrs. Peg Fate.

My fondest hope for this endeavor is that it may inspire some idealistic youths to worthy public service, especially in my native hills where the need for education and conscientious leadership is so great.

ALBERT GORE

Carthage, Tennessee
July 1972

Contents

CHAPTER I

Attitudes of the South

"THE SOUTH." There are two ways of looking at the South: *What* is it? and *Who* is it? The observer with preconceived notions on the subject usually asks the first question—and is left with a confused jumble of facts and myths. I prefer the second question, for the South is the people who live there—and to understand them, one must begin with their origins.

When my son was thirteen, I drove with him on a weekend trip to Williamsburg, Virginia, and nearby Jamestown. I wanted him to see the names of the settlers who had landed at Jamestown, one in particular about whom he had not yet learned.

These intrepid pioneers had established the first permanent English colony in America in 1607, thirteen years before Plymouth Rock. There in 1619 the first representative legis-

lative assembly convened to set the pattern for self-government in America. There, too, in the same year, the first
Negroes in America landed, coming as indentured servants.
James Bryce, the great British commentator on the United
States, called the Jamestown settlement "one of the great
events in the history of the world—an event to be compared
for its momentous consequences with the overthrow of the
Persian Empire by Alexander; with the destruction of Carthage by Rome;—one might say with the discovery of America by Columbus."

Here in the South was the cradle of our self-governing institutions. And I wished my son to witness that one of these
pioneers bore his name.

Together with their trade, skill, or other classification, the
names of the settlers were engraved on a plaque. Among
others, there was listed:

EDWARD BRINTO, MASON

THOMAS COWPER, BARBER

THOMAS EMRY, CARPENTER

THOMAS GORE, GENTLEMAN

I stood watching from the corner of my eye for my son's reaction. Finally, he said, "Dad, we've slipped a little, haven't
we?"

We must have, because many years later, at the conclusion
of the Revolutionary War, two Gores, brothers and privates,
were mustered out and given a grant of land in the scrabbly
hill country of what is now Overton County, Tennessee.
Then a part of North Carolina, it was a rather rough terrain
characterized by marginal clay soil, steep hills, shaded coves,

and clear creeks. There was no river transportation; "bottom land" was scarce.

One of the early Gores had the civic motivation—or was it just good business judgment?—to donate the land on which the courthouse was constructed, while retaining the surrounding property. This brought a measure of good fortune; but life in the hilly and mountainous regions—whether in the Appalachians, the Smokies, or the Blue Ridge—was meager and usually the result of hard work. In other areas an easier way to prosperity developed—slavery. Although the great majority of people throughout the history of the South never owned slaves, the slaveholders rapidly gained more land and more money, and came to dominate the local culture and politics.

I know of no Gore ancestor who was a slaveholder; indeed I know of only a few upland families who were. Is it any wonder, then, that when fundamentalist preachers later came into the area to preach in Brush Arbors and to inveigh against slavery, saying it was un-Christian and wrong, that they found a warm, sympathetic reception in the places where slaveownership was not profitable? These yeomen farmers were competing with slave labor. Sturdy individualists and fiercely independent, the uplanders were doubtless as eager for the better things of life as their descendants are now, but they could not compete successfully with the slaveowners who controlled the rich plantation lands; and since economics and religion have a convenient way of developing affinities, the sentiment against slavery came to have a religious meaning.

Today, as then, political realities in the South, as in every other region, flow from the history, the customs, and the culture of the people. In this sense the South is like every other section of our country. Yet the South is distinctive in many ways, including its politics—which have frequently been tumultuous. Consider, for example, one of the most striking political developments of our time—the reversal of positions of the two major political parties on the issue of race relations —the issue that has underlain all politics of the South and that even in 1972 submerges all others. It was the Republicans— the party of Lincoln—who had fought slavery and undertaken to integrate the newly freed blacks into Southern politics and society during the Reconstruction Period. Yet in recent years, it has been the national Democratic Party that has tried to secure civil rights for blacks and to integrate them into American society with equal rights. And it had been the Republican Party, together with "conservative" Southern Democrats, which has sought to exploit racial prejudices—inflamed as they are by the crowded conditions of our cities, problems of school integration, and by competition for industrial jobs.

In the new politics of the right, the people of a state or region are carefully surveyed not to determine their needs or aspirations, but to assess their fears, hates, and prejudices and then an expensive propaganda campaign is tailor-made to exploit the worst in them. This strategy was much in evidence during the 1970 elections and it can be seen clearly again in 1972.

Even so, the progressive forces of tolerance and social conscience have reason for hope in the South because, despite some 1970 losses (my own included), they scored significant victories in most Southern states, as we shall later see in detail. In fact, a movement away from reaction and toward a progressive populism was clearly discernible in the 1970 voting patterns in the South and in the 1972 state primaries. This trend is surely apparent in the 1972 Presidential campaign.

Nixon's 1968 "Southern Strategy" to compete with George C. Wallace became in 1970 a blatant attempt to capture the Wallace vote for Republican candidates for the United States Senate and for governor. In 1972 the strategy was shifted to greater emphasis on school busing, housing problems in the suburbs, tax favoritism, and an appeal to shallow chauvinism by proposing still larger expenditures for the defense industry.

Richard Nixon not only took pains to limit the grounds for Wallace's possible attacks on him but competed for the racist element of Wallace's constituency. It was not by accident but by astute political design that "forced integration of the suburbs" became code words for racism. If President Nixon did not coin the phrase, he adopted it and gave it circulation. Though housing and transportation of schoolchildren are genuine issues, their treatment in the context of racial terminology is only a variant of many past appeals to bigotry.

A huge chunk of the Nixon budget deficit, a $6-billion increase in the armed services budget, is more nearly associated with an appeal to the extreme rightist sentiment than to genuine needs of national defense. The big war industries will get along very well with this, thank you. This surely means large campaign contributions, too. The traditional Southern attraction to violence is assuaged by this, just as Nixon's needless and cruel prolongation of the Vietnam war, and his incredible pretension of winning the war while withdrawing from it, is a prayer to the ghost of Robert E. Lee.

Yet on other than racial and sectional appeals, Mr. Nixon executed a 180-degree switch to more liberal positions on welfare reform, proposing a guaranteed annual income, and on a *rapprochement* with Communist power centers.

The Wallace threat itself shifted, too. He no longer stood in the schoolhouse door. Though he made the welkin ring with attacks upon busing "our little children to kingdom come," he marked his campaign with a firmer New Deal brand of populism.

Among the Democrats, other than Wallace, there were major shifts toward the liberal side of the ideological spectrum. Even bland Senator Edmund Muskie, the early front runner, made a gradual but dramatic movement from chauvinism to frank acknowledgment of error, to condemnation of the war as a "moral wrong," and finally to championship of a succinct, peaceful settlement, the forerunner of a firmer liberal policy on priorities. Thus a traditional mainstream politician, over the period of his unsuccessful candidacy, emerged as a representative not of the old guard but of the progressives in the Democratic Party—only to be outflanked on the right by the inimitable Hubert Humphrey and on the left by George McGovern, who, far more than any other, shrewdly sensed the spirit for change in the Democratic Party.

The Democratic candidates favored for the Presidential nomination by the more conservative element—Congressman Wilbur Mills of Arkansas and Senator Henry Jackson of Washington—never gained positions of serious contention. Though both were highly regarded by the leaders of their party, the voters in the Democratic primaries were looking for more affirmative, progressive leaders.

The result of the 1972 primary campaigns, then, was a confirmation and an acceleration of the progressive trend which I saw manifested in the Southern elections of 1970. Yet only a few Southern delegates joined McGovern's march to the Democratic Presidential nomination. Should the tide of change rise in the South and carry with it traditional Democratic political loyalties, as it did with FDR's New Deal, the South could become a crucial 1972 battleground.

The history of Southern politics, then, holds vast meaning for the political struggle being waged now in every state of the Old Confederacy. "The South," wrote V. O. Key, Jr., in 1950, "remains the region with the most distinctive character and tradition." That is still true, yet the student of the South and of its politics will not venture far before he discovers a vast diversity of interests. This diversity had, and still has, its geographic, economic, and social roots and its political bearings. Any realistic evaluation of Southern politics of the past or the present must reckon with many identifiable groups in the social structure and the varied geography of the region. But the natural content, perspectives, and history of Southern society make it increasingly clear that the basic ingredients of Southern politics have always been emotions and attitudes about race. The "unity" of the South has been at the same time both real and illusory—real when racial issues were in the foreground, but illusory when economic issues gained prominence. This political paradox can be summed up in the epithet "poor white." They will answer to either name—but not to both at once.

Who were the pioneers from which the Old South was formed, from which the aristocracy came, from which the poor whites came? Many historians have argued that men of position and power in the old country did *not* embark on those frail ships "for a dismal frontier," as Wilbur Cash called it, "where savages prowl and slay, and living is a grim and laborious ordeal."

The laborer faced with starvation; the debtor anxious to get out of jail; the apprentice laborer, reckless, eager for adventure and even more eager to escape his master; the peasant weary of the exactions of milord; the small landowner and shopkeeper faced with bankruptcy and hopeful of a fortune in tobacco; the neurotic haunted by failure and despair; and, once in a blue moon, some wealthy bourgeois smarting under the snubs of a haughty aristocracy and fancying himself in the role of a princeling in the wilderness—all—all of these kinds came. But not the monied, not the gentleman of rank, not the cavalier who was happy in the drawing rooms of his native land.*

Like most other pioneer Americans, the Southern pioneers believed in fundamental Christian religious doctrines, in equality in political freedom, in individualism, and in a frontier variety of social justice. The "equality" they believed in, however, did not include equality for black slaves—a paradox which may not have occurred to most of them although it did to Thomas Jefferson. Blacks aside, the political ideals of Jefferson inspired these hardy frontiersmen to self-government, to the beginnings of public education, public roads, and the use of the instruments of government to protect the weak and to restrain the strong. As if they drank freedom from their cool mountain springs, frontier backwoods Southerners were powerfully affected by the doctrines of popular sovereignty— "God-given" rights of men, and of individuality and freedom which constituted the principles of the Revolution.

Many a backwoodsman, born in a log cabin of poor parents, became an "aristocrat" upon his success as an entrepreneur or as a lawyer. President Andrew Jackson, for example— born of obscure parentage in a log cabin in the Carolina mountains, a swashbucklering but poor young lawyer—succeeded financially and came to own a beautiful estate and a magnificent ante-bellum home with white columns surrounded by magnificent trees, and he had countless slaves. In

* Wilbur Cash, *Mind of the South.*

the frontier manner, he was thereupon considered an aristocrat. His way of life included the duello, the paternalistic
obligations of the master, and the cavalier styles regarded as
befitting of his station. The Virginia aristocracy was relatively
small. Professor Douglas Dowd has argued that it included
only some four or five thousand of the greater planters. They
were complemented, however, and largely supplanted by the
strong, the able, and the ambitious emerging from the back
country, and the more enterprising and fortunate among the
white tenant-farmer group.

The criterion for social status in the Old South was largely
a matter of property, particularly land, and not especially of
grace in social exchange. Because so many of the new aristo-
crats who achieved higher social status by accumulating land
and slaves were relatives of the still struggling but less fortunate common whites, there was a sure feeling of solidarity
among *all* whites.

The three commonly recognized bases of Southern civiliza-
tion were: 1) slavery; 2) the plantation and its major crops—
cotton, tobacco, and rice; and 3) the code of chivalry. The
plantation system enabled a class of large landowners to see
themselves as "gentry." Slavery enhanced their sense of superiority and led many of them to believe they were a natural
ruling class. The remaining white population of the Southern
backwoods, small farms, and tiny villages constituted the
majority.* Tens and hundreds of thousands of them were
farmers on the hill lands, less productive bottom lands, and
poorer cotton lands. Doubtless, many were jealous of the

---

* Just before the Civil War there were 8 million whites living in the South
—that is, in the eleven states that became the Confederacy. Of these, less than
400,000 owned slaves and many of these owned only one, two, or possibly three
who worked with the family in the fields and woods or served as domestics
in the home.

planter who did own cotton land—or (in South Carolina) rice land, or (in Louisiana) sugar-cane land. Yet they were not without worldly goods. Many had good saddle horses, of which they boasted. They had roughhewn cabins, a garden, perhaps a cow, and products from the field and forest. Elegance was beyond their means, but many of them lived well by the standards of the day. And if the less fortunate among them were called "poor whites," one must consider that this term was a relative one. They were also called "hillbillies," "Georgia crackers," and now and then "white trash"—particularly by the black slaves who worked as domestics and were inclined to refer to them scornfully. The feeling of rejection was mutual between them.

People took from the "aristocracy" what they could use—manners to which they could adjust, and those values which they could afford. Southerners delighted in hospitable manners and customs. Southern hospitality became a matter of often exaggerated pride. Notions of honor and decorum, obedience to the austere principles of devout religion, were valued by rich and poor alike. They also enjoyed—on occasion—a good stiff draught of corn liquor, a square dance, the fiddle and the banjo, singing schools, and picnics with "dinner on the ground." It was characteristic of the Southern frontier manner that it placed no particular value upon rank—it was what a man had and what a man could do that determined his worth. Feats of personal courage and unusual physical prowess, were second only to possessions in importance. One's neighbor might have more land or slaves but one might outfiddle him or best him at a turkey shoot, at a square dance, or at a rail splitting, and this demonstrated a certain right to equality.

The common white man in the South, then, was what Cash

called a "hell of a fellow," and he prided himself upon this status. His life consisted of more than daily drudgery; work was not every day. In most places the church was the center of his social life, and on Sunday he took his wife and little ones there (or maybe she took him) and invited others to "go home with us for dinner." The leisure of Saturday gave him time to dream or to brood, sometimes to gamble, sometimes to drink, but sometimes to help build a new church or a cabin for a neighbor who had been "burned out."

It is both tragic and ironic that the South, which had endowed the new American republic with such a spectacular galaxy of enlightened leaders—Presidents Washington, Jefferson, Madison, and Monroe, together with Chief Justice Marshall, for instance, were all Virginians—fell for so long into the grip of a leadership subservient to minority and exploitative interests.

The South's story has been largely, but not entirely, a story of its betrayal by political and cultural leaders. Central to this story has been and still is the basic division in Southern life: the cleavage between white and black. But in tracing the origins of this primal fault it is not enough simply to cite the interest of a white slave-owning sector in the continued subordination of the Negro, as important and obvious as that interest was, for the racial cleavage became deeply imbedded in human psychology and emotion as well as in the South's social customs and tradition.

A more powerful instrument than mere economic interest had to be forged and nurtured by the dominant planter elite during the ante-bellum years in order to bind the mass of white yeomen in defense of the South's "peculiar institution." Religion, always a profound influence, was twisted by political demagogues and even by church leaders to support slavery. To the uneducated populace, God was successfully portrayed in support of white supremacy and as standing firm with the "Southern way of life." From one pulpit to another word went forth that paganism and infidelity were sweeping the world elsewhere but that the South would "stand firm in the faith." One of the most eminent churchmen of the South, Dr. Farmwell of New Orleans, called slavery a "providential trust"—God's plan, undoubtedly, for bringing the heathen black to the land of opportunity, to enlightenment and faith, and thus (if the black really had a soul) to eternal bliss. The Baptist, the Presbyterian, and the Methodist churches, which had early been dominated by racial egalitarian pastors, denied the new doctrinal nostrum, but the Southern leaders would have no more of this. And, as the Civil War approached, they stopped at nothing short of a *Southern Baptist* Church, a *Southern Presbyterian* Church, and a *Southern Methodist* Church more agreeable to their aims. Eventually, but not without much soul-searching, there was developed in the South, especially in the plantation areas, a religious base for slavery, for racial segregation and discrimination.

The mountainous areas of east Tennessee and Kentucky— where the nonslave-owning whites found affinity between their relative economic backwardness and a religious belief that slavery was wrong—became the early center of the Southern abolitionist movement. Farther west, in the valleys of the Mississippi and Tennessee Rivers, slave-owning was not only an index to prosperity, but a matter of social and political standing. So, even by the early 1800s, a sharp division developed between the east and west within these states—a division that still manifests itself in the ballot box. And farther south, there was division, too, within Alabama and Georgia where the hill country in the northern parts of those states was not nearly so strong for slavery as in the southern areas.

But the sharpest division of all, of course, was country-wide: between the states of the North and East, on one hand, and the states of the South, on the other. For a while the South had an ally in the newly developed West, but Southern political leaders, driven by their slave-owning supporters, sacrificed their ally in the fight over the Missouri Compromise, and gradually they became isolated.

Meanwhile, what of the Negro? Most of the slaves brought from Africa came from a 3000-mile stretch along the west coast. Some had been kidnaped by Europeans and Africans, some were sold into slavery for infraction of native laws. Regular markets were established in Africa where slave traders from Europe could traffic in slaves, many being kept in forts and trading stations built near the coast or in the open markets where they were sold at private treaty or at auction. Branded and chained, the newly purchased slaves were rowed to ships anchored at sea where they were stacked in holds for the dreaded "middle passage" across the Atlantic.

In the new land, the slave faced unspeakable travail and hardships, suffering conditions that must have produced a despair of the human spirit beyond imagination. It should not be surprising to learn that there were repeated insurrections and attempted escapes. There are more than 200 recorded revolts by small groups of slaves before the Civil War. Two of the most publicized revolts, both long-planned, were led by Denmark Vesey in South Carolina in 1822, and by Nat Turner in Virginia in 1831. Vesey's plot was betrayed by a slave and ultimately 37 blacks were executed. Turner and his followers struck viciously at the Travis family, murdering all of them, and then moved from plantation to plantation, killing 55 whites in thirty-six hours. As word of this insurrection spread, 3000 enraged whites proceeded to slaughter more than 100 slaves in retaliation, and to execute Turner and his lieutenants.

The influence of slavery upon the social process of the Old South was deep and thorough. In certain ways the Negro affected the white man as much as the white man affected the Negro—subtly influencing manners, language, music, emotions, attitudes, and culture.

Opposition to slavery in the North intensified with time and with the repetition of horror stories about the evils of slavery, the most notable being Harriet Beecher Stowe's *Uncle Tom's Cabin.* Of course, there were good masters and often there was real affection between master and slave—particularly in instances where blacks and whites worked the land together or where blacks worked as domestics in the house. But while the whip and the lash may not have been the usual pattern, they were used all too often. And, in any case, nothing can alter the fundamental judgment that slavery was wrong, that it was "brutal and ugly." Slaves had no rights; they were *slaves* and they could never forget it. As more and more people realized the enormity of this tragedy, the abolitionist movement gained strength.

In one of our truly epochal political campaigns, Abraham Lincoln rode the rising tide against slavery into the Presidency. He gave this one issue a moral tone that inflamed the sentiment against slavery.

Southern leaders, fighting back, had more than their share of moral paradoxes. Their heated, convoluted effort to come to grips with slavery resulted in much hypocrisy and patent dissembling. The South was placed on the moral defensive before the nation and before the world, and this produced attitudes among Southerners that resisted either logic or reason, as did the whole idea of secession and war, which was clearly impending. This psychology had a deep impact upon the blacks—fearful of the present, fearful of the future, and fearful of everyone around them.

The natural effect of white supremacy on the white himself must have been equally profound. The result, according to Cash, "was the perpetuation and acceleration of the tendency to violence." In any event, the militancy and belligerency of the South became accepted as a part of its image, if not its real character. Just how all this was translated into the brutality and barbarism of lynching is difficult to fathom. More than 300 persons are said to have been hanged and burned by mobs between 1840 and 1850. Yet less than 10 per cent of these victims were Negroes, a slave being a costly possession, with an average price of about $500. The other 90 per cent were "poor whites."

Not surprisingly, the strongest support for slavery, for secession, and for the Civil War came from the rich delta landowners in states with the most plantations and slaves. Strong opposition came from the upper South, from the old Whigs, and from common white farmers who did not own slaves. Throughout the South, the decision on secession was bitterly contested. Nearly half the counties in Alabama, for instance, voted against secession in the state convention. Winston County in Alabama followed the logic of secession and declared itself an independent state, with embarrassing results to the Confederacy. (Incidentally, Winston County has been a Republican county ever since.) Many highland counties all over the South—in the Appalachias and the Cumberlands, in the Ozarks, and in the piney-woods hills of northern Louisiana—opposed secession, several seeking to become independent states. Slaves flocked to the Union armies in droves and took up arms against their former masters, thus forever giving the lie to the self-serving myth that blacks were predestined for and actually happy in servitude. Many whites, too, joined the Union army. Sometimes, among white families, one brother went with the North, another with the South.

It is unnecessary here to recount either the horrible destruction of the bloody Civil War or the valor displayed by the soldiers of both the Union and the Confederacy. What we should consider is the resultant attitudes among people of the South and among non-Southerners toward the South. Four years of fighting, four years of common experience, four years with a common foe, four years of destruction and bitter ultimate defeat, brought a unity in the South that had not been possible before. In the hour of its defeat, the Confederacy was born.

After its defeat, the Confederacy rallied to defend a new cause—the myth that the "Old South" had suffered an unjustified defeat in a war to preserve a gracious and glorious "way of life." Few myths have been so enduring. According to legend, the ante-bellum South was a grand society with cultured and handsome gallants who moved as graciously about the drawing room as among lovely ladies through trellised and tailored rose gardens, and later repaired to the dueling grounds to engage in matters of honor with the nonchalance of accepting an invitation to a supper party. According to this image, the Old South was a land of large and spacious mansions, beautiful lawns, magnolia trees, handsome horses, mint juleps—a romantic culture characterized by benevolent paternalism, a society that was free of guilt complexes and never found it necessary to justify slavery. After all, the slaves had been happy in their servitude under their benevolent masters.

As with most myths, there was an element of truth in it.

There were indeed rich planters (though not many of them were cultured and generous), and they had a gracious way of life. But there were other elements in the Old South that Southerners had chosen to ignore. These elements—the poorer whites and black slaves—were at the center of the myriad social and economic problems that faced the South after the Civil War.

Instead of tackling these problems forthrightly, the political leaders of the South who traditionally had been associated with and sanctioned by the planter class, chose instead to defend the "Lost Cause"—the myth. Yet, in total defeat, Southerners were without the means to be grandly romantic. The planter who had doted upon the prestige of land and slaves no longer had slaves and his land lay untilled. The South, in many ways, was being treated as a conquered province, and it deeply resented this. Though Andrew Johnson, a Southern Democrat and Lincoln's Vice-President, tried to be compassionate toward the South after becoming President, his opposition in the Congress, led in the House by the powerful Thaddeus Stevens and in the Senate by Charles Sumner, insisted that Republican political regimes, composed of carpetbaggers, local scalawags, and newly freed blacks, be imposed upon the states of the South. Reconstruction was, in the main, a period of exploitation, corruption, and vengefulness, though some constructive democratizing improvements were made, including the introduction of blacks to political freedom and participation.

Stories of corruption, pilfering, ignorance, and repression by the ill-informed blacks and Yankee carpetbaggers who were holding public office by fiat, became commonplace in most Southern households. These stories intensified the Southern opposition to the Yankee, to the Republican Party, and to the carpetbagger. Most of all, they intensified the hatred and fear of "the cause of it all"—the Negro. A decade and a half of Reconstruction came to be emblazoned in the white Southern memory and psyche as an era of unparalleled and unmitigated oppression and corruption.

Many modern historians, while not denying the corruption, have insisted that rarely if ever in the history of mankind have the losers in a major civil war been treated with the leniency that was accorded Southern whites, only one of whom was executed (the commander of the notorious war prison at Andersonville). On at least one point, however, there is general historical accord: by 1876 the North and the Republican Party had tired of the whole affair, and, upon the occasion of the Tilden-Hayes dispute of 1876, the South was "redeemed" from radical Republican rule and left to order its own internal affairs as best it could.

The Compromise or Redemption of 1877 was engineered by conservative Democrats and it left them the political heirs of the planters. They came to be known as the "Bourbons"— after the royal house of Spain whose reactionary members "learned nothing and forgot nothing." They envisaged a "New South," with burgeoning industry and commerce. But, at best, their understanding of the massive socioeconomic problems facing the South was limited. Their basic goal was to lure Northern capital and industry southward by promising what was to become a standard package: tax benefits; a large, docile, and nonunion pool of cheap labor; minimal restrictions and regulations; and sympathetic local governments and police. But the basic problem was that the masses of cheap laborers—white and black—were unlikely to view their new peonage as a blessing. Always heavily outnumbered at the polls by the increasingly impoverished farmers and la borers, the Bourbons especially feared an insurgent coalition of poor whites and blacks.

To meet this very real threat, there quickly evolved a symbolic "New South" creed, woven from several mutually supportive strands, all of them binding the newly solid South tightly to the Bourbon-controlled Democratic Party. Central to this process, paradoxically, was the glory of the "Lost Cause."

The Bourbons—the "Redeemers"—cultivated a reputation as Confederate brigadiers whose honor could not be questioned and to whom loyalty was essential. No matter that there were few real ties between the new merchant-industrialist elite and the old planter class, despite the implications of the Bourbon label. The fact that conservative "Redeemer" state treasurers in Virginia, Georgia, Tennessee, Alabama, Arkansas, Kentucky, Mississippi, and Louisiana were later found to have embezzled hundreds of thousands of dollars in public monies—one, Louisiana's mercurial Major Burke, absconded to Honduras with more than $1.7 million—did not deter the conservative Democrats who had ousted radical Republican regimes. They ruthlessly retrenched state expenditures on even such crucial public services as the fledgling school systems, and slashed state taxes—especially business taxes. They were largely safe from the reach of popular discontent because of their prestige and, more importantly in the long run, because the South's new one-party system effectively strangled the competitive interplay of candidates and the real issues in Southern political life.

While historians have marveled at how long and irresponsibly both major parties continued to fight the Civil War with rhetoric for decades after the smoke had cleared—the Republicans "waving the bloody shirt" of treason at the Democrats;

the Bourbons echoing the Republicans in urging their constituents to "vote as you shot"—political scientists have be-
moaned the destruction of the two-party system throughout
the South. Before the war, Whigs and Democrats contested
close elections in a meaningful two-party system. But the one-
party system, in which a party nomination in the spring or
summer primary elections of the dominant party became tantamount to election, produced shifting factional squabbles,
based more on personalities and emotional themes like
"nigger-baiting" than on real issues, and invited moneyed interests to play behind the scenes. Tragically for the South, this
one-party dominance was practiced with a vengeance in the
post-Reconstruction decades, as the hated Republican Party
of Reconstruction was quickly reduced to a corporal's guard
of mountain whites and Negroes. Bourbon Democratic politicians allied themselves with speculating entrepreneurs, from
the statehouse to the merchant-lawyer courthouse crowd—
generally to the mutual enrichment of both (and of Northern,
English, and other outside investors). This coalition siphoned
large profits out of the economically colonized region, leaving
it capital-starved for decades.

Despite the booster rhetoric of the industrial promoters of
the New South, by 1900 the Southern share of U. S. capital
and manufacturing was *less* than it had been in 1860! And
King Cotton also had suffered a devastating decline. Whereas
the 9-million-acre crop of 1873 had sold at 14¢ a pound, the
bumper 23-million-acre crop of 1894 had bottomed at a shud-
dering 4¢ a pound. Since the break-even point for cotton at
that time hovered around 7–8¢, the insolvency of the South's
one-crop economy and chronic overproduction was driving
Jefferson's once-noble yeomen into the misery of massive
tenancy.

With the withdrawal of Federal troops by the Hayes Administration, the South regained mastery of its own fate. But instead of striving to create a new order, its politicians set out to restore the South of mythology—without slavery, of course, but with a peonage system as near to slavery as possible, sometimes worse. Devastated, defeated, despondent, without money, without markets, without tools, without strong moral leadership, the South struggled haltingly to its feet.

During the same period, a tide of emotional reaction struck down many of the rights which had been accorded the Negro. The Democratic Party became the party of the white man—a party that was against the North, against the Yankee, against Federal intervention. Many white plantation-owners—with their allies, the merchants and bankers—opposed any participation by the blacks in politics, and after the Federal troops were gone, they set about systematically to deny them political rights. They did this with the one-party system, with the white primary, with state constitutional amendments prescribing literacy tests and other requirements for voting, and with the poll tax, which disfranchised not only the blacks but many poor whites as well. This scheme was resisted by many Southerners, particularly by those in the uplands and the mountains of Tennessee, Kentucky, and North Carolina where the Republican Party had remained strong. Yet, in general, the South truly was the "Solid South." The Democratic Party primaries became white primaries, though there were exceptions from state to state and from community to community.

This dedication to white supremacy became overwhelming in its economic, social, and even religious manifestations. The unity of white Southerners in virtually every sphere was intensified. Opposition to "outside agitators," the "Damn Yankees," was its purifier. The defense of white supremacy, though not so fully formulated as the argument for slavery had been, remained essentially the same old proslavery argument in a new guise. It became what Ulrich B. Phillips, an authoritative writer on the Southern way of life, called "the central theme" of Southern culture. It was, wrote V. O. Key, Jr., "a watchword of no exact meaning; broadly it includes the practice of residential segregation, the custom of social separation, the admonition of sexual isolation, the reality of economic subordination and the habit of adherence to the caste etiquette of black deference toward white." Even the poor whites supported white supremacy, perhaps even more emotionally than the planters, and dissent from it in any and all forms was fiercely resisted and resented. Tolerance "was pretty well extinguished all along the line and conformity made a nearly universal law," wrote Wilbur Cash. Any questioning or doubting was equated with disloyalty to the South and a challenge to the Southerner's ego. Therefore, doubts and doubters, dissent and dissenters must be resisted just as if they were "outside agitators." The deep-rooted individualism and keen sensitivity that prevailed throughout the South now engendered fierce opposition to outside influence in *any* form. The psychological effects of this social discipline were inescapable. And there was a widespread belligerency about this—a belligerency that resulted all too easily in violence. Dissent became not only politically impossible, but dangerous as well.

In the years following Reconstruction, violence increased throughout the social order. Men were edgy, wore chips on their shoulders, and quickly resorted to firearms. An honor questioned must be defended. This honor complex became a factor in normal community life and had its influence upon the conduct of the police and the administration of justice. A martial and vigilante attitude became ingrained in Southern society. The historian Frank E. Vandiver has said:

> I agree that the South was, is, and probably will be, different from the rest of the country. I do not think that difference is necessarily evil. But I do suggest that response to challenge is a theme in southern experience which is perhaps more constant than others. It focuses the deep currents of extremism in southern blood, it explains the political, social, military, even economic behavior, and—to me, at least—it comprehends the South.

This "response to challenge" can be found in the reaction of a teen-age boy to "a dare" or in the chivalric emotion of a Southern male if his honor is questioned. Even before the Civil War, the South had gained the reputation of being composed of brave and belligerent men. The Battle of King's Mountain in the Revolutionary War is enshrined in Southern folklore, not to mention Cowpens and Eutaw Springs, or the Mexican War. (It was in this war that Tennessee gained the title of the Volunteer State. A call went out for 3000 volunteers, and 30,000 turned up. This is still a source of pride and patriotism in Tennessee.) The reaction to challenge, like the reaction to fear, may often be one of violence.

In the South after Reconstruction, the prevailing fear became fear of the blacks, and that fear was in a strange way centered upon sex. Protection of the Southern white woman became a challenge to Southern white manhood, a matter of honor and gallantry. Southern womanhood must be kept inviolate, protected against miscegenation, and saved from rape. Rapists deserved nothing less, and must receive nothing less, than the violent punishment of lynching. On this there was but little dissent. Agreement about protecting womanhood prevailed everywhere—in the mountains, in the hills, in the bayous, on the plantations. During this period lynchings became widespread, brutal, and sadistic. And, unfortunately, the Southern "leaders" were often in the vanguard of the posses. These Bourbon leaders were predominantly former shopkeepers, loan sharks, and businessmen who had acquired land and wealth in the aftermath of the Civil War. They were even less democratic than the old planter class, depleted by death and impoverishment, and the new Bourbons lacked the compassionate and humanitarian paternalism often shown by the former.

These new leaders of the South corrupted and adulterated many aspects of its culture. In politics, graft and naked force were widely evident. The leaders resisted the use of government power for the benefit of the people, advocating instead tax exemption for new industries (together with excise taxes on the poor), and subsidies to business, railroads, and other special interests. They paid lip service to the cult of the Confederacy, but they were primarily interested in economic gain. They voted Democratic at home, but in economic thinking were aligned with the most conservative wing of the Republican Party. The Southern Democrat–Northern Republican coalition was forged from economic affinity. "Behind the cotton and racist curtains," Vandiver wrote, "procrustean leaders sought a split-level prosperity; one which would fatten the rich and starve the poor." They talked of balanced budgets and no public debts.

They fought every liberal idea, and they fought the few liberals who managed to get in office. Any show of progress, any liberal intent must be suppressed; and suppression was accomplished by appealing to the voters' fear of the Negro—

to white supremacy, in other words. And in later years, if this didn't work, labor leaders and social reformers would be tarred with the Bolshevik label.

Working people and small farmers, both traditional supporters of the Democratic Party, were virtually without political power or influence, being ruled and ruined for the benefit of a small minority of people. To me, one of the South's mysteries is why the mass of the people followed such blind leadership for so long. Perhaps it was that the common man in the South had traditional habits and had been trained to follow the leader. That he should follow so docilely, even in the throes of poverty, is powerful testimony to his abysmal education, to his misplaced faith in his self-appointed leaders, and to the illogic of his racial antagonisms. This was less true of my own people in the hills and mountains, of whom I am intensely proud. Though they were only a segment of the South, their kind existed not only in the Appalachians but in the Blue Ridge, the Ozarks—and in the uplands of most states. One difference was that in the hills and in the mountains the people had never had the slave-master complex to begin with, and the cry of white supremacy did not stir them as it did in the delta areas—although its effect even here should not be taken lightly.

It may have been impossible for a Southern leadership to survive which did not at least pay homage to the South's solidarity on the subject of white supremacy. This was a great pity, for there was a crying need for enlightenment; the desertion of responsibility is a frightful price to pay for holding public office. Conscience and courage might have stemmed the tide toward reaction, economic depression, and political oppression, but conscience and courage were seldom found in Southern Bourbon politicians.

As the nationwide depression of the early 1890s increased these stresses to the breaking point, the once-magic rhetoric of the "Lost Cause" and "Redemption" began to lose its hold. A protest coalition of poor whites and blacks, that nightmare of the Bourbons, became a reality as white and "colored" branches of the Farmers' Alliance merged to form a phalanx of more than 2 million people geared toward political action in the Populist or People's Party.

The dramatic story of the Populist revolt is one of soaring hope and shattered dreams. This was the most serious effort yet attempted to put together a real majority in the South since the time of Jackson. Economic and social factors, ideologic and religious convictions combined in this political rebellion against the vested power of the Bourbon minority, their abuse of power, and their betrayal of the public interest. Populism was frightening to the established conservative Southern Democrats and to their alliance with Northern Republicans, for it threatened to bring an effective coalition of workers, farmers, preachers, teachers, blacks, and other dispossessed people to redress the inequities in the republic's social and economic order. The Populists made a strong bid with considerable early success. But the momentum of heady Populist victories in the early 1890s foundered in 1896 on the shoals of Bourbon corruption and violence, and the politics of racial hatred triumphed once again.

For in defeating Populism, Southern reactionaries played upon latent racist fears and prejudices. Unfortunately, this issue proved sufficient to arouse the average white even more powerfully than economic and class exploitations. "The traumatic experience of the 1890s," wrote Dewey Grantham, "demonstrated how even the more democratic currents in a region so powerfully affected by tradition and racist mythology could be turned into reactionary channels." Tom Watson, Populist leader from Georgia and his party's Vice-Presidential candidate, had told his black and white followers, "The accident of color can make no difference in the interest of farmers, croppers and laborers . . . you are kept apart that you may be separately fleeced of your earnings." But if Watson's coalition sounded like good economic sense, Bourbon appeals to racial solidarity made more psychological sense. This shrewd minority must be given credit for political acumen, because nothing was lost in their victory, save honor.

And to insure that such a bitter and emotionally exhausting donnybrook should not be repeated—that Southern whites in the future could afford to differ politically without black votes making the margin of difference—the Bourbons undertook to, and did, disfranchise the blacks. The techniques were relatively simple, although occasionally ingenious. The 15th Amendment, designed to franchise the blacks, was an obstacle of small consequence so long as one avoided explicit mention of Negroes in the disfranchising statutes or constitutional amendments adopted by the states. The arch-conservative Supreme Court of the turn of the century took no action to prevent this perversion. The disfranchisers turned to "racially neutral" devices such as the "understanding clause," the grandfather clause, literacy tests, the poll tax, and to the primary election, where the Democratic Party was regarded as a private club open to whites only. Concomitantly, the South erected the elaborate caste structure of Jim Crow, with racially separate facilities for public transportation and accommodations.

The disfranchising movement of 1890–1910 effectively purged the South's black voters from the rolls, but in one important sense it *was* "racially neutral" in that hundreds of thousands of poor white voters also were effectively barred from the franchise. It was bad enough that in the new century the South's public discourse should so largely ignore her very pressing social and economic problems and degenerate instead into competitive demagoguery. But disfranchisement so withered the Southern electorate that the profession of politics became a preserve of privilege. The spoils of office, and electoral participation, were restricted largely to the white middle and upper classes, a small minority in a relatively poor and largely agrarian region. By 1924, for instance, the once proud electorate of South Carolina had been appallingly reduced in voter participation even in Presidential elections to only 7 per cent of the potential! The rest of the South did little better.

So the achievements of Populism, though its goals were soundly based in economic and social justice, were spasmodic and short-lived. The people who had supported them became disillusioned and bitter. Southern Democrats who had openly joined the Populist movement got their fingers burned. The ultimate betrayal of the movement, through its leaders' failure of action and lust for personal aggrandizement (and, I think, through political cowardice and vindictiveness), was a bitter chapter in Southern politics. Populism might have succeeded if the actions of its leaders in office had been faithful to their promises. But instead, one after another abandoned their friends and then turned upon their followers, both poor white and black.

Nevertheless, the Populists could point to early—and substantial—victories in the legislative assemblies of eight states; in the elections of six governors and some forty congressmen, and in the lasting influence of their ideas. One authority has said that the Populist movement "was perhaps the single most important liberalizing force the South nourished during the late Nineteenth Century." I believe the record supports this conclusion. Though some writers, notably Richard Hofstadter in his *Age of Reform,* maintain that Populism was illiberal in that it harbored anti-intellectual and anti-Semitic tendencies, I believe that Populism was an outstandingly liberal movement. Among the issues on which Populism based its appeal were: an equal division of educational funds, an equitable tax rate, opposition to favoritism for business, and outrage at the malodorous operation of the convict-labor system. Also, it favored local option elections, equitable money policies, and forward-looking farm and labor programs. Do these issues sound illiberal? Not to me.

Populists took credit, and I think rightly so, for a revival of the principles of Jefferson and Jackson. The Populist credo was to a great extent embodied in the New Deal, in the Fair Deal, and in the Great Society—and we now find them in the platform of the Democratic Party in 1972. Why? Because principles that serve the real interests of the mass have a basic similarity, whether they are acted upon in the nineteenth or the twentieth centuries, and whether the name of the party is Democratic, Populist, Progressive, or Liberal.

During the Populist period, the South generally was more liberal than many other sections of the United States. A tradition of radicalism and liberalism remained (scattered) throughout the South, and in times of economic stress it could still be exploited, as Roosevelt discovered and as others may discover again. Progressive movements in the South have affected the attitudes and aspirations of not only Southerners but all Americans—perhaps far more than we realize.

Except for Populism, brief as it was, minority rule prevailed in the South from Reconstruction to the New Deal.

And by the beginning of the twentieth century, the Negro was segregated, largely disfranchised, and denied every opportunity to gain equality, justice, or genuine freedom. The cruelty of the system was unbelievable yet real. Its scars will be long-lasting.

I do not mean to insist that the South was wholly devoid of progressive achievement during those dark years. Even the notorious demagogues—men like "Pitchfork" Ben Tillman, James Vardaman, Theodore Bilbo, Tom Heflin, the Arkansan Jeff Davis—were reformers after their own crude fashions. They occasionally left on the statute books such modest achievements as attempted insurance reform or railroad regulations. But their laws tended on the whole to be easily evaded and blunted by the powerful corporate lobbies— banking and insurance, railroads, brewers and distillers, mining and lumber, fuel combines, schoolbook publishers, large merchants and industrialists generally—to whose muscle (and not infrequently graft) the pliant one-party legislatures, tempted governors, and purchasable commissioners too often succumbed.

It is true that the Progressive Movement also came to the South, but not until the 1920s, and then rather timidly, dressed largely in the gentlemanly clothing of "good government"—which translated as honest but minimal government. Its executive budgets, even its farm-to-market road-building and school-construction programs, made only a small dent in the South's chronic poverty. "Business Progressivism" spurred industrialization in the South: textiles, lumber, chemicals, metals, light tools. But, as novelist Stark Young wrote, "the changing South is still the South." Perhaps this was his way of saying that the change had occurred to things, not to people. The economy was being reconstructed, but the social mores and the people's attitudes had not been restructured. Its tragedy, its poverty, its defeat, its frustration, its failure, its guilt over slavery, and its social mores remained. Nevertheless, progressives welcomed signs that the South was beginning to inch toward the mainstream of the national economy.

Politically, the Republican Party in the South was still closely identified with the Negro, and was overwhelmingly rejected by the whites (though I must always make an exception of the traditional white Republicans in the Appalachian Mountains, about whose partisan tenacity I learned the hard way). The Republicans had at times shown spotty tendencies to abandon their alliance with the Negro, but this had been tentative. The Democratic Party, on the other hand, was unquestionably the party of the whites.

Meanwhile, the growing centralization of power in the national government (and the relative decline of state and local governments) was bringing a change in the character of federalism. With the improvement of transportation and communications, more problems assumed national characteristics. This change, which has accelerated throughout this century, was a major public issue in the South very early on—"States' rights" were sacred words held over from ante-bellum days. One choice was federal action, federal programs, and federal intervention to assure that the programs are carried out effectively and economically. The other was laissez-faire federal government. In the light of developing conditions a plea for home rule was a plea for apathy. Let the states do it, if it should be done at all; let the local government do it alone, if it is to be done—which really meant that very little of anything would be done. The acknowledged virtues of states' rights and home rule, which understandably had—and still have—a strong appeal, were ardently advocated by the conservatives. The doctrine of states' rights they practiced, however, was only a smoke screen for inaction.

Even today, the conservative is convinced that strong state governments are infinitely more desirable than a strong federal government. This dates back to Thomas Jefferson's idea that the closer the government is to the people, the easier it is to control. But the key to the question of control is: "easier for *whom* to control?" For the conservatives, state legislatures were easier to control than Congress or the national administration. A governor was nearer at hand, easier to reach, and a local legislator even easier. That is, of course, a virtue of local government. Governors and state legislators *should* be easier to reach—but control by the few all too often accompanied this ease of access. During the early years of this century, the planters, the merchants, the relatively few industrialists, and the bankers of the South (especially the bankers) exercised the prevailing influence, and what these conservatives really wanted, of course, was inaction. At the state level they could confuse and diffuse, prevent programs or modify their administration. At this level they could prevail, and conservative special interests made sure that the state government assumed only those powers of which they approved.

Liberals and progressives, on the other hand, pleaded for solutions to problems, and argued that the federal government, with its vast resources and regulatory power, was the proper source of programs for regional and interregional developments. This "new federalism," as they called it, steadily pulled the South into national involvement. Paradoxically, the Southern one-party system played a significant and affirmative role in this connection. Though a one-party system was organized in the South primarily to maintain white supremacy, the resulting unity strengthened the South in the national arena. This strength was not always used for the common good, naturally, but at times it was.*

Meanwhile, economic conditions remained poor for the mass of people. Unorganized workers and small farmers were struggling with high interest rates, large debts, and depressed incomes. The Republican Administrations in the early years of the century fostered very few economic policies which promoted their welfare.

Liberals, wearying of the theoretical laissez-faire pleas of the conservatives, continued to urge positive action. People were crying out for change. Their hopes were renewed by the turn of events in New Jersey, where Governor Woodrow Wilson, a transplanted Virginian, was attracting nationwide attention as a progressive governor. (A Southerner had not been elected President since James K. Polk.) Handsome, articulate, and liberal, Wilson appealed to the progressives of the South. Liberals in the South were happy with the opportunity to support a man of his eminence and one who was "a winner"; they provided enthusiastic support for his nomination.

To make it sweeter, the Wilson Administration started off with a distinctive Southern coloration. Five members of his cabinet were born in the South, and Southern Congressional delegations were in a position to play a strong part in his leg-

---

* Within the Democratic Party, it should be remembered, the South had a veto on nominations for President, by virtue of the two-thirds rule which existed for many years in the Democratic National Convention. Unable to nominate a candidate on its own, it could prevent nominations. This power was nearly always consciously exploited by the conservatives to protect the status quo in the South and was at times a deciding factor in Democratic nominations. The federal action inherent in "new federalism" was denounced by the conservatives as federal intervention, or at least an implicit threat of federal intervention.

islative program since many Southern senators and congressmen were chairmen of important Congressional committees. Moreover, a few of these chairmen had been agrarian radicals in the 1880s and were attuned to Wilson's program of antitrust action, banking regulations, tariff reduction, and farm reform programs. But other Southern legislators of conservative commitment, urged on by their financial and political supporters, began to muscle in. President Wilson and his lieutenants found themselves reluctantly compromising with the Southern conservatives and neglecting the liberal factions which had been instrumental in giving him the nomination and election. Southern conservatives, observed the biographer Douglas S. Freeman a few years later, had "a disconcerting way of conquering their conquerors." Their adroitness and callousness were illustrated by their facility in raising and exploiting spurious issues designed to divert public attention from more pressing social and economic problems.

But the most obvious political development in the South attendant upon Wilson's election was a change in the character and position of the two political parties. Democratic Party leaders, despite their conservative inclination, *had* to compromise with Wilson, and Wilson, in turn, was forced to compromise with them. This had a democratizing effect upon the Southern power structure, and moved it closer to the mainstream of American political life.

However, World War I soon darkened the skies and lessened the chances that the progressive forces might establish a democratic, liberal program of social action on the home front. Southerners—conservative and liberal like—supported the war enthusiastically, true to the historic pattern and traditions of the South. On the battlefield, the famed and indomitable 29th Dixie division once again wrote chapters of valor, stirring Southern pride and patriotism.

But as the war wore on and casualties mounted, the "War Party" brand once again was burned upon the Democrats—even in the South. "He got us into the war," they said of Wilson, especially in the Southern hills. After the Armistice, this antiwar sentiment grew, and the Democrats were in trouble. Wilson's bad health, the disruption of the economy, the uncertainty of national politics, the continuing bitterness about our involvement in a European war and our great losses—all of these things spelled danger. Though most political observers at the time of the Armistice thought Wilson was a triumphant hero as he courageously journeyed to Europe and put forward his peace proposals, trouble was brewing at home, especially among Republican senators. It was not entirely surprising, therefore, that the Republican victory which elected Warren G. Harding was sweeping. In Tennessee, for example, a Republican was elected governor. Even Cordell Hull, later to become Roosevelt's Secretary of State, was swept out of his Congressional seat.

The free rein given business and financial interests during the Harding and Coolidge Administrations brought riches to some and ruin to others, but the Republican goose was hanging high. Without consumer protection, corporate regulation, or even a concerned public, the people fell victim to the rapaciousness of special interests. Times were hard throughout the South generally, but the old cotton areas were worst off. The agricultural depression set in early, and many farmers who had borrowed excessively under the stimulus of increased demand for food and fiber during the war now found themselves encumbered by high mortgages and falling prices —brought on by excess production and dwindling markets. The South was heavily dependent on foreign markets and these were beginning to dissipate under high tariffs. This hit hard at the South which exported half its cotton production, half its phosphate, and one third its tobacco. Prices fell to depressing lows. Southern farm boys left in droves for Detroit and Akron and Chicago and Cleveland—any place to find a job. Farm land fell in value, just as did farm commodities, and many mortgages were foreclosed. Eastern financial institutions, particularly insurance companies, were large holders of farm mortgages, and they now became large holders of farm land. The disastrous national depression that later followed the 1929 stock-market crash was more of the same for the South, only worse, since it had suffered depressed conditions for almost ten years.

It was during these uncertain, constantly difficult times that I grew to young manhood, struggling for a college education, alternating between working at odd jobs, teaching in rural schools, and attending the University of Tennessee and what is now Middle Tennessee State University. My salary as a teacher in 1926 was $75 per calendar month, and I was considered fortunate. This was my "Prosperity" during the period of "Normalcy."

I must admit that I became a political activist very early. Since childhood I had dreamed of being a lawyer, and maybe even a successful politician, and I never allowed this dream to dim for very long. In any event, I was electioneering against Herbert Hoover before I was old enough to vote.

Al Smith, a big-city Catholic and an advocate of the repeal of prohibition, was unappealing in the South, except that he was a Democrat. But I was for him and I worked hard for his election in my local county. When a visiting congressman came to speak at the little high school of which I was principal, I introduced him and thus made my first political speech for Al Smith.

Religion was the really hot issue. I recall going to the county seat to hear a Baptist preacher speak in the court-house. There were so many people I could barely get in. He spoke of Romanism and Rum, War, and Ruin. "Normalcy" was still the magic word: in my community this meant "no war, no rum" (legal, that is), and "no Catholic in the White House." Hoover carried Tennessee. Though Hoover did not do very well in the Deep South, particularly in the rural areas, in the uplands and in the backwoods areas, nevertheless sentiment had shifted heavily toward the Republican ticket.

Hoover's election was a source of great rejoicing to conservative elements throughout the country, even in the South, despite its economic plight. Hands-off Republican policies had been confirmed. The economy was in the hands of its despoilers. The stock market and the speculators went wild. But the pliant Hoover Administration soon proved to be an economic disaster.

In the panic that followed the 1929 crash, my father, who had become uneasy about his small savings and had scattered them in deposits in three small neighboring banks, lost every penny as all three banks closed at the same time. Fortunately, my father had paid off the mortgage on his farm, but even though he was debt-free, there was no money for family needs. I helped him drive livestock from the pasture to the corral for shipment to Nashville. Alas, the livestock did not sell for even enough to pay the trucking bill! I made a crop of tobacco that year and received $89 for my entire year's work. So I, too, went job-hunting to towns in Tennessee and to the Northern cities. Finally I found one driving a peddling truck, selling used and cheap new furniture, stoves, linoleum rugs, and now and then a radio, or swapping a radio for an organ. My salary was $12.50 per week. My favorite meal at the city café was Mrs. White's homemade vegetable soup.

With the fury of a raging storm, the Depression and panic swept the entire country, growing worse by the day. Nothing was spared—nothing and nobody: bankruptcies, bank closings, failures, suicides, locked doors, joblessness, bread lines. Hoover repeatedly predicted that prosperity was just around the corner, and this became a laughingstock as conditions grew worse and worse.

When Franklin D. Roosevelt came upon the scene, I, along with many others of my time and nearly all my friends saw him as the leader we needed to bring about a new deal for the whole country, and especially for the dispossessed. Jubilant over the opportunity to support him, I helped organize Young Democratic Clubs in my county and in surrounding counties, and I exulted in the battle because I felt the country needed a change from our terrible economic hardships.

A political revolution was clearly in the wind; change was demanded even in the South. The race question, so far as I recall, was scarcely mentioned throughout the 1928 campaign. Blacks were still Republicans. And besides, the people were preoccupied with their economic plight, with bread and meat and rent and jobs—a chance to live—and they wanted a new deal. The election of Franklin D. Roosevelt rolled like an irresistible tide.

CHAPTER II

My South Changes

MARCH CAME none too soon in 1933. Several friends and I gathered around the radio in the barbershop in Carthage and heard Franklin Roosevelt declare, "All we have to fear is fear itself." The strength of that matchless voice and the confidence and determination in his words seemed to reach to every part of our community and to awaken hope where none had been. The call for action fell on willing ears, and the South, like the rest of the nation, eagerly awaited its orders to move forward. The Harding-Coolidge-Hoover dry spell had been a long one, and it had brought the area—and the nation —close to economic collapse and revolution. Desperate fears of further economic ruin plus a frightening amount of political ferment threw even the Bourbon politicians into the arms of the New Deal, at least temporarily. Indeed, during the early days of the New Deal it seemed that the South would finally become a full-fledged participant in our national life. Except for the upper crust, who whispered reservations, and the few remaining hard-shell Republicans, the South embraced the Roosevelt programs. Among my acquaintances, enthusiasm was deep and genuine. The populism of the late nineteenth century had not been stamped out in the South, certainly not in the Tennessee hills where my family lived. And Roosevelt capitalized on these roots of social justice. He nourished them on pure water and cheap electricity—and they quickly sprouted.

The Roosevelt landslide had brought an unprecedented Democratic majority to Congress (313 Democrats, 117 Republicans, and 5 Independents in the House of Representatives; in the Senate there were 59 Democrats). These large majorities gave swift and overwhelming approval to the Roosevelt program in the first one hundred days of the Congress. The South played a key role because the one-party system of the South and the seniority rule in Congress had placed Southerners in important positions as chairmen of the committees and in party leadership posts in both House and Senate.

Early in 1933, Democrats in the House of Representatives established a steering committee to push through the vital measures that Roosevelt had requested. During the First Session of the Seventy-third Congress, bills were brought to the floor under a "closed rule" ten times. A "closed rule" prohibits any congressman from making amendments to a bill and limits the time for debate on it, which means that the members vote on the bill without change, yea or nay. Nearly all of the early New Deal economic measures were presented to the

House in this gag-rule fashion, and under the prevailing circumstances there was little practical political choice for congressmen but to pass them. This kind of undemocratic procedure, even when used in an emergency, is questionable because it prevents the collective judgment and will of Congress from being applied during the legislative process and stifles any opportunity to improve the laws. (Later, after the powerful Rules Committee became dominated by conservative Democrats, I saw this procedure used to stymie the programs of both Roosevelt and Truman.) Yet under the circumstances, it was accepted not only by congressmen but by the people as well. In my area, the hill country of the South, there was scant patience with Roosevelt's few critics, especially among Democrats.

At about this time, I was elected county superintendent of education in small, rural Smith County, Tennessee. County warrants (checks) for teachers' salaries and school supplies were nonnegotiable for cash. I remember one young teacher who regularly sold his salary warrant of $100 for $60 cash. I managed to remedy this, but many, many other things were completely out of my reach. At school after school, I saw suffering and need among the children of destitute parents. Still, there was a ray of hope among those parents and I shared it—we had faith in the leadership of the new Administration.

In Congress, there was a readiness to take action, even to surrender much that had been regarded as cherished prerogatives of the legislative branch. Many would later regret this shift of power to the executive branch, but under the stress of the times, the Congress appeared even more anxious and unorthodox than Roosevelt. Far from favoring the business and banking interests (as Congress had done during the "normalcy" period of the Harding-Coolidge-Hoover era), the new Congress was ready to approve an income-tax amendment requiring the publication of income, to pass the TVA Act and the National Industrial Recovery Act, to grant authority to devalue the dollar, and to abandon the gold standard. Above all, congressmen and senators were eager to relieve economic distress and to support programs designed to stimulate the economy. People desperately wanted work, so the Congress enacted bills to create jobs. "Our greatest primary task," Roosevelt said, "is to put people to work." The Works Progress Administration provided welcome relief not only for laborers but for unemployed artists, teachers, writers, and even technically trained people. (In my home county, I sponsored a WPA project to level the high-school football field by pick and shovel. Incredible as it may now seem, the playing field, atop a clay hill, was some eight feet lower on the "down-hill-drag" corner. [That was our favorite touchdown corner.] Dirt-moving machinery may have been more economical, but we did not have the machinery and the real purpose of the project was to provide jobs for destitute people while also accomplishing something of value.) Many a proud man stood in line to get these menial jobs because their families were in need. Other Administration programs, like the Civilian Conservation Corps and the National Youth Administration, provided needed relief for the young.

Naturally, there was the usual amount of local politics involved in these programs. For example, the powerful political organization in my state (then headed by "Boss" Ed Crump and his lieutenant, Tennessee's senior senator, Kenneth D. McKellar) had exclusive control over the numerous managerial, supervisory, and clerical job appointments. These were choice plums then, and political obligations were the pits—as I was later to learn.

The New Deal had barely begun before the Bourbons started to desert it. Southern opposition congealed around the conservative business interests and the politicians who catered to them. The Southern States Industrial Council, a sort of Southern carbon copy of the National Association of Manufacturers, became an early focus. This curious organization was composed of many of the ultraconservative financial and business interests who had wielded power in the South since the Redemption. These men called themselves "Southern Democrats" or "Jeffersonian Democrats" or "States' Rights Democrats," thus drawing the important distinction between sectional and national party loyalty.

The first object of their ire was the National Industrial Recovery Act, in particular its proposal to modify the wage differential between North and South. To explain: hourly wages in the textile industry in the North were 38.5 per cent higher than in the South, and immediately after the imposition in 1933 of the NRA's textile code, this difference was reduced to 15.9 per cent, thus lowering Southern profits. Other improvements in wage and working conditions advanced by Roosevelt also brought opposition from council members. In 1934, for example, Roosevelt announced his intention to retain the principles of collective bargaining, minimum wages, and the ban against child labor.

At the Southern States Industrial Council meeting in Birmingham in 1934, the industrialists planned a resistance to the fair-wage policies for Southern industry. One of the speakers went so far as to hint at another act of "secession" if the wage differentials between the North and South were eliminated. The *Chattanooga Times* reported:

Applause greeted Theodore Swann, a Birmingham chemical manufacturer, when he said: "Sherman's march to the sea was no more destructive than the NRA is going to be to the South. Before it is over, we may have secession." W. D. Moore, president of the American Cast Iron Pipe Company here said: "Only by combined and unified efforts can we stem the tide that is running against the Southland today."

Later in the year, the council met in Chattanooga and announced opposition to the collective-bargaining provisions being discussed for the National Labor Relations Board, and any minimum wage provisions.

I myself became concerned as to what future course the South and my state would take when many politicians and business leaders in Tennessee withdrew their support of Roosevelt after the 1932–1933 crisis seemed to have safely passed. A number of Southern political leaders began to shift their support to the reactionary businessmen with their narrow viewpoints and their quite irrational opposition to any Roosevelt proposal. The comments made and actions taken not only by businessmen but by newspaper editors and community leaders during the Chattanooga meeting of the SSIC were characteristic. They spoke of new Southern opportunities but warned against government "competition" and expressed the fear that the Roosevelt trend toward more active government participation in the marketplace would ruin the South. The average Southern businessman or industrial leader, it seemed, all too often associated Southern progress with the continued impoverishment of labor. The exploitation of labor, whether slave or free, has been one of the constants in orthodox "Southern-conservative" psychology and philosophy throughout our history.

The council adopted a report demanding continued wage

differentials between North and South. Southern labor must be kept free from the influence of union organizers—free, in the language of the report, from disturbances by "professional activities of outside agitators." How up-to-date that sounds! Speakers demeaned Southern labor, holding (according to William B. Hesseltine in *The South in American History*) that the "inferior workmen" of the South justified and necessitated a lower wage in the South than in the North or East. (Bear in mind that these business and community "leaders" were talking about *white* Southerners, for Southern industry then had virtually no place for blacks.) The Council proposed a "subnormal" weekly wage of $9.50 for men, $8.00 for women, and $6.00 for children. A child was thought to be worth two thirds as much as a man in the textile mills, and perhaps he was.

Southern politicians who catered to these business interests took up the chant: "low wages" and "continued wage differentials." They backed owners and managers right down the line in their fierce resistance to union organization of the mills, and they provided steady opposition to the passage of minimum-wage laws. In Georgia, striking workers were thrown into virtual concentration camps by Governor Eugene Talmadge. Yet only a few of the politicians who cheered these actions openly fought Roosevelt's other domestic programs in 1934. (One who did was Virginia's Senator Carter Glass, who called the New Deal "an utterly dangerous effort of the federal government to transplant Hitlerism into every corner of the nation.") Still, many of them were disturbed. And no wonder. They were closely allied to large financial interests, and had not Roosevelt said, "the measure of the restoration lies in the extent to which we apply social values more noble than mere monetary profits"?

At any rate, by 1935 the Southern States Industrial Council had grown bolder, and it held a well-attended dinner in Washington, D.C., about which *The New York Times* reported on April 2:

"The Southland since its birth has placed moral and spiritual values above mere economics and is still unwilling to sacrifice them," John E. Edgerton, president of the Southern States Industrial Council, told an audience of Southern Congress members and their guests here tonight at the Council's annual dinner. "Whether ours is the best blood, the best language, the only God and the soundest basic philosophy is a matter which others have been granted a right to, and may, dispute," Mr. Edgerton drawled amid applause. "We think they are, and so strongly do we think so that we are not willing to trade any of them. That does not mean that we will not at all times welcome into our midst any other of whatever race or creed who come with peace in their hearts and high purpose in their souls to help us with the self-compensating tasks that belong to a free and progressive people." He declared that communistic and socialistic missionaries "have come among us" and "have told of how unprogressive we are."

But this time, Southern labor fought back and—with national leaders who did not desert them as the Populist leaders had done some forty years earlier—they began to make some solid gains. Federal legislation, particularly the National Labor Relations Act of 1935 and the Fair Labor Standards Act of 1938, encouraged both unionization and a fair wage.

Although Southern opposition to the Roosevelt domestic program mounted among Bourbon politicians, they continued to support his foreign program, which retained almost solid approval in the South. In fact, some of his strongest and most unwavering support for foreign trade was found there, where increased exports of cotton and tobacco alleviated economic conditions and brought acclaim for the Cordell Hull Reciprocal Trade Program. After watching the South's foreign markets dry up during the 1920s, Southern leaders, including Hull (my fellow townsman and political mentor), had reached a consensus on a solution. Hull, acting under the new authority of the Reciprocal Trade Agreement Act which he had sponsored as Secretary of State, began to negotiate some trade agreements with Latin American countries. As a result, U.S. exports to those countries quickly jumped an amazing 40 per cent. This alone was enough to guarantee support for the Roosevelt-Hull foreign program in the South.

In fact, most Southerners favored a more aggressive foreign policy in all areas, and as Roosevelt moved during his second term to play a stronger hand against Germany and Japan, his support in the South even grew, just as it diminished in some other parts of the country, especially in the Middle West. Historically sympathetic to Great Britain, militant in tradition, and all too often self-righteous, many Southerners were eager to demonstrate the superiority of the United States, and they were ready for World War II long before Pearl Harbor. (In his first term, President Roosevelt had been slow to cooperate with Britain and France, and he didn't seem very impressed with the need for checking Hitler. Secretary Hull, for his part, was interested in international relations but more from a domestic and economic point of view. This is understandable, I believe, given the plight of the American economy in the early days of the New Deal. In any case, this order of priorities had met with popular approval.)

Roosevelt did not do very much to ease the social plight of the Negro in his first term, either. He sent no civil-rights bills to Congress. The concept of a fair employment practices commission was talked about—enough to anathematize it in the South—but not until 1941 did the President finally establish it, and then by executive order. The military forces remained segregated (with the Negro largely relegated to labor battalions in the Army and messboy in the Navy), and segregation was still practiced in much of the federal bureaucracy. In the South particularly, there was little economic opportunity for the Negro except in the most menial of jobs.

One can say, in fact, that Roosevelt was tender-footed about any question involving racism. He did not even recommend an antilynching bill. As a politician, he realized that he had to have the legislative help of Southerners to enact his economic reform programs—which were his top priorities.

> I did not choose the tools with which I must work. Had I been permitted to choose them I would have selected quite different ones. But I've got to get legislation passed by Congress to save America. Southerners, by reason of the seniority rule in Congress, are chairmen or occupy strategic places on most of the Senate and House committees. If I come out for the antilynching bill now, they will block every bill I ask Congress to pass to keep America from collapsing. I just can't take that risk.*

For the life of me, I could never understand why congressmen and senators opposed an antilynching bill, yet the very suggestion of it threw many Southern politicians into a tantrum. I never believed that such an attitude could please more than a craven few, but this minority was vocal and powerful.

Though Roosevelt was slow in openly identifying himself with Negro projects and programs, he was quietly working to change the attitude of the federal government toward the

*Walter White, *A Man Called White* (New York: The Viking Press, 1948), pp. 169–70.

Negro. By 1936, a "Black Cabinet" of Negro advisers contained over thirty members, including Robert Weaver and Mrs. Mary McLeod Bethune. The moral leadership for racial justice was furnished by Mrs. Eleanor Roosevelt, the dynamic wife of the President.

The Negro in the South began to undergo changes in attitude that were at once obvious and subtle. As his economic opportunity improved, he began to switch his (then relatively few) votes to Roosevelt and the Democratic Party. But more important, I believe, he began to change his attitude toward himself. This is, of course, a difficult process to chronicle. Perhaps it all began with the arrival of the boll weevil. Strange as that sounds, there is strong evidence that that much maligned insect did almost as much to emancipate the Negro as Lincoln.

The boll weevil first appeared in Texas in 1892, and by 1923 it had blanketed the cotton South. Entire areas of the old cotton kingdom were wiped out—abandoned. And as the fields were abandoned, so was a way of life. Sharecroppers and tenant farmers began to move off the land and into urban centers. At first the Negro drifted toward Southern cities such as Richmond, Atlanta, Memphis, and New Orleans. During World War I, many had moved north when jobs opened up in defense industries. Then the Depression accelerated this move from the land. Going from bad to worse, the Negro (as well as the poor white) began to prepare himself for social change. By the early 1940s, mostly because of pressure from black leaders like A. Philip Randolph, but also out of a genuine sympathy for the oppressed, Roosevelt began to give direction and force to that change. And when it became apparent that a vast social reorganization was destined to occur, the power structure of the South, once again failing its leadership responsibility, vigorously resisted it.

Roosevelt gradually offered firmer moral leadership through those desperate years. I think we are often inclined to underestimate the crucial importance of leadership in a democracy. In virgin democratic theory, every man is his own master and makes up his own mind about issues, candidates, and ideologies. But in actual practice, we act in groups. We are members of a club, a church, a lodge, a union, a political faction or party. Thus politics has become the art of manipulating groups in order to accumulate political power. In such a pluralistic system, leadership is essential. Without it, the individual flounders in a sea of meaningless choices.

There was a crying need for strong leadership in the South, but most of the "leaders" were heading in the wrong direction, caring more about exploitation of both poor white and poor black. Even the best of these were often reduced to the lowest common denominator of racism—in all its subtle and not so subtle ramifications. Most Southern politicians—progressive and conservative alike—felt compelled to holler "Nigger" from time to time, and to align themselves with the conservative establishment and thus support exploitation of lower-income groups. But Roosevelt embodied hope for all poor people, and this hope may have been more important in the long run than the proposal of civil-rights bills, which, during the New Deal would not have survived a Senate filibuster anyway. In response to Roosevelt's appeal, blacks flocked to the Democratic Party even more rapidly than they moved north.

The Congressional elections of 1934 were an overwhelming endorsement, an overwhelming mandate for Roosevelt. In the House, the Democratic total increased from 313 to 322 while the number of Republicans declined to 103. In the Senate, the Democrats gained 9 seats for a total of 69 while the

Republican number declined to 25. The popularity of Roosevelt with the great mass of the people was greater than ever, and many congressmen, fearful of losing their places on his coattail, once again clambered behind him. The winning elements were the same as they had been in 1932—hope of recovery from the economic Depression, affection for Roosevelt, and confidence in his leadership.

This result was not surprising to me. As state campaign manager of Congressman Gordon Browning's unsuccessful race for the United States Senate in 1934, I learned firsthand about Roosevelt's hold on the people. Yet when the new Congress convened, strong opposition developed. A small group of Democratic senators, not all of them Southerners but largely influenced by Southerners, had come to consider the New Deal "radical." These included Senators Carter Glass and Harry Byrd of Virginia, Thomas Gore of Oklahoma, Josiah Bailey of North Carolina, and Millard Tydings of Maryland. (There were other Southern senators and congressmen, such as Hatton Sumners of Texas, Howard Smith of Virginia, Edward Eugene Cox of Georgia, who opposed the New Deal from time to time, but they were not so outspoken.)

Senator Glass was a small, peppery gentleman, who had published a newspaper in Virginia before coming to the Senate. Scarcely anything about the New Deal pleased Glass. He gave his first outburst against Roosevelt when the President declared a bank holiday. Author of the Federal Reserve Bank Bill, Glass felt aggrieved enough to blast, "I think the President of the United States had no more valid authority to close or open a bank in the United States than has my stable boy—it looks to me as if Hoover carried the country to the edge of the precipice and this Administration is shoving it over as fast as it can." (The National Recovery Administration was anathema to him. He called the Blue Eagle the "Blue Buzzard.") And in 1935 he wrote, "Now is about as good a time as anybody could find to die when the country is being taken to hell as fast as a lot of uneducated fools can get it there."

Then came "Black Monday," May 27, 1935—when the Supreme Court delivered a series of opinions against the New Deal, chief among them the decision that struck down the NRA by unanimous vote. Angered, Roosevelt hit back hard, denouncing the Court for taking the country back to "horse and buggy days." Not content with mere rhetoric, he launched a new legislative and programmatic initiative, which came to be called the "Second New Deal." While the first New Deal had dealt largely with agricultural and industrial recovery, the Second New Deal initiated an economic-planning and reform phase, not only economic planning for the future, but more democratic taxes and more regulation and discipline of big capitalism in order to preserve and stimulate small business and new initiatives. The most controversial issue, and easily the most divisive one in the Democratic Party, was a tax proposal which the President had previously refused to recommend but now turned to with zest. It included a graduated corporation income tax, a steep increase in the inheritance tax, an intercorporate dividend tax, an increased surtax on large personal incomes, and a gift tax on fortunes. (Shades of McGovern in 1972!)

This, of course, raised the hackles of the rich and of big business. Their long-held suspicions of "that man in the White House" were confirmed. Roosevelt had said in his annual message in January 1935, that, "in spite of our efforts and in spite of our talk, we have not weeded out the over-privileged and we have not effectively lifted up the under-privileged." While such messages "set up goals in human terms that the average man could grasp for," as John Gunther described it, it was maddening to those who squirmed but at the same time felt satisfied with the description of "overprivileged."

The wealthy elite in the South were further infuriated when the President made a speech about the "pseudo" society of the South: "When you come right down to it, there is little difference between the feudal system and the fascist system; if you believe in one you lean to the other." As if this were not enough, he soon spoke again in even more determined tones: "It is my conviction," he said, "that the South presents right now the nation's number one economic problem—the nation's problem, not merely the South's." Of course, the President was speaking the truth, but it was not at all what conservative Southerners wanted to hear.

Another highly controversial measure, strongly opposed by the private utility interests, was the Utility Holding Company Bill, one section of which their lobbyists labeled the "death sentence." The country had been shocked by disclosures of the involved and corrupt corporation holding-company operations of Samuel Insull of Chicago. Moreover, high electric-power rates aroused popular anger with the private power "trusts" who had fought against the TVA and, generally, against all New Deal measures. Wendell Willkie, president of the Commonwealth and Southern Corporation, had been particularly active in this regard. And opposition to these economic measures brought to the surface still more anti-New Deal senators and congressmen—notably Senator Walter George of Georgia, Congressman George Huddleston of Alabama, Senator "Cotton" Ed Smith of South Carolina, and others. These dissidents combined with Republicans to give the President a very tough time on these two measures.

Senator George, a dignified, eloquent, and forceful Southerner, was rapidly growing in power and prestige in the Senate. He was unabashed in his acknowledgment of his closeness
to "business interests in Georgia." Reputedly, his closest
friends and political supporters were officials of the powerful
Coca-Cola Company and of the Georgia Power Company.
Later, I served in the Senate with Senator George and I never
heard anyone express any doubt about his affinity with big-
business interests. In any event, in 1935 he found both the
Roosevelt tax program and the Utility Holding Bill extremely objectionable, and—one of the most powerful orators
of the Senate—he spoke against them with great vigor and
effectiveness.

All of this opposition created a great deal of speculation
about Roosevelt's political fortunes in the 1936 election. Perhaps there was never any prospect of a serious test—at least, I
never thought so—but if there had been, the Republican
nomination of the lack-luster Alf Landon completely dissi-
pated it. Roosevelt, running serenely on his past record and
his personality, scarcely mentioning his opponent, solidifying
his position with the mass of whites, and broadening the
Democratic base in an outright appeal to the blacks—
"Among American citizens there should be no forgotten men
and no forgotten races"—was re-elected by a landslide,
swamping Landon and carrying every state except Maine and
Vermont.

Perhaps the 1936 campaign's most remarkable factor was
not so much the unprecedented majority as it was the awakening of a political conscience in millions of people who had
previously been more or less indifferent to national politics,
and, perhaps most significant of all in the long run, the now
decisive switch of blacks from the Republican to the Demo-

cratic Party. This held a vast portent not only for the future of the New Deal and the Fair Deal, but also for all future Southern and national political struggles.

In 1936, I strongly supported the campaign of my friend Gordon Browning, this time a successful candidate for governor of Tennessee, and after the election I was oppointed to the position of commissioner of labor in Browning's cabinet. This brought me into closer contact with labor and business throughout Tennessee, and it broadened my contacts in other states, too. One of my responsibilities was the inauguration of the unemployment-compensation program that had been enacted by the state in response to the National Unemployment Act. This took me to Washington from time to time and into contact with the Roosevelt Administration. The current controversy at that time was the Fair Labor Standards Bill (the minimum-wage law), introduced in the House in May 1937. It was evident from the beginning that there was little Southern support for the bill in 1937, even though it was sponsored by a Southerner, Senator Hugo Black.

After a tortuous committee course, the bill was hotly fought on the floor of the House. Representative Eugene Cox, conservative Democrat of Georgia, spoke vigorously against it: "The passage of this measure is the worst thing that could take place at this time. It would throw a million out of work." Represenative Martin Dies of Texas went further. "There is a racial question involved here," he said to a chorus of rebel yells from the floor. "Under this measure what is prescribed for one race must be prescribed for the other. And you cannot prescribe the same wage for the black man as for the white man."

The Southern States Industrial Council, following its accustomed pattern, waged a determined fight against the bill.

It passed a resolution in an Atlanta meeting which stated that it was not only "economically unsound" but would "throttle industry." Though the bill only provided for a minimum wage of 25¢ per hour, to be stepped up in three years to 40¢, it suffered recommittal by a strong vote. Of the 99 Southern representatives voting, 81 voted to recommit the bill, which meant that the bill was dead for 1937. But Roosevelt was not content to lose this fight. The bill was brought up again in 1938, and this time it passed by a large majority, finally becoming effective on October 24, 1938. And there is no record to show that it "throttled" industry. (The same arguments were still used against another raise in minimum wages in July 1972.)

Despite growing opposition, the feeling of the South at that time, as I caught it, was one of growing confidence that we could solve our problems with a man of will and action in the White House. For my own part, I exulted in the search for solutions and longed for an opportunity to go to Washington and have a part in the great drama. My chance came when, early in 1938, the congressman from my district, J. R. Mitchell announced his candidacy for the United States Senate. Immediately, I announced mine for Congress and resigned as commissioner of labor to begin my campaign, only to find the "federal crowd" opposing me, on a factional basis, because of my support of Governor Browning. But after a vigorous campaign I won anyway—and by a good margin—in the Democratic primary. In the general election I was unopposed.

I recall one incident of the campaign with respect to the Wage and Hour Law. During the course of the primary a businessman and leading citizen in Marshall County, Tennessee, befriended me and gave me active political support. After my nomination in August, I was invited to speak at the Rotary

Club in his county seat, where he introduced me quite generously, saying I would be a "sound, safe representative, avoiding the wild-eyed schemes of the New Deal." He particularly pointed out the Fair Labor Standards Bill as one of those "unwise schemes" that would hurt the South. He called upon me to explain "in the course of [my] remarks" how I would effectively oppose such measures. What a spot I was in! I was not opposed to such measures as the minimum wage. I did the best I could, what with the tender sensibilities of my friend, but my remarks were very disappointing to him and I don't think he ever quite forgave me. (Later, he opposed me when I ran for the Senate.)

It was in this same year that Roosevelt, in his only real effort to eliminate his opposition within the Democratic Party, undertook to purge Senators George, Tydings, and Smith. This unsuccessful attempt aroused bitter sectional resentment, and I felt its influence in my own campaign. But strangely enough, it was not in any way harmful to me because it tended to weaken the influence of the federal jobholders who had been brought to bear against me by the Crump-McKellar forces. This was ironic, because my deepest political commitment was to ease the plight of the very people for whom the Roosevelt programs were aimed. But such were the factional politics of the day.

Job patronage was then an index of political power and the control of this patronage in state after state had a profound influence in sustaining the loyalty of party leaders—perhaps more so in the South than elsewhere because for so many people there—tenant farmers, Negroes, and badly paid office workers—a New Deal job offered the first real hope they had had to escape the misery of the long Depression. It was widely reported that when Roosevelt took office, 50 per cent of his mail concerned jobs. Though Southern politicians might have ideological qualms about the New Deal or might have strong ties to the business leaders who were so decidedly antagonistic to it, the urge to be the distributor of these sought-after jobs and projects held many of them in line. "States' rights," always a rallying cry for the do-nothings or the defenders of the status quo, seemed less important in the Depression than jobs and developmental assistance. Roosevelt needed Southern Congressional support, and he knew perfectly well the power of patronage and did not hesitate to use it. At times, this practice served to entrench the conservatives and hamper liberals. Yet, as Dewey Grantham writes in his excellent book, *Democratic South,* "if the New Deal did not dislodge those who dominated the power structure of the South, it threatened them as they had never been threatened before." This was a truly dangerous dilemma for Southern conservatives—a dilemma that was further exacerbated by Northern Democrats, and the increasing activities of civil-rights organizations, and organized labor, which had come to great power through the patronage of Roosevelt.

As a new congressman from the hill country of Tennessee, proud of my independence, I thought the New Deal had gone too far in some respects and, also, from a strictly personal angle (which I now realize I should not have considered), I was irked because the "federal crowd" in charge of the WPA and other federal programs in Tennessee had used questionable tactics against me. For further aggravation, the public housing administrator, Nathan Straus, gave me condescendingly short shrift, if not downright rude treatment, when I asked some critical questions about a public housing bill before my committee. This led to my first invitation to the White House. I had heard many reports about Roosevelt's charm and ingratiating manner, about his knack of being jocular with those who opposed him. It was reported that even an old recalcitrant, such as Carter Glass, sometimes melted under Roosevelt's charm. Senator Kenneth McKellar of Tennessee said, "Yet [when] he is called in, the President calls him Carter and it is a delight to hear them talk to each other. They are both fine at repartee, and the utmost good humor has always prevailed when I have seen them together." According to one anecdote I had heard in the Congressional cloakroom about Roosevelt and Glass, they were riding together to some ceremony in Roanoke, Virginia, when the President said, "Carter, for once I have you going along with me." "Yes, Franklin," Glass retorted, "for once you are going in the right direction."

I went to the White House with my new briefcase full of documents, ready to explain to President Roosevelt what was basically wrong with his Public Housing Bill. I reached for it a time or two but never even got it opened, as the President talked about everything else but the Public Housing Bill. He was gay and amusing and then eloquent. He wished, he said, to maintain a balance in government and that the government act as a benevolent arbiter of conflicting interests, but, most of all, he dreamed of relieving small farmers, field hands, and workers from the desperate economic conditions of their lives. He expressed the view, which I had never heard before, that eventually we would come to have an annual wage and full employment. This was such music to the ears of a young Populist from Tennessee that after the meeting was over, a Presidential aide accommodatingly retrieved the briefcase I had left behind in the Oval Room.

Because of faulty concepts, such as eligibility restricted to those of steady and substantial income, I led a successful fight

against the Housing Bill. But very soon I became quite un-
comfortable with the coalition that opposed it, composed as it
was of irreconcilable Southerners, a few moderate Democrats,
and nearly all the Republicans. There was surely no secret
about the coalition. It had a bipartisan high command, and
it operated quite effectively in obstructing progress in both
House and Senate. This was not where I belonged and I soon
became independent of it.

Although Roosevelt's economic issues stirred the deepest
resentments in the House of Representatives, there were
other divisive issues, too: the court-packing bill, his attempt
to purge Senators George and Tydings, etc. These had contributed to a bitterness about the New Deal which, I discovered upon my arrival in Washington in January 1939, had
hardened considerably since 1937, when I first had had contacts there. Unfortunately, it also had taken the taint of sectionalism.

Being "against" Roosevelt became a popular national pas-
time for conservatives. No parlor conversation was complete
without a gibe at "that man in the White House." In the
South, it was only natural that the opposition to him might
coalesce around the idea that Roosevelt was an enemy to "the
Southern way of life." Such a coalition, although much discussed, never took place; the majority of the voters remained
with Roosevelt. A Tennessean who came back from Europe
because of the Spanish Civil War, found that wherever she
went she was exposed to condemnations of Roosevelt and
what "he's doing to the South." She asked, "But who's *for*
him?" "Nobody," she was told. "Then who voted for him?"
she asked. "Everybody," she was quickly assured.

The war in Europe was increasingly threatening, and the
popular attitude toward Mussolini, Hitler, and Tojo was in-

creasingly hostile. Roosevelt turned his attention to the war, and moved to aid Great Britain and France while preserving the forms of neutrality. This softened his opposition in the South, where sympathy for Great Britain was particularly strong and where many professed a ready belligerency. Then, too, production of war supplies improved economic conditions, and this helped to ameliorate Southern discontent with Roosevelt.

In February 1940, Administration leaders asked me to make the lead-off speech on the second day of debate on a bill to repeal the arms embargo. I felt as if they were exploiting my independent status and my closeness to my fellow townsman Secretary Hull, but I leaped at the opportunity nonetheless. The point I tried to make was that provision of aid to Great Britain would strengthen our own defense. I found in later years that tying our own defense to aid for our traditional allies had strong appeal to my Scotch-Irish Southern hill-country constituents.

After the 1940 election,* inflation became a serious threat. I took a part in the government's efforts to control inflation and through my work, established a warm relationship with Roosevelt, whom I had come to admire extravagantly. (Incidentally, the way in which he succeeded in controlling inflation of prices, wages, and interest rates was remarkable, and I was later to cite his success many times in my criticism of the

---

* Roosevelt's foreign and economic policies bolstered Southern support for his renomination and re-election for the unprecedented third term, albeit over the bitter opposition of a minority. This was a disappointment to other Democratic aspirants, including James A. Farley, the powerful chairman of the Democratic National Committee, and Secretary Hull. There had been much talk of Hull for President, a position he earnestly desired, and then later there was talk of him for Vice-President, but he did not wish to be nominated for the Vice-Presidency and authorized me to convey this sentiment to the convention in Chicago.

high interest rates that prevailed in the Johnson and Nixon Administrations.)

When the war finally broke upon us, the whole country unified in support of the war effort, no one section more solidly or more enthusiastically than the South. Leaving aside its global and military consequences, the war's effects on the South were far-reaching. The pool of excess labor seemed to vanish almost overnight, as military camps sprang up in the pine barrens and industry geared up for production increases. Consumer demand grew; prosperity soared. Even so, opposition to Roosevelt's social and economic programs continued, and with talk of a fourth term for the wartime President it became more intense. But his renomination and re-election were never in question with the majority of workers, particularly those who had decent paying jobs for the first time in their lives, for they were emotionally tied to Roosevelt.

One beneficiary of the wartime economy was, of course, the Negro. His absolute and relative gains were immediate and substantial. He never again would have to return en masse to the cotton fields or to penurious domestic service. An improved economic status was now his to keep; and the Constitution, after all, was plain in its expression of the rights of citizens. The courts, under the spur of Roosevelt appointees, had begun to act more forthrightly on these issues. The "separate but equal" doctrine laid down by the Supreme Court in 1896 was being undermined by one decision after another. More and more thoughtful people, in the South as well as elsewhere, were coming to see that there was no such thing as "separate but equal." Separatism, enforced by the coercive power of government, could never produce equality. And the facts were plain to see that equal opportunities were not being given to blacks and whites. Even the physical facilities were patently and obviously unequal, and enforced separatism was rank oppression.

I drove back and forth between my homes in Tennessee and Washington quite often during my early years in the House, and I never crossed the ridge just south of Pulaski, Virginia, without noticing the physical facilities provided the public by the State of Virginia at the scenic overlook there. On top of the ridge, commanding a magnificent view of the valley, was an overlook with parking space and rest-room facilities. Down the hill at an elevation of some 100 feet less was the "colored" area, where the Negro traveler who was paying the same gasoline tax I was paying to help build and maintain the highways could park his car, look out over the valley, and use his own "separate but equal" toilets. It always seemed to me that there was a lot of symbolism, as well as plain, ordinary, everyday cruelty in that.

The sense of deep personal loss, as well as sadness, resulting from Roosevelt's death at Warm Springs, Georgia, was nationwide. Certainly, I knew, it was genuine in the South. For though many Southern political leaders, particularly those who were indebted to the conservative business groups for their political support, had grown hostile, the mass of the people never wavered in their affection. Roosevelt—glamorous, charming, inspiring and dedicated—remained the people's hero.

Succeeding Roosevelt was a task too great for almost anybody, more particularly a man of ordinary talents and background without Roosevelt's charm. But President Harry Truman was gritty and gutsy, and this attracted admiration, even in the South where his social views, such as fair-employment practices for the blacks, were widely deprecated.

Eventually, President Truman, who had always been a civil-rights supporter in the Senate, became an activist for civil-rights legislation. Where Roosevelt had been noncommittal or silent, Truman was a determined doer. This infuriated the Bourbons in the South. Not even the Korean War, though very strongly supported in the South, was sufficient to quell the furor when Truman called for enactment of a strong civil-rights program. The reaction was immediate and drastic, with threats of political reprisal loudly voiced from many quarters. Nevertheless, Truman insisted on a strong civil-rights plank in the Democratic Party platform for 1948. And then came the big convention blowup. Several delegations in whole or in part walked out—left the convention and ostensibly the Democratic Party!* The States' Rights Party, quickly dubbed "Dixiecrat" by the press, was formed with South Carolina's governor, Strom Thurmond, as its Presidential candidate.

The Dixiecrats were nothing more or less than the old Bourbon leaders of the South who believed that by "hollering nigger" and waving the flag they could once more control the Southern states. The immediate objective was not to defeat Truman—an event which they, along with most political observers, assumed would occur anyway—but to force the decision into an electoral college box while they sat on the lid. This short-term objective was not beyond possibility, nor was it foreordained to failure. Governor Thomas E. Dewey, the Republican Party nominee for President, was in a minority position; Truman looked weak, placed as he was in the shadow of

---

* The 1948 movement had almost surfaced in 1944. At the Democratic National Convention in that year there was a surge of anti-Roosevelt sentiment, and some or all the delegates from seven Southern states gave their votes to Harry Byrd in protest against Roosevelt's program. In three states, a slate of anti-Roosevelt "Democratic" electors got on the ballot.

Roosevelt; the die-hard New Dealers and the party's left wing were thumping for Henry Wallace and generally lining up for an attack from the left. So the prospects of a Dixiecrat attack from the right looked pretty good—if they could carry the "Solid South." Of course, any more lasting accomplishment by such a backward-facing splinter movement was clearly doomed to failure, but the possibility of an electoral-college imbroglio was frightening.

Fortunately, not enough Southerners were willing any longer to follow blindly this advance to the rear. Unlike the Populists of the 1890s, the Southern rank and file in 1948 had leadership at the national level that did not betray them. With a few notable exceptions, the followers of the Roosevelt-Truman political philosophy stood firm at the state level. The Dixiecrat-Bourbons had thought it would be otherwise. These little men, with Thurmond out front (the same Thurmond who has more recently changed parties once again and who has led President Nixon into ambush with his inglorious Southern Strategy), thought that once more the Southern workingman, the "red-necks," the Ku Klux Klansmen, would follow them and in the process intimidate any white politician who sought to intervene. There was, of course, no question in the minds of the Dixiecrats of their ability to continue to scare the Negro away from the polls. But these would-be betrayers of the South could not pull off their ploy. Truman received 303 electoral votes, Dewey 189, Thurmond 39, and Wallace none. Moreover, the Dixiecrats failed to hold their forces together for a long-run effort.

Most Southern politicians close to Washington took little part in the Dixiecrat movement, with the notable exceptions of Senator James Eastland and some congressmen from Mississippi, "Boss" Crump of Memphis, Tennessee, and lesser

figures scattered through the South. Many people who disagreed with Truman on the race issue were deeply loyal to
the policies which had led to economic progress under the
New Deal. So, many Southerners who basically were perhaps
white supremacists continued to support the New Deal-Fair
Deal for economic reasons and out of traditional party loyalty. Indeed, in some Southern states, particularly Tennessee,
the 1948 elections gave an impetus to liberalism and progressivism. It was in the same year that Estes Kefauver was elected
to the Senate and Gordon Browning, with whom I had been
closely associated since 1934 and who, while somewhat on the
conservative side, was a national party loyalist, was elected for
another term as governor. Although the state as a whole had
long been plagued with racism, especially in the western
parts, the openly racist Dixiecrats got less than 74,000 votes
against over 270,000 for Truman electors. Yet this disaffec-
tion from the Democratic Party in a state with a normally
substantial and vigorous Republican population (about 40
per cent of the electorate) portended trouble ahead in two-
party contests.

In 1948, the Dixiecrats carried only four Southern states,
and even in these—Alabama, Louisiana, Mississippi, and
South Carolina, our most depressed and most heavily (mainly
nonvoting) Negro-populated states—they masqueraded as
Democrats, using the Democratic emblem or label. In Alabama, the Dixiecrat electors were on the ballot as official
Democrats and got 171,443 votes out of a population of some
3 million (1950 census), almost 1 million of whom were
largely voteless blacks. But the Congressional politicians
there, led by Senator Lister Hill, soon had the state back on
good terms with the national party. In Louisiana, where the
population was 2.7 million in 1950 and included almost 900,-

ooo Negroes, the Dixiecrats got 204,290 votes. Truman electors received 136,344 and the Republicans got 72,657. The Long family, which preferred to work within the National Democratic Party and to distribute its favors although maintaining many positions contrary to national party policy, had that state back in line very soon. In 1948, Earl K. Long, brother of the "Kingfish," was elected governor and Russell Long, son of the "Kingfish," senator. In Mississippi, the Dixiecrats received only 167,538 votes out of a total population of slightly more than 2 million, almost 1 million of whom were Negro. Given the paranoia of Mississippi's leaders, and particularly the defection of Senator Eastland and some of the congressmen, there was nothing that could be done to rescue that state, and it still remains America's South Africa. In South Carolina, the Dixiecrats got 102,607 votes from a state with a population of about 2 million, of which more than 800,000 were black. But even there, the home of Strom Thurmond, the Dixiecrat movement had but little staying power. (Two years later, Thurmond ran for the Senate in the Democratic primary, not on the Dixiecrat ticket. He failed to defeat Senator Olin Johnston but later was elected as the nominee of the very Democratic Party he had tried and is still trying to destroy.)

The importance of the Dixiecrat movement lay in the fact that Southern Bourbon political leaders finally made an open break with the Democratic Party *in order to maintain white supremacy,* while before 1948 they had chosen to bear "present ills" rather than to risk a break in the solid Southern front of white Democracy. There always had been considerable reluctance to split the white vote, and many factional leaders would compromise on any point in a showdown in order to preserve the fiction of the solid party. But the Dixiecrats forced an open break and thus opened the door to a regularized two-party system in the South. Having done so, they then moved in the direction of national Republicanism. They made no distinction between the "national" Republican Party and some state or sectional euphemism such as "States' Rights Republicans" or "Texas Regularcans." The transition seemed to need no half-way stations. The cheerful readiness with which a "Jeffersonian Democrat" could become an Alexander Hamilton-Barry Goldwater-Nixon-Agnew Republican suggests the prior existence of either an affinity of views or kindred interests! In the long run, the Democratic Party might gain from the departure of these incompatible elements and by forthrightly taking its stance as the traditionally liberal, progressive party of the people.

I think both the Dixiecrat movement and the trend of Southern conservatives to support Dwight Eisenhower stemmed initially from the Southerners' disagreements with the economic and social policies of the Roosevelt and Truman Administrations. This is not to question Eisenhower's personal popularity—not at all—but a careful examination of the "Dixiecrat to Ike" trend in the areas that supported Thurmond indicates something deeper than the likableness of a pleasant personality. Throughout the South, especially in Texas, Tennessee, and Florida, this type of conversion to Republicanism became respectable, even fashionable, among suburbanites with big mortgages on small houses. Though this social tilt may wear thin in the face of the hard domestic realities, many have become hard-core reactionaries through this influence.

It had been the New Deal-Fair Deal insistence on economic and social justice for *all* Americans, particularly for equal treatment of the Negro, that was the seminal agent of party change. Roosevelt helped the underprivileged and lifted millions from despair to hope. Truman took overt steps toward economic and social equality, and insisted in 1948 on running on a strong civil-rights platform, and Southern politicians knew he meant it.

Neither the defeat of the Dixiecrats nor Eisenhower's heroic glamor meant that the South had turned its back on racism. Racism remained the ugliest and the most effective factor in Southern politics.

CHAPTER III

The Period of Massive Resistance

Now THAT the Depression of the 1930s was but a memory and appetites for militarism were at least temporarily sated by World War II and Korea, political leaders of the South faced what to them was the gravest of threats to the Southern way of life—racial integration.

After 1948, it was believed by some and fervently hoped by many others (including myself) that the South had come further than it really had in the area of race relations. It was true that economic gains had been made by blacks throughout the South, particularly in the cities. Even political gains were being realized as more and more Negroes were able to vote (the all-white primary was rapidly disappearing); a few had even been able to win office. Gradualists among Southern leaders felt that—given enough time, say something in the nature of another fifty years—the South would be indistinguishable from other parts of the country in treatment of and attitude toward blacks. But such well-meaning, if mistaken, people did not reckon on the effect of "forced" school desegregation, integrated housing, and equal-employment practices. Nor did most of them even see it coming. Some hard-line white supremacists did see it coming, however, and they had begun preparing to prevent it. When, on June 5, 1950, the Supreme Court handed down a trio of decisions dealing in one way or another with the separate-but-equal doctrine, knowledgeable segregationist leaders knew well that the days for that doctrine were numbered.

One crucial decision involved Herman Sweatt, a young black man, who had tried to enter the law school of the University of Texas and whose application had been rejected because of his race. (Texas had a separate, and unequal, Negro law school.) Lawyers for Mr. Sweatt, in addition to attacking segregation per se, argued that the Negro law school was inferior and that Sweatt's constitutional right of equal protection of the laws could be satisfied only by admission to the regular state university.

Predictably, the Supreme Court held that the Negro law school was not equal to the state university, that "the University of Texas Law School possessed to a far greater degree those qualities which were incapable of objective measurement but which made for greatness in a law school." The admission of Sweatt was ordered by the Court. Since virtually all black schools in the South were actually inferior to the corresponding white institutions, this case obviously constituted a basic threat to the whole separate-but-equal fiction. And the Court's opinion had a particular sting for Southern politicians in Congress because it was rendered by Chief Justice

Fred Vinson, long a beloved member of the Southern Congressional bloc, and a favorite friend of Speaker Sam Rayburn and other members of the establishment hierarchy. Congressional cloakrooms, where Southerners predominated, rocked with discussion of the Sweatt case, and I listened to much of it. "Boys, this is it, look out," the senior and very respected Representative from Georgia, Carl Vinson, remarked with perhaps a more accurate assessment than he realized. But as plain as its implications were, the Sweatt case provided very little psychological preparation of the public for the extension of the ruling to elementary and secondary schools. It was, after all, a case involving only one university and only a single student placed in unusual circumstances. What was increasingly apparent to legal scholars was generally unsuspected by the public.

The McLaurin case, decided on the same day, involved plain, old-fashioned Jim Crow segregation. McLaurin, a black, had been admitted to the graduate school of the University of Oklahoma, but was segregated there in every respect—even to the point of having to sit in a separate room, apart from white students, where he was privileged to listen through an open door to the lectures. The Court held this kind of separate-but-equal mockery unconstitutional, too. On this same historic day, the Court also prohibited segregated arrangements in railway dining cars.

These three cases, while not receiving the public attention later to be focused on the decision on public-school segregation in 1954, clearly indicated there was little time left to the "Southern way of life," if by that hackneyed phrase was meant the continued discrimination against black citizens by so-called legal institutions and means by which the Negro was kept in a subordinate position. Another Georgian, Roy Har-

ris of Augusta, a political power in Georgia throughout the
forty years of the Talmadge era, saw the handwriting on the
wall. "We anticipate," he said, "that they [the Supreme
Court] will go all the way and say that there can be no such
thing as separate and equal facilities." (Incidentally, a press
dispatch caught my eye as I was writing this chapter. It was
reported in *The Washington Post* of March 11, 1971, that
Roy Harris had tried to get Dean Rusk fired from his job as
professor of international law at the University of Georgia.
Harris made a motion that the Board of Regents not renew
Rusk's contract on the grounds that, among other things,
Rusk's daughter had married a Negro. The Regents voted 8
to 4 to renew Rusk's contract—illustrating that Georgia,
under the leadership of the relatively enlightened business
community of Atlanta, has come a long way despite its Har-
rises.)

Though Senator Herman Talmadge, an able legislator,
does not say too much about segregation these days around
Washington, when he was governor of Georgia he upheld segregation to the last ditch. In 1949, for instance, when some
black parents petitioned the courts for equal educational facilities, Governor Talmadge said heatedly in a radio address,
"This litigation is the opening wedge to break down segregation in the Southern states." He attacked "Northern agitators"—this is part of the ritual—and added, "As long as I am
governor, Negroes will not be admitted to white schools."
With the strong backing of Roy Harris, Talmadge became an
early exponent of the "interposition" of the power of states
against the federal government. He was by no means alone in
displaying disrespect for the federal courts and in counseling
disobedience and unlawful conduct by the people. Other
Southern politicians—most of them, in fact—took the same

irresponsible course: betraying, misleading, and misrepresenting the enlightened best interests of the people and catering to the worst and lowest common denominators of racial prejudice, lawlessness, and fear.

There may have been some political "heroes" in this cause, but few, if any, were to be found among white Southern politicians. I know I cannot include myself. Though I had publicly acknowledged the existence of discrimination (to do so was then a mark of a Southern progressive) and had avoided race-baiting, I was by no means a torchbearer for racial equality in my first campaign for the Senate in Tennessee in 1952. Instead, I based my appeal for black support primarily upon a liberal economic record—full employment at decent wages, social security, TVA, health, housing, etc.—and let the sleeping dogs of racism lie as best I could. When campaigning with a long-time personal friend, Henry Vaughn, then as now an official in Tipton County on the banks of the "Great Muddy" in west Tennessee, where the Mississippi delta culture still prevailed, we made a stop at a crossroads community where I "pressed the flesh" of all with the customary warmth. When we were back in the car, Vaughn said, "You just lost that box." "How?" I inquired, astonished. "By shaking hands with the niggers," he said.

I rejected this indignity and continued to shake hands with blacks and to solicit their support throughout the campaign. I termed myself a moderate on the race question, but I neither made any forecasts about the Supreme Court decision in the pending *Brown v. Board of Education* case nor talked about what it might mean. I never broached the subject of racial integration. I did campaign hard, and apparently effectively, on the economic and social issues with which the mass of working people, both black and white, could identify.

My opponent in that campaign was the late Senator Kenneth McKellar, a distinguished and honorable gentleman of the old school. Not once in the course of a long campaign did he stoop to racism. Instead, he and his supporters concentrated on the traditional values of power, patronage, prestige, and his record of service, especially extolling the power of his seniority in the Senate, chairman of the Appropriations Committee, and president pro tem, the Senate's position of highest honor. Since the Tennessee Valley Authority, so very important to Tennessee's economic development, depended upon appropriations from Congress, these were telling issues. I was hard pressed to answer the charge that if elected I would be only a powerless freshman, starting at the foot of the class. My tactic was to look to the future, to talk about long-range plans and programs, obviously beyond the life span of a man already eighty, thus indirectly making the point of his advanced age without ever once making specific mention of it, which would have been considered indelicate given his venerable position and record. My references to his record were always praiseworthy—but always in the past tense.

This issue of power and promise between us was dramatized by a contest of campaign doggerel that many Tennesseans found amusing. There suddenly appeared on utility poles, roadside trees, barns, and in storefront windows a placard which read:

> THINKING FELLER
> VOTE FOR MCKELLAR

The first few times I saw this I found it amusing, but I soon discovered that it was effectively making the point that his seniority and power counted in the Senate. There had to be a retort. My wife has finally consented to share with me the onus of its authorship. Beneath each such McKellar placard we placed one which read:

THINK SOME MORE
AND VOTE FOR GORE

This is not to imply that the race problem was entirely absent from the campaign. Far from it. The political machine of Ed Crump in Memphis had been built on a large, controlled Negro vote. With this vote as a base, Crump (a native of Mississippi) had built an incredibly powerful political machine that totally dominated the city and he soon controlled the politics of state offices, too. One might find it incongruous that Crump, having founded his power on the Memphis black vote, supported the Dixiecrat ticket in 1948. But President Truman wanted the blacks to be free and equal and to have a free vote. "Boss" Crump's power could not survive *free* and *independent* voting by blacks, who composed about 40 per cent of Memphis's population. I had campaigned hard in Memphis for both white and black support for the anti-Crump candidates in 1948: Browning and Kefauver. I worked hard in Memphis in my own campaign for both white and black independent support, and managed to eke out a bare majority in the city, even though this was McKellar's home. And this assured me the Democratic nomination, which was then tantamount to election in Tennessee.

In the November general election, I campaigned hard for the national Stevenson-Sparkman Democratic ticket. Because the Republicans in Congress had been fighting the Tennessee Valley Authority so hard, we made TVA a campaign issue in Tennessee. General Eisenhower, well coached by his Republi-

can newspaper supporters in Tennessee, was unequivocal in
his support of it. On October 15, he told his Tennessee audience, "Certainly there will be no disposition on my part to
impair the effective working of TVA." Again, just before the
election on November 2, a telegram from General Eisenhower
was highlighted in the Tennessee press.

> TVA has served well both agricultural and industrial interests
> of this region. Rumors are being maliciously spread in TVA
> areas that I propose not only to decrease the efficiency of the
> operation but to abandon it, which is grossly untrue and utterly
> false. If I am elected President, TVA will be operated and
> maintained at maximum efficiency. I have a keen appreciation
> of what it has done and what it will be able to continue to
> do in the future. Under the new administration TVA will
> continue to serve and promote the prosperity of this great sec-
> tion of the United States.

Yet not long after Eisenhower's inauguration I began to
hear rumors that could not be dismissed as "grossly untrue
and utterly false." After a trip on Eisenhower's plane Senator
Lyndon Johnson told me of a conversation he had inadver-
tently overheard during which the President said, "We will
sell the **** **** thing." This provoked me, and while I
could not at the time publicly relate what Senator Johnson
had told me, I alerted a number of key people in the seven-
state area about it.

And indeed, within less than six months, President Eisenhower eliminated from the new budget funds for the construction of badly needed generating facilities in the western
portion of "that great section of the United States" served by
TVA. With a genuine penchant for reducing complex problems to slogans, the President began to associate TVA with
"creeping socialism"—augmented by a later reference to the

provision of "cheap power" by TVA as "this curious thing in socialist theory. . . ." Curiouser and curiouser! (The President's White House operative was A. H. Wenzell, an employee of the First Boston Corporation, who later disagreed with his chief's "creeping socialism," and opined instead, "I would call it galloping socialism.")

Edgar Dixon and Eugene Yates were corporate executives of Middle South Utilities, Inc., and the Southern Company, large utility combines in the mid-South area. Though well known in corporate circles, they were relatively obscure so far as the general public was concerned. But their names were to become household words. The controversy over what came to be called the Dixon-Yates contract began to take shape on May 11, 1953, when George Woods, chairman of the First Boston Corporation, came to Washington to see Joseph Dodge, Director of the Bureau of the Budget. Mr. Woods wanted to get the government out of business—never, of course, with any thought that his own company might gain from the process. So, Mr. Woods deputed A. H. Wenzell as First Boston's man in Washington—in the White House itself and at government expense. Wenzell set about his work in such an aura of secrecy that Budget Bureau people were cautioned not to let anyone know of his presence, particularly anyone connected with TVA. By September 3, Wenzell had completed a report. A copy was delivered to the President by the director of the Bureau, and a copy was also sent to former President Herbert Hoover, whose "task force" report on TVA had followed the Wenzell line closely: its recommendation had been to sell TVA's power and fertilizer facilities to private investors.

The Dixon-Yates strategy began to take more specific form. Although it involved TVA and the people of Memphis most directly, officials of neither the city nor the TVA were consulted. Pains were taken to withhold information about the deal from Congress and from the public. Those who would rob the people of their public property do not openly proclaim their intentions from the rooftops. They set about it shrewdly, with subtle orchestration by Madison Avenue, and approached their victims without forewarning.

Fortunately, a few of us had been alerted (Estes Kefauver, John Sparkman, Lister Hill, John Sherman Cooper), and we struggled against the insidious attackers, who were well armed with power, wealth, and slogans. We dramatized it into a national issue. But it was only the outraged cry of the public, after the machinations of people with power, position, and high finance were finally revealed, that laid this scheme to rest.

Meantime, the courts had moved slowly but inexorably toward the climactic *Brown* decision. The NAACP chief counsel, Thurgood Marshall, and others had concluded rightly from the language of the Supreme Court's opinions in the three 1950 cases that insofar as the Court was concerned the separate-but-equal doctrine was dead. Suits which had been filed petitioning equal facilities were then withdrawn and reworked to call for complete elimination of the dual school systems in the South and elsewhere. (It should not be forgotten that school boards in Kansas, Delaware, and the District of Columbia were defendants in three of these cases. Official school segregation was not then exclusively a problem of the South, nor is it now.)

In 1954, the fateful *Brown* decision, which left the legal structure of the caste system without a constitutional foundation, was finally handed down, ninety-one years after the Emancipation Proclamation. Perhaps anticipating a severe reaction to it and unwilling to act hastily in dismantling a system built up over a century, the Supreme Court refused to order immediate desegregation and postponed for almost a year a final schedule that would put the decision into effect. Then, after lengthy rearguments had been heard and copious briefs had been submitted by the interested parties and their allies, the Court unanimously announced that the system of school segregation should end "with all deliberate speed." There had been more "deliberateness" than "speed" in the functioning of the Court itself, and clarity was the victim of exigency in its decree.

Those who feel that the members of the Supreme Court and the federal judiciary in general are not astute politicians, without regard for public opinion, are badly mistaken. The Court knew full well the far-reaching results of the decision it was determined to hand down, and it sought to prepare the public for it. Chief Justice Earl Warren, a consummate politician in his own right as governor of California and Republican nominee for Vice-President in 1948, must have wished to avoid a split decision on such a momentous issue, for he went to great pains, evidently at the price of watered-down language, to achieve unanimity on the Court in both the basic decision and in the implementation decree.

In fairness, it should be recognized that the Court's position was a very delicate one. There had been a bitter battle in Congress during 1950 over the Fair Employment Practices Act. The House had passed a weak bill, but the Senate had filibustered it to death; President Eisenhower, a Texan by birth, had skirted the issue in his campaign in 1952.

In the Deep South, the passions, the energies, and the great abilities that should have helped revitalize American democracy had long been frozen by the threat of racial upheaval.

Popular feeling in the South ran high on the subject of racial discrimination. Violence, radicalism, racism, and religious fundamentalism ran perilously close to the surface. Though the ideological and legal bases for segregation were disappearing, white Southerners, still clinging to the vision of a South that really never was and encouraged in this folly by their own political leaders, were by no means prepared for the basic changes that the Court's decision required.

While all this was going on, Senator Joseph McCarthy of Minnesota, Congressman Martin Dies of Texas, and other self-annointed patriots were stirring up hysteria about communism and "anti-American" subversion. There was, then, a deep uneasiness throughout the country, and particularly in the South, where any attempt to reduce the power of employers over employees was regarded by conservatives as a radical movement, if not an attack upon private property. The propertied class had been aroused by the battle over the Fair Employment Practices Act, and for many of them, as well as for the less fortunate and less learned, the school desegregation litigation seemed of a pattern with these earlier threats to the basic social fabric. There was added frustration in the realization that the Supreme Court was completely (or so it seemed) immune to threats and entreaties from the electorate. McCarthyism offered a convenient explanation for the unrelenting pressure for social change—it was a Communist plot! As the political tone was more and more set by those who adopted the loudest and most extreme position, it was not long until mere silence became the hallmark of Southern liberalism on racial matters.

My own reaction was to refer publicly to the Brown decision as the "law of the land" and carefully to couple this timid declaration with a description of myself as a moderate. This brought the wrath of Southern segregationists down upon my "compromising" and "gradualist" head. "Moderation means gradualism," declared Roy Harris, "and gradualism means race mixing." Ross Barnett, governor of Mississippi, equated a Southern moderate with a burglar who "comes into your house and tells you that if you give him just a few of your valuables, he'll go away. Just sort of a 'token' burglar." Representative John Bell Williams of Mississippi (later to be governor) explained, "The self-styled moderates are simply saying they believe in a little bit of pregnancy." Even the late, highly respected Richard B. Russell of Georgia felt called upon to say, "There can be no such thing as token integration. This is merely a device of the race mixers to obtain total and complete integration." Maybe there was some truth in these statements—as in most demagoguery—but this hot and rancid political stuff was an open invitation to extremism, which made moderation a hazardous political course.

Research into public attitudes at the time showed widespread Southern opposition to the *Brown* decision. Melvin M. Turnin and his associates at Princeton University reported that when white respondents in Guilford County, North Carolina, were asked what action they would take if schools were desegregated, 77 per cent said they would "amend the U.S. Constitution." Another team of researchers probed Southern white attitudes as to segregation, moderation, or integration. Sixty-four per cent of Southern whites favored strict segregation, 28 per cent favored a moderate approach to the problem, with only 7 per cent favoring integration. Public-opinion polls published in the popular media generally agreed with these findings. The American Institute of Public Opinion found that 80 per cent expressed disapproval of the *Brown* decision. Prospects for immediate popular acceptance of the decision as the law of the land were, therefore, dim, and the political outlook for the moderate or gradualist was hardly good. Even "education," which I always offered along with "time" as a possible solution to "our dilemma," was shown to be less influential than I had hoped. Though education had been shown to have a direct correlation with racial tolerance, not until the white Southerner had advanced beyond high school were the odds better than 1 to 3 that he would be other than a "strict segregationist," and the majority did not attend college, still fewer graduating.

The independent or liberal Southerner, if these terms can be used fairly to describe a person of emancipated intellect and a sense of public responsibility, generally contented himself with avoidance of racial demagoguery and active identification with other issues. With me, the other issues were public works, TVA, taxes, nuclear energy, economics, and international questions. With my colleague Estes Kefauver, they were crime, monopoly practices, TVA, drug prices, and Presidential aspiration. Lyndon Johnson concentrated on the areas of power broker, tax favoritism, and military affairs.

But backward looks and a turning away from the very real problems of the real world characterized most Southern politicians during this period. The past must be preserved or in some instances restored, they argued, and it could not be preserved if, as Senator Eastland put it so succinctly in the Senate in 1954, the Supreme Court were to be allowed "to destroy those great institutions and the great culture which are in full flower in the Southern states—the culture of the Anglo-Saxon."

The nostalgic, backward look went so far as to revive wide advocacy of the pre-Civil War doctrine of "interposition." John Calhoun would not have been pleased, I think. He could have told his latter-day, would-be disciples that it was impossible to interpose the power of any given state between the federal government and a local school board so as to prevent the execution of court orders by the board.

Throughout these trying days, President Eisenhower could have been an important force for reconciliation, so great was his prestige and popularity. In the South, Eisenhower was not generally subject to criticism for "playing politics," as most of our Presidents have been, and this tolerance and generosity on the part of the public toward him extended to the civil-rights issue. But he failed to exercise the powers of his office for the moral leadership that was needed to set a proper tone for national observance of the Court's decision, and this undermined whatever tendency there was to accept the decision. In fact, it was freely rumored in Washington, and soon it was widely reported, that in private the President had expressed his disagreement and dissatisfaction with the Court decision. The President's public statements on the subject were vague and indirect, and the idea quickly got around that the Administration would do nothing to enforce the school desegregation decree. At a press conference when the President was asked about this, he answered in his not unusual way, "It might have been that I said something about 'slower': but I do believe that we should—because I do say, as I said yesterday or last week, we have got to have reason and sense and education, and a lot of other developments that go hand in hand in this process—if this process is going to have any real acceptance in the United States."

No pattern of administration leadership or assistance in the enforcement of Court orders was forthcoming, then. Massive resistance, the Southern battle cry, was thus encouraged by (and to some extent resulted from) the President's lack of leadership. Southern state officials and courthouse groups needed but little encouragement to dig in and resist, and they surely took heart from Eisenhower's attitude.

The resistance movement had actually begun in some states well before the 1954 decision. In 1953, for instance, Governor Herman Talmadge proposed to the Georgia legislature a plan according to which the public-school system could be converted to a private system and tuition grants be paid by the state for children to attend private schools. The Georgia Commission on Education was created to be something of a strategy and propaganda organization for this new endeavor.

In Mississippi, a pupil-placement law was enacted and the Legal Educational Advisory Committee established. South Carolina, too, under the leadership of Governor James F. Byrnes, once a highly respected politician and statesman but then embittered after his break with President Truman, had started early in 1952 on "preparedness measures" designed to avoid and evade desegregation.

Interestingly enough, Louisiana and Alabama took no action prior to 1954. In Alabama, Senator John Sparkman had to run for re-election in 1954, and he undoubtedly did what he could to cool matters. In Louisiana, the Longs were firmly back in the saddle and they were interested, among other things, in offshore oil rights, a "giveaway" which Eisenhower had endorsed in 1952, and they wanted to keep close to the federal government in order to reap this harvest.

Although nearly all Southern governors and most other public officials spoke the language of massive resistance, there was actually little formalized inclination to defy Court orders in Florida, North Carolina, and Tennessee. And except for the Byrd machine, about which I shall write later, Virginia might also have continued on a moderate course. In Tennessee, good sense prevailed for a while. I was proud of Tennessee's governor, the late Frank G. Clement. At the very outset, Clement stated that Tennessee's public schools would "continue to operate for the benefit of all of our children." And he was to demonstrate his political courage later on when an effort made in the Tennessee state legislature to pass a pupil-assignment law was defeated with his help.

According to Fred Travis, long-time political reporter for the *Chattanooga Times,* Clement and his advisers were throughout concerned with the governor's national image. Travis reported at least one strategy conference to discuss whether Clement should enhance his national reputation by moving toward the liberal side, or whether he should solidify his position in Tennessee by abandoning the moderate position he had taken on race matters and moving to the right in line with most other Southern governors. So far as I ever knew, Clement himself did not at that time waver from a progressive, law-abiding position.

Indeed, Governor Clement was in great demand as a speaker and received wide national acclaim. He definitely had stars in his eyes as the 1956 national election approached. He and his supporters made a determined and successful drive for him to be chosen as keynote speaker at the Democratic National Convention. The hope was that he would bowl the convention over with a Cross of Gold speech and become the Vice-Presidential nominee. (There was frequent mention of William Jennings Bryan's oratorical feat of 1896.) At the convention, I was on the platform, seated beside the Democratic National Committee chairman, who was following a text of the governor's speech. Clement finished his prepared text, the audience was pleased, but he was far from through. Seemingly unable to deny the audience further declamations, he launched into one of his oratorical extravaganzas. Knowing what was coming, I remarked to the chairman, "Hold your hat; next to fried chicken we Southerners suffer most from oratory." Twenty minutes later, the chairman was tearing his hair. The endless speech blew Clement's carefully nurtured plan to "take" the convention and thus become its Vice-Presidential nominee—an ambition Senator Kefauver and I shared.

"Too Much Talent in Tennessee?" had been the title of an article in the March 1955 issue of *Harper's Magazine*, written by Tennessee's noted author Wilma Dykman. She forecast a contest of some kind between Governor Clement, Kefauver, and me, perhaps at the 1956 national convention, and now all of us, and thousands of other Democrats, were in Chicago at that convention. Senator Kefauver was again a candidate for President. Clement had been endorsed by the Tennessee delegation as a favorite-son Presidential candidate. I, too, was thinking about the Vice-Presidential nomination. This made for a unique and unprecedented state triangle of ambition, pride, and politics.

My candidacy was quiet and unannounced, but I had arrived in Chicago with very powerful support, actively urging my "selection." Everyone assumed that, as usual, it would be a "selection," by the Presidential nominee in conference with a few key Democratic leaders. My champions included the late Sam Rayburn, Speaker of the House and the presiding officer of the convention; former President Harry Truman; and a number of my Senate colleagues and former Congressional colleagues, including my closest Senate friend, Senator Mike Monroney of Oklahoma. My situation with my own Tennessee delegation and constituency was more delicate. I had enthusiastically supported Senator Kefauver's Presidential candidacy in 1952 and I had publicly announced support of his candidacy in 1956. (Loyalty to a fellow Tennessean and to my Senate colleague required my support of him over a non-Tennessean.) But while Kefauver had again done well in the primaries, he had not done as well as in 1952, and by convention time his chances for the Presidential nomination seemed slim.

The rivalry between Kefauver and Clement within Tennessee and the Tennessee delegation was fierce. The Clement faction was clearly in the majority in the delegation, which operated under the unit rule, but Kefauver's supporters were both hopeful and determined. I had no particular group of my own, but I was the second choice of both groups. I was forced to play a waiting game, but the fierce infighting threatened to destroy the chances for all three of us.

Outside the delegation, the situation was developing quite encouragingly for me. Though I was keeping a low silhouette, a number of my friends from all over the country were working quietly but effectively. For my own part, I was saying nothing about a candidacy but was appearing before the platform committee in support of positions about which I felt strongly, and, of course, I was warmly greeting delegates and party leaders in the traditional convention fashion. The platform committee announced that it had approved my proposed plank on atomic-energy policy. This boosted me a little, and a few leaders began publicly to suggest my availability. A news dispatch from Chicago said, "Gore is emerging behind the scenes as the most generally acceptable of all the possibilities."

With the renomination of Adlai Stevenson, as had been widely predicted, all attention at the convention was on the Vice-Presidential "selection," about which there was now a keen contest. Senator Hubert H. Humphrey was running hard and was rumored to be confident that Stevenson favored him. Senator John F. Kennedy had the solid support of the New England delegation and much support from large-city delegations in various parts of the country, and they were pressing Stevenson to select him as his running mate. Supporters of Kefauver were loyally urging him as the best and most helpful running mate. The same was true of Mayor Robert F. Wagner, Jr., of New York. On top of all this, Governor Clement made a public announcement of his Vice-Presidential candidacy. "Governor Clement," reported the Memphis *Commercial Appeal,* "spent an hour and twenty-five minutes with Mr. Stevenson in the latter's hotel suite Wednesday night. While he said he neither asked for nor received any commitment, it appeared significant that he became an active candidate for the Vice-Presidential post after the meeting."

I, too, had my hour with Governor Stevenson and I left with the strong feeling that I was his most likely choice. We were friends and we talked with candor at some length. From our conversation I believed his personal preference might well be Senator Kennedy, but that the question of his Catholicism was very troublesome. I got the definite impression, too, that he simply was not going to select Kefauver as a running mate, whatever. He felt some deep irritation about some events in the primaries, and the candidacy of Governor Clement was operating against Kefauver (and me). Governor Stevenson walked slowly with me to the door where we stood and continued the conversation. He asked where I might be reached by telephone, writing the number on an envelope. The last thing he said, with his hand on my arm, was, "Albert, it may be you." I could scarcely feel the floor as

I walked down the hall, lighted with photographer's flash-bulbs which looked to me like stars in the clouds of tobacco smoke.

Then, at the convention, came the shock—Stevenson's announcement that he would neither make the choice of a running mate nor indicate any preference to the convention. I was dumbfounded and disappointed; standing in my tracks looking first at the floor and then at the ceiling.

Everything was bedlam. It was impossible to get a taxi or an elevator or to reach anyone by telephone. All around I was running into friends who would inquire, "Are you going to get in?" Senator Kennedy, I heard, had decided to seek the nomination, and soon literature boosting Kennedy was being distributed to delegates' rooms. This made many suspect collusion with Stevenson. I wondered if he had some advance notice of Stevenson's action. Senator Humphrey had decided to go before the convention, I heard. And so had Mayor Wagner. "Throw your hat in, Albert," a delegate from North Carolina yelled. "Your chances are as good as anyone's." My excitement was increasing. Governor Clement, I learned from a telephone call, was in a huddle with his supporters.

Delegates who had supported Senator Kefauver in his losing bid for the nomination were now clamoring for the consolation prize for their fallen hero. There was a news report that he was leaving the city, another that he would run. I stopped by my hotel for a moment and Kefauver telephoned. He was running and, to my surprise, asked me to place him in nomination. I then felt my chances were as good as his (if Rayburn would go for me they might be better), and he must have been aware of my interest in the possibility. I just said, "I think I had better not, under the circumstances." It was not an unpleasant exchange; we understood each other well.

Finally, about 1:30 in the morning, I met with my friend Sam Rayburn, and he said he was for me. I felt confident this meant the big Texas delegation was behind me, and I told him I would let him know my decision early the next day. In a taxi going back to my hotel I could still hear Adlai saying, "Albert, it may be you." And I began to think it might be me after all.

Only one thing stood between me and a candidacy before the convention—my own state delegation. I talked to several members. A majority was clearly committed to Clement so long as he was an announced candidate. Though it was then very early in the morning, I telephoned Clement and found him still awake. I began to wonder if anyone was sleeping in Chicago. I asked him point blank what he was going to do; I told him of the encouragement I had received, and of my interest in letting my name go before the convention if I could have the support of the Tennessee delegation. "Are you going to stay in?" I pointedly asked. He hesitated, but gave me no answer except to say, "If there is a change, I'll let you know."

Early that morning he called as I was shaving and said he had decided to withdraw his name, but he did not offer to support me. Nevertheless, this freed the Tennessee delegates and I decided to ask for their support, which I did in a speech before the delegation. In the course of my remarks I pledged that if it should appear that I could not win, but that another Tennessean could, I would then withdraw. I closed my remarks, though, by saying, "I believe I can win and I ask your help." The delegation took a vote and gave me solid support on that basis. I then asked my neighbor, Lieutenant Governor Jared Maddux of Cookeville, to place my name in nomination, which he did eloquently.

At the end of the first ballot, I was in a fairly strong third position with wide-ranging support, though most of my votes had come from the Southern and border states. Kefauver and Kennedy were out in front. Humphrey and Wagner dropped out, but additional support had been pledged to me. I believed that if I could hold my own through the second ballot, Kefauver and Kennedy would then be deadlocked and I might gain the nomination on the third ballot. When the second roll call started, Arkansas, to my surprise, switched from me to Kennedy. Kefauver and Kennedy were picking up most of the Humphrey and Wagner strength, but Kentucky, which had supported Humphrey on the first ballot, switched to me and other delegates told me they were going to do the same. I thought I still had a chance until I signaled to Senator Johnson, with whom I was on cordial terms, by raising my hand toward him with a quizzical lifting of the brow, and he shook his head slowly for a negative reply. I knew what had happened. The Texas delegation had feared that Senator Kefauver would be the nominee, to which they were strongly opposed, and they switched to Senator Kennedy to try to prevent it. The Texas switch to Kennedy brought the convention into roaring excitement. Many delegates were clamoring and shouting for recognition. Kennedy's nomination then appeared imminent, unless I could quickly throw a long forward pass. I stood high on a chair and waved for recognition to Speaker Rayburn, who was presiding. He immediately recognized me, the crowd suddenly quietened, and I shouted into the microphone:

> With gratitude for the consideration and support of this great Democratic National Convention, I respectfully withdraw my name and support my distinguished colleague, Estes Kefauver.

Bedlam! I never heard such a roar. My loyal friends of Okla-

homa switched to Kefauver, as did Kentucky, and then one
delegation after another supported Kefauver and he was the
nominee in a matter of minutes.

It had been a fast and furious battle; one of the most exciting moments of my life. I had had very little time and no
organization except friends who had quickly rallied round
after Stevenson threw it open. My total expense was only a
few taxi fares and telephone calls. And, like a fever from a
summer cold, my excitement soon abated.

The experience provided me with an invaluable lesson in
the inner workings of political-campaign organizations—a
lesson that was to prove useful in performing my immediate
Senate duties. In 1955, I had been appointed chairman of the
Senate Election Subcommittee. Senators Mike Mansfield of
Montana and Carl Curtis of Nebraska served with me on the
subcommittee. This subcommittee was authorized to investi-
gate federal election campaigns, to exercise surveillance over
them, and to consider election charges and contests. The Senate provided the subcommittee with funds and the power of
subpoena.

Although campaign finances had long been a national
problem and sometimes a national disgrace, no thorough investigation of the subject had ever been made. The subcommittee determined to make such an investigation of the 1956
election campaign, and early in that year I began quietly to
organize a competent staff of experts for the purpose. John
Moore, a capable young attorney from Maryland (who later
became a judge in Maryland), was staff director. Dr. Alexander Heard, a professor of political science from the University
of North Carolina, became the subcommittee's chief consult-
ant. (Heard is now chancellor of Vanderbilt University, and

was co-author with V. O. Key, Jr., of *Southern Politics,* the most important work on that subject of the period.)

In order to gain credibility and establish our nonpartisanship, we resolved to begin our study by investigating a fund-raising function of my own party. When the Pennsylvania Democrats gathered in Harrisburg at a $25-a-plate dinner to hear Adlai Stevenson, I sent a telegram from the subcommittee demanding all records of ticket purchases, receipts, and disbursements. My fellow Democrats were not amused and the reaction was somewhat greater than I had anticipated. But it soon abated when they realized that functions and operations of both political parties would be impartially investigated.

As the investigation progressed, we were able to identify the contributing source of more than $33 million spent by the major forces in the 1956 campaigns. Undoubtedly, the total amount was much higher than this figure. The breakdown of known expenditures was as follows:

Republican	$20,685,387
Democratic	$10,977,790
Labor	$ 941,271
Miscellaneous	$ 581,277

The largest single expenditure in this election was for television and radio time. During the period from September 1 to November 6, the two major parties spent a total of $9,501,000 on television and radio for all political offices. Again, this figure represents only what we were able to document; there was no doubt that more money was in fact spent on the media. The actual breakdown of contributions may not have disclosed very much that was new, but it surely did dramatize the economic polarization of politics. Republican contributions came primarily from wealthy individuals and people associated with the large corporations, while labor's contributions went primarily to Democratic committees and candidates.

What was more significant, however, was the geographical distribution of political contributions. New York was the major source of individual contributions to both parties—as one would have expected; but one might not have expected it to be so overwhelmingly, so preponderantly, in support of Republicans. Contributions of $500 or more made by individuals in New York to Republican candidates and committees totaled $2,382,047—almost equal to the total aggregate of $2,820,655 of such contributions made to Democratic candidates in *all* the states (including New York).

Though the investigation of campaign contributions and expenditures was conducted as a nonpartisan undertaking, campaign chores were something else. I actively supported the Stevenson-Kefauver ticket in many speeches over the country. Stevenson, a man of honest and inquisitive intellect, had suggested that we should seek an agreement to stop atmospheric tests of nuclear bombs. This position was both sound and farsighted, but it boomeranged on him badly, for it was a new issue that the people did not understand, and, besides, it related to national security—a field in which Eisenhower's credibility was unassailable. Since I was a member of the Joint Committee on Atomic Energy and felt very strongly about this issue, I was asked to support Stevenson's position on a national television hookup, which I gladly did.

After the program, speaking invitations poured in from across the nation. One of these was from Senator Lyndon

Johnson to come to Texas to speak to a state-wide rally at Austin. Johnson's close friend Senator Earle C. Clements of Kentucky had given him a favorable report on a speech I had made in Louisville. He was very anxious to carry Texas for the Democrats, and he believed the atom-test issue was hurting the ticket. So, to Texas I must go.

The night's gala occasion in Austin was really a big affair. Speaker Rayburn and several other Texas congressmen were there, with many rising young stars like John B. Connally and Ralph Yarborough. Johnson had arranged a state-wide television hookup for my speech, but he took a generous portion of the scheduled time in his introduction. I didn't mind that, only as *I* talked I could hear him whispering to my wife that I was taking too much time to warm up my audience with a little humor at the beginning. Johnson was in no mood for humor; he wanted me to tell Texans about issues like radioactive fallout, strontium-90 poisoning, the danger of fetal deformations, etc. That evening, we drove some fifty miles to Johnson's home on the Pedernales to spend the night—an interesting and sometimes exciting experience. One minute he would be driving seventy or eighty miles per hour (during a break in the conversation or while I was talking) and then Lyndon would slow to a perking rate, with first one hand and then the other on the steering wheel as he talked and gesticulated to add emphasis to his points. Lady Bird and my wife, Pauline, rode in the back seat, where Lady Bird sparingly dispensed refreshments to the conversationalists in the front. Though we had settled most of the country's problems by the time we reached the ranch, the four of us tarried beside the pool for a few moments and mourned the election outlook for the Democratic Party.

Despite all that could be done, Eisenhower ran well in the

South in 1956 as he had in 1952, overwhelmingly defeating the Stevenson-Kefauver ticket. He carried those Southern states which had strong built-in Republican support, such as Tennessee with its big Republican vote in east Tennessee. But in the solidly Democratic Deep South, a county-by-county analysis shows that Eisenhower made his best showing in the Black Belt counties; that is, in those counties which had the most Negroes and, therefore, the strongest anti-Negro white sentiment.

To the private glee of many Southern reactionaries who nevertheless still called themselves Democrats, the South— the white South, the only South that mattered to them— rapidly became more conservative and attempted to solidify all Southern factions in this position. The typical white Southern political figure, particularly around the courthouses, felt that no sacrifice was too great to maintain the social order, to keep the races separate socially and genetically pure. Most Southern political leaders had learned that it was impossible to win in any contest of force and power with the federal government. They were confident, however, that they could maintain white supremacy in the South by state force and state power so long as the federal government stayed out of the picture—that is, the executive branch of the federal government (since the federal courts had only limited means at their disposal to enforce their decisions and decrees).

Sentiment for massive resistance grew by leaps and bounds. The shock troops, the political cadre, were the Citizens Councils. They were formed to intimidate the Negro and to keep whites in line. Swift and vindictive treatment was meted out to blacks who ventured to ask for compliance with federal law. In a broader context, the Southern plan called for the councils to become a political force somewhat outside the regularly institutionalized political organizations, although some of the same people were involved in both the local political organizations, particularly the courthouse gangs, and the Citizens Councils. The council movement was not uniform and varied in effectiveness from state to state. But one thing was sure. They were able to organize and exert pressures so that several political leaders moved toward a harder line on race than they might otherwise have chosen—for instance, Senator Lister Hill of Alabama. In other cases this organized pressure group gave politicians an excuse to adopt positions they actually favored, but which in calmer times they might have felt reluctant to express or implement.

For whatever combination of reasons, the Southern revolt against the national government grew, and it was strongly expressed in the halls of Congress. And this was a somewhat new twist. While the 1948 Dixiecrat movement had been confined largely to state and local politicians, in 1956 the leaders of the Southern revolt placed a high political value on conformity of all politicians, making it a cardinal political sin for a Southerner to break rank. The whole scheme of massive resistance through interposition was based upon an assumed solid Southern official phalanx, both within each Southern state and by the Southern delegations in Congress. This left little room, if any, for independence or tolerance of dissent. Social ostracism, economic sanctions, and political punishment were the weapons. These were chilling winds. I know; they blew on me steadily.

In the Congress the whole movement for racial integration, including the *Brown* decision, was denounced as "the offshoot of a diabolical plot first hatched in Soviet Russia by Communists nearly three decades ago." Congressman E. C. Gathings of Arkansas filled forty pages in the *Congressional Record*

with charges against the NAACP. Senator Eastland, chairman
of the Internal Security Subcommittee, was active in linking
patriotism to the status quo, and in identifying the forces for
change as subversive. He held hearings in Memphis on "Communism in the Mid-South." Congressman Ed Willis of Louisiana, as chairman of a subcommittee of the House Un-
American Activities Committee, took up where Martin Dies
had left off. He probed "Communists Activities and Infiltra-
tion in the South" in Atlanta. This studied effort to brand the
movement toward racial integration as subversive and un-
American was virtually the unanimous voice of the neo-
Bourbon South.

The outward manifestation of the Southern revolt in Congress was the so-called Southern Manifesto (its real title was
"Declaration of Constitutional Principles"), a bit of low doggerel which hardly lived up to its high-flown title but which
was by no means taken lightly in the South.

It was a dangerous, deceptive propaganda move which encouraged Southerners to defy the government and to disobey
its laws, particularly orders of the federal courts. Clever in its
over-all approach, the manifesto condemned the decision in
the *Brown* case by the nation's highest court, even though
unanimous, as being a "violation of law"! As if this were not
enough, it emphatically affirmed the Southern position as one
in support of established law and order. It was the Supreme
Court, not those who vowed to defy its decision, who had
substituted "naked power for established law"! Those who had
altered the status quo by due process and by court decision
were the violators of law and order. If the Negro kept to his
place, there would be no disruption, no illegality, no problem. The manifesto appealed to, or warned, political leaders
outside the South to move with caution for the time might

come when they, themselves, would be "the victims of judicial encroachment."

As one might guess, the originator of the idea for the manifesto was none other than Strom Thurmond. He was unwilling to take his poor showing in 1948 as the final word, and he had managed election to the Senate as a *Democrat* in a white-supremacy-type campaign in South Carolina. In the Senate, he became a busybody against any and all civil-rights movements, measures, or suggestions. With the manifesto, he had the support of such respectable senators as Byrd of Virginia and Russell of Georgia.

Harry Byrd was one of the kindest men who ever lived, and a gentleman. He may have been somewhat ruthless at times in his younger political days, and perhaps a little antediluvian in his social and political views, but when I knew him best—after 1957, on the Senate Finance Committee, of which he was chairman—he was gentle and generous. He had habitually taken a somewhat simplistic view of the world and its problems, and for a few years before he left the Senate, though beloved, he was in his dotage. But in 1956, Senator Byrd still enjoyed great prestige. When he endorsed Thurmond's idea for the manifesto, the massive Byrd machine of Virginia swung into high gear and took over the leadership of the interposition strategy. Senator Byrd was quoted in the press as stating that the "Manifesto [is] part of the plan of massive resistance we've been working on. . . ."

Senator Richard Russell, another prestigious Southerner, was unenthusiastic about the manifesto, but he, too, was soon sadly caught up in the movement, as was Georgia's venerable senior senator, Walter George, then a candidate for re-election. Perhaps the Talmadge faction, breathing hard on his neck, put pressure on George, for he became not only an endorser but a champion of the manifesto. Senator Russell and some other Southern senators rewrote the resolution, though changing it little. It was then signed by nineteen Southern senators and eighty-two Southern congressmen, and introduced in both Houses of Congress with fanfare and oratory. Twenty-four members of the House refused or neglected to sign the document. On the Senate side, Kefauver and I flatly refused to have anything to do with this effort to mislead and betray our constituents and the South. In my view, a political leader performs a distinct disservice when he encourages a course of conduct which he knows full well cannot succeed and which, even should it achieve partial success in the short run, would definitely be contrary to the long-run interests of the people of his state and country. Lyndon Johnson, who had been made Majority Leader largely through the influence of Russell and other Southern senators, maneuvered to avoid the manifesto, and a decision was made by the Southern caucus to avoid asking him to sign it. I was not thus favored. Thurmond presented it to me on the floor of the Senate, in full view of the press gallery. I took one quick look at it and gave a flat "No," handing it back to him with some disagreeable emphasis because he already knew I would not sign it.

Much of my constituency was outraged at me. "We expected as much of Kefauver," many of them said, "but not Albert." I replied that my grandfather had tried unsuccessfully to secede from the Union in 1861, and I had no wish to emulate him by endorsing and encouraging interposition in the middle of the twentieth century. Actually, I regarded the manifesto (what an irritating and pretentious name!) as the most unvarnished piece of demagoguery I had ever encountered. Moreover, I was convinced that my fellow Southerners—and that is how I regarded them—were deliberately and callously misleading their people, and that nothing but tragedy and sorrow could come of this open defiance of the law, this cheap appeal to racism. But this was not how many of my own people saw it. I was thus placed in the anguishing position of either violating my conscience or appearing to be "against the South." But I never once thought of putting my name to it. Ever thereafter, bigots hurled the "anti-South" epithet at me, and my refusal to sign the manifesto was to be the principal weapon used against me in a hard-fought campaign for re-election in 1958—as it was against any white who did not conform.

Interposition was seriously proposed as a legal and constitutional means to nullify the Supreme Court decision. Its advocates rested their arguments upon States' rights and upon a commitment to use state power—police and state guards, if necessary—to prevent implementation of federal court orders. They hoped that, with the acquiescence of Eisenhower, they could face down the courts. It would be made unlawful in each Southern state for a school official to obey a federal desegregation order. State law and orders would thus be interposed between the local institution and federal court orders.

Interposition became a favorite subject for discussion and resolution in every Southern state, though unanimity of governors was never quite achieved. Four states—Alabama, Georgia, Mississippi, and Florida—carried the doctrine to its logical conclusion by pronouncing the *Brown* decision null and void, as the Southern Manifesto had done. To my embarrassment, the Tennessee legislature passed a "Manifesto of Protest," as did some other states, but it stopped short of endorsing interposition.

I soon came to realize that more than racial prejudice was

involved in the drive for interposition. Protection of white supremacy was paramount, of course, but it was also a determined affirmation of States' rights in other important fields, particularly taxation and regulation of economic concentrations. For instance, the Resolution of the Florida Legislature declared:

> . . . said decisions and orders of the Supreme Court of the United States denying the individual sovereign states the power to enact laws relating to espionage or subversion, criminal proceedings, the dismissal of public employees for refusal to answer questions concerning their connections with communism, "right to work" protection, and relating to separation of the races in the public institutions of a State are null, void and of no force or effect.

In Texas, where oil supremacy was the equal of white supremacy, the doctrine of interposition had a strong appeal, and it was in Texas that its first dramatic test came, in the fall of 1956, when Governor Allan Shivers intervened (with Texas Rangers) to prevent the execution of federal court orders with respect to two schools. Without any manifest support from President Eisenhower, the federal judicial authority gave way to state force in both instances.

These victories of state force over court order, following the removal of Autherine Lucy from the University of Alabama by state police earlier in the same year, heartened the champions of interposition and seemed to validate the statement of Senator Byrd (not a lawyer) in February of the same year, that:

> If we can organize the Southern states for Massive Resistance to this order, I think that in time the rest of the country will realize integration is not going to be accepted in the South. In

interposition, the South has a perfectly legal means of appeal from the Supreme Court order.

Fortunately, not all resistance to law and order prevailed. Governor Clement of Tennessee sent state troopers to the Clinton High School not to prevent Negro children from attending school, but to preserve order and to escort black children to their classes. And then there was the turbulent, year-long bus boycott by blacks in Montgomery, Alabama, that ended in desegregation of the buses and in making Martin Luther King a national figure.

In one significant instance, President Eisenhower did act decisively, though belatedly and somewhat apologetically. That was at Little Rock, Arkansas. There, on September 2, 1957, Governor Orval E. Faubus, undoubtedly aware of the massive resistance victories of his neighbor in Texas, ordered the Arkansas National Guard, in effect, to prevent desegregation of the city's Central High School. Though Faubus stated and reiterated that he was neither opposing integration nor defending segregation and that he had only called out the troops "to maintain and restore order and to protect the lives and property of citizens," he followed a course of action which supported segregation.

Faubus found himself riding an accelerating wave of popularity whereby his political options were sharply narrowed. Racial demagoguery had flared to new depths in Arkansas, in Washington, and throughout the South. The Little Rock School Board, trapped between a federal court order and the Arkansas National Guard, appealed to the federal district court and to President Eisenhower for instruction and for action. Emotion-packed and tragic days followed, dragging on into weeks. It must have been an agonizing experience for Eisenhower, what with his now known antipathy to the *Brown* decision and his wide political support among segregationist elements in the South. On the very morning after Faubus had called out the guard, Eisenhower said at a press conference: "You cannot change people's hearts merely by laws. Laws . . . presumably express the conscience of a nation and its determination or will to do something. But the laws here are to be executed gradually." He offered neither constructive suggestions about the challenge to the federal authority at Little Rock nor solutions to the problem. But on September 5, he firmly stated, "The Federal Constitution will be upheld by me by every legal means at my command"— only to qualify it the very next day through an Administration spokesman who issued a statement that President Eisenhower was still opposed to the use of federal troops to enforce court orders. Finally, on September 24, the President federalized the Arkansas National Guard and saved the federal judiciary from another defeat in the South.

Though one dramatic thrust did not compensate for years of lack of leadership, it did serve to put to a dramatic end the spurious doctrine of interposition. The best explanation of President Eisenhower's reluctant but finally decisive action has been written by Emmet John Hughes, perhaps the most perceptive chronicler of the Eisenhower years, who wrote:

> The President, so slow to take firm federal action in support of civil rights, could and would respond with dispatch to a public challenge to presidential and constitutional authority. He could never view the first matter as anything but a dubious interpretation of law by the Supreme Court, trespassing close to a defiance of human nature. But the second question stood in no doubt: it was an issue of the dignity of the nation and its sacred founding documents.

If Eisenhower's personal attitude and slow action on race questions were pleasing to Bourbons of the Deep South, the economic policies of his Administration, particularly the tax policies of his Secretary of the Treasury, George Humphrey, were equally so. For a reversal of the Roosevelt-Truman economic policies as well as social policies was the constant goal of Southern conservatives.

A sharp division on economic policies has long existed among Southerners. In periods of economic distress, the appeal of liberal economic issues has been strong enough to predominate even over the race issue—during the Populist revolt and the New Deal, for instance. But just as the New Deal-Fair Deal era was our longest sustained period of liberal economic policies, the reaction has been characterized by prolonged and unusual pressures. Southern conservatives who had waxed rich during the recovery and prosperity of the Roosevelt Administrations seemed hell-bent for reversal of those policies lest too many others climb the ladder. Most of all they wanted to "broaden the base" of taxation, by which they meant to lower tax rates on high incomes and put the burden on the many, preferably by sales or hidden excise taxes. (I have long noticed that rich white men attribute the problems of race relations to the lower-income groups. "They [poor whites] have to compete with them [poor blacks]," the saying goes. But it had been the poorer whites who had usually supported economic policies that eased discrimination and racial tension, while it was the class of whites whose economic interests put them in support of reactionary candidates who indulged in race-baiting.)

Freedom—political and economic—is an imperative, but freedom to starve is not its necessary concomitant. Economic justice is a prerequisite to social justice. The former implies considerably more than merely the correction of physical abuse and degradation. One must go far beyond the eradication of acute want if each citizen is to participate fully in the total social and cultural life of his community. And this requires revenue. The next question is: Who pays it? My goal has been a graduated tax on income—"taxation according to ability to pay," as Cordell Hull, author of the income-tax amendment, described it. To the degree that our tax laws vary from this yardstick of social and economic justice, they are, in my view, regressive.

Other tools that the government can employ in achieving maximum economic justice include money management or, broadly speaking, the government's monetary policy. In this area, too, the Republican Administration of the 1950s was true to form: Treasury Secretary George Humphrey, a noted rightist, and that big bankers' tool William McC. Martin, Jr., then chairman of the Federal Reserve Bank Board, reversed the low-interest-rate policies of the Roosevelt and Truman Administrations. Southern conservatives enthusiastically joined in this misrepresentation of the interests of their credit-starved constituents.

Those of us in the South who regarded ourselves as progressive or liberal on economic issues and as moderates on social issues had a difficult time of it for those eight years. This was particularly true of me in a border state. The end of my first term was approaching, and I faced a re-election fight in 1958, already branded as a deserter to the South on civil rights and as a liberal on taxes, public works, regulation, and power.

But before that the 1957 Civil Rights Act was debated and passed. Despite strong opposition from my state, I voted for the bill, since I thought it in a sense constituted Congress's answer to the turmoil rocking the South. The measure was a mild one, largely ineffective as judged by most. But it did place the Congress on the side of social justice, and in the era of "massive resistance," the mere passage of civil-rights legislation was itself worthy of note. Not only was this 1957 measure the first modern civil-rights law enacted by the Congress, but it created a new attitude toward filibustering in the Senate. After the long debate on that Act, those who favored filibusters were on the defensive, and this tactic steadily lost support and tolerance.

From an economic as well as a social point of view, I considered the rapidly growing use and effectiveness of money in politics to be a threat to genuine democracy of the people. Since my 1956 investigation of campaign finances, I had advocated passage of a law forbidding the use of private money by anyone, including a candidate, in federal elections. Since in our entire federal government only 537 officials—the President, the Vice-President, and the Congress—are chosen by the people, the ballot boxes in their elections should be freed completely from private subsidy. I finally got the Senate Finance Committee to approve my bill to provide for federal funds for federal elections for those candidates who would neither accept nor spend private money, but I was never able to pass it in the Senate because the coalition of Southern Democrats and Republicans opposed it and all other measures that would effectively curb or control money in politics. So I knew that plenty of money would be available for my opponent in my next election contest.

Sure enough, the "Southern Manifesto" was the first prop of my well-financed 1958 Democratic primary opponent, the conservative former two-term governor of Tennessee, Prentice Cooper, who waved the *Congressional Record* in which the "sacred document" was printed (minus my name, to him a truly cardinal political sin), pledged that his first act as Tennessee's next senator would be to sign the manifesto—at that point waving it with increased vigor. I promptly ridiculed the document with all the wit and sarcasm I could summon, and this proved an effective way to deal with it. The *Nashville Tennessean* stanchly supporting my candidacy, sent a reporter on a search for the document Governor Cooper, if elected, had said he would sign. Like the Holy Grail, it was nowhere to be found, which added piquancy to my treatment of the issue. "Perhaps Strom Thurmond is saving it for his Presidential Library in Aiken, South Carolina," I mused out loud.

The "anti-South" tag was much harder to deal with—indeed impossible for me to shake off—and this gave me much trouble, particularly in west Tennessee. Also, a massive publicity effort was mounted—billboards, newspapers, TV, radio —to brand me as non-Tennessean in attitude, having an affinity with the iniquitous East instead of the South. This, too, proved sticky because by then I had made my short-lived but substantial bid for the Vice-Presidential nomination, and had been all over the nation on speaking itineraries. Billboards blazoned a slogan: "Tennessee needs a Senator FOR, not FROM Tennessee."

I played up my role in exposing and ultimately defeating the Dixon-Yates contract. Moreover, the promise of benefits from the twelve hundred miles of interstate highway to be built in Tennessee under the terms of the Gore Bill (the National Interstate Highway Bill, which I had authored, was always thus spelled with capital letters and enunciated distinctly by my supporters) was most helpful. I went to the people cataloguing not only what I had done and what I had accomplished and what I had tried to do for Tennessee, but also for America, "of which Tennessee is a proud and im-

portant part." I made no public reference to my national political ambitions, carefully keeping those meager but conscious inner stirrings to myself.

It seemed to be working out pretty well, but I experienced
one serious fright in the campaign. Orval Faubus won an almost unprecedented third-term nomination for governor in
neighboring Arkansas by a sweeping majority—only a few
days before the Tennessee primary-election day. The *Arkansas Gazette* editorialized:

> The moderate position formerly espoused by many Southern
> political leaders, and by this newspaper as a matter of principle,
> has been rejected by the mass of voters in this upper Southern
> state and is now clearly untenable for any man in public life
> anywhere in the region.

Dixiecrat supporters of Governor Cooper shouted with glee
and renewed their waving of the manifesto. My supporters
redoubled their efforts, as did I, and we won the primary by
a comfortable majority. Even so, the potency of the race issue
—symbolized by the code words "Southern Manifesto," "anti-
South" and "non-Tennessee"—had its effect, particularly in
west Tennessee, where Cooper ran strongly and where, I was
later to learn, the labels left lasting scars on me.

One thing this campaign showed, as Senator Kefauver had
also demonstrated, was that a liberal Democrat could win the
nomination in a Tennessee primary in a hands-down two-
man battle. But the potential for trouble in the general election was clearly apparent—a combination of Republican
strength (it had normally been about 40 per cent of the vote)
with the Dixiecrat element of the Democratic Party and
economic conservatives who were affronted by my liberalism,
especially on tax policies. Two things eliminated this poten-

tially serious threat before November of that year. First, the
Republicans failed to nominate a serious contender against
me and, second, the Democratic nominee for governor was
the late Buford Ellington, an ex-Mississippian of extremely
conservative views, who had won the nomination by a razor-
edge vote in a four-man race during which he had declared,
"I am an old-fashioned segregationist." There was much dissatisfaction in the Democratic Party about Mr. Ellington's
nomination—not only among the liberal and progressive elements but also among moderates and many factional leaders.
Ellington's precarious position was recognized by the popular
former governor, James Nance McCord, who announced his
candidacy as an Independent in the November election.

Ellington needed me to blunt the Independent threat before it gained strength.

I had always been intensely loyal to the Democratic Party.
So, I promptly endorsed Ellington as "the nominee of the
Democratic Party." Furthermore, I campaigned the state side
by side with Ellington in joint appearances. The band wagon
began to roll, and victory for both of us was assured.

During a bus ride after a night engagement where I had
"laid on the wood," for the ticket, I confided to Ellington that
I might have an interest in preferment at the 1960 Democratic
convention. Ellington promptly said, "I'm for that." I thanked
him and chalked it up in my mind.

Nationally, the Democrats scored a resounding victory in
the 1958 Congressional elections. The country was suffering a
serious economic recession for which the economic policies of
the Republican Administration were widely blamed. Eisenhower, though still beloved as few men in our history, was
losing some of his magic appeal, and his illness and approaching retirement had further eroded his influence. His Admin-

istration was coming to a premature end. Drift characterized both policy and program of his later months in office. A general malaise prevailed.

Who could be surprised by signs of unrest? Prominent governors were flouting the law of the land, a large segment of Congress openly defied the unanimous decision of the nation's highest court, and the country's chief executive failed time after time to support the legal decrees of the federal courts. An era of disorder, lawlessness, and disrespect for governmental institutions was clearly predictable. And when it came, as we now know, the advocates of interposition were the first to demand "law and order."

Eisenhower's final act, perhaps his most lasting contribution, was his warning to his countrymen of the dangers inherent in the burgeoning "military-industrial complex." Much about this remarkable man had been praiseworthy, likable, and downright good. I shall ever have a deep admiration for his refusal to send U.S. combat troops into Vietnam in 1954 to save the French from defeat at Dienbienphu when it was urged upon him by Vice-President Nixon, Secretary of State John Foster Dulles, and the chairman of the Joint Chiefs of Staff, Admiral Radford. One will never know, but historians can meditate upon the knowledge and possibly the anxieties which prompted this good and simple man of military renown to conclude his service with that prophetic valedictory warning.

CHAPTER IV

Turbulence, Triumph, Tragedy

AN UNSURPASSED IRONY of the turbulent period of "massive resistance" in the South was the perversion of political language, whereby reactionary politicians came to cherish the label of conservative, while those who advocated or were willing to accept the decisions and decrees of the Supreme Court who sought to protect and, indeed, to conserve the citizens' guarantees under the Bill of Rights, were derisively called liberals—or subversives, or revolutionaries, or just plain "nigger-lovers."

How brief are our memories and how fickle are political loyalties! It is a documented fact that during the New Deal Southerners were *more* inclined than all other regional groups to regard themselves as "liberals." In 1937, when asked in a public-opinion poll, "If there were only two political parties in this country—one for conservatives and one for liberals—which one would you join?" 61 per cent of Southerners replied "liberals," as compared with 47 per cent of New Englanders, 51 per cent of Middle Westerners, 50 per cent in the Plains states, 51 per cent in the Rocky Mountains, and 54 per cent of Far Westerners. During the Depression and New Deal years, of course, the primary connotation of liberalism was economic, not racial, and during those grim years the prostrate South had received considerably more than its share of federal assistance. But by the late 1950s, liberalism—to the Southern mind—had become narrowly synonymous with racial integration.

Segregationists, on the other hand, claimed "conservative" for their identification. I remember hearing Senator James Eastland of Mississippi say, in very flat tones, many times, "I am a conservative," and he authenticated the terms of the movement.

Senator Eastland was always courteous and polite to me, and in many respects he is a generous and estimable man, surely a "man of his word," as the saying goes in Congressional cloakrooms. He was one colleague, however, with whom I did not engage in conversation on the race question, though I frequently listened to him both in Senate debate and in cloakroom dialogue. The gulf between us was too great for mutual discussion to bridge—not that I was a white knight for civil rights. I wasn't anything more, really, than a moderate who believed in the Constitution, who respected and supported duly constituted courts of the land, and who had compassion for oppressed fellow Americans. But my recollection of his chilling remarks on the subject of race, and his frequent use of extreme and inflammatory terms, held me back from dialogue with him.

Southern politics has always suffered from an inordinate amount of blackguardism, but the advent of racial integration brought about a new era of name-calling. No longer was it sufficient for a politician to master simple invective; a new lexicon of code words became tools in the hands, or rather in the mouths, of the demagogues. A "subversive" was either "anti-American" or "anti-Southern," depending upon the victim. The "Southern way of life" was white supremacy, which meant keeping the "nigger in his place." "Pinty headed," "pink," "outside agitator," and even "intellectual" became terms of opprobrium as used by those who denounced the "National Democratic Party" as "liberal" and "anti-South," self-styling themselves as "Jeffersonians," "Southern Democrats," or sometimes just "conservatives." They were fond of saying, in referring to the "National" Democratic Party, "it left me, I did not leave it."

Of course, intemperateness of language and attitude was by no means monopolized by Southerners. Many people from outside the South, including politicians, were not only extreme in their denunciations of the South, but increasingly hypocritical in their refusal to acknowledge, much less deal, with racial discrimination in their own constituencies. A "Southern politician" was a "racial bigot." The white South felt put upon and, not without justification, became angered; instead of concentrating on correction, it entrenched and fought back.

In keeping with the semantic corruption, Southern politicians advocated and Southern legislatures actually perverted the law to accomplish illegal ends, so that the whole process became a mockery of justice, confusing and blurring the lines between legality and illegality in a region where the tradition of violence and militarism was already deeply embedded in social mores. All this demonstrated, I thought, an irresponsibility on the part of Southern political leaders and a widespread lack of commitment to the rule of law among the very people who were soon to call loudest for "law and order."

In response, the declining confidence in, and respect for, law by the blacks was ominous. The icebergs of their resentment and impatience were everywhere apparent, but the true proportions of the revolt were neither clearly visible nor comprehended. One thing is certain, however. The Negro had had a political awakening. And it was high time. Blacks had long constituted a largely nonvoting minority nationally and a large, virtually voteless, segment of population in the South. But after Truman's victory with overwhelming Negro support in Northern cities, the Negro vote became a principal topic of political conversation and strategy everywhere. After the Voting Rights Act of 1957, Negro influence in Southern politics began slowly to increase.

In this confused, rapidly changing context, the Presidential race to succeed Eisenhower began. The prospects for the election of a Democrat appeared so promising that jockeying for position among possible nominees began earlier than usual. The candidates were off and running as early as 1958, though each felt obliged to maintain the traditional stance of a noncandidate. (This continuing coyness in American politicians, about who is and who is not running for office, reminds me of nothing quite so much as the ritualistic mating dance of the gooney birds I once saw on Midway Island.)

The Presidency of the United States, to me, is so awesome an office and it so dwarfs the human being that at times it seems preposterous for anyone, or particularly for one's friend, to aspire to it. In the process of daily living, all men of my acquaintance fell short of fitness for that exalted spot. Yet it is a vital part of the American Dream that any one of us may seek the office on an equal footing, and that one from among us shall win it. In my early political days, I thought no one could ever replace Franklin D. Roosevelt. He fulfilled all my requirements. Then I witnessed the elevation to the Presidency of a man from Independence, Missouri, with ordinary talents and earthy experiences and attitudes, and I saw him become a very good President.

By 1958, every potential candidate for President in either party was one with whom I had crossed verbal swords on equal terms, at least in my view. And this, naturally, had a bearing on my attitude when observers began to mention my name as a Presidential potentiality. My first reaction was an incredulous, "Who? *Me?*" But then I thought about all those other "potentialities"—Jack, Lyndon, Stu, Hubert Horatio, Estes—and I must admit that I thought I could do at least as well as any of them, maybe better. After all, there is no modest way to seek the Presidency. So my pulse quickened.

Since I was carrying a full load as an active senator, running for re-election to the Senate in 1958, and doing all within my power to help assure that the Democrats would capture the Presidency in 1960, I found myself busy on all fronts: international, national, and local. Perhaps a brief account of my flirtation with Presidential ambition can serve to illuminate the issues and personalities involved in that most interesting election of 1960.

The better to acquaint myself with foreign affairs, I made an extended overseas trip in late 1958 which included two weeks in South Vietnam. There, I came to have grave doubts about our policies in Indochina, and the government of South Vietnam which we supported. Each day there these doubts grew. Senator Gale McGee of Wyoming, with whom I

was traveling, and I spent almost a day with Ngo Dinh
Diem, whom the United States had installed as head of state,
and an evening with Diem's brother and his wife, the beautiful and controversial Madame Nhu. At a Washington press
conference in January 1959, after our return, I expressed concern that Diem's "authoritarian policies seem to be growing
instead of diminishing," and that "some costly mistakes"
should be corrected in our aid program, which I described as
"loose, confused, and disorganized." In addition, I pointed to
danger signals of corruption in the use of American aid by the
Saigon government. Strangely enough, Senator McGee disagreed with nearly all my observations, including those on
the program of so-called land development, which I called an
"economic monstrosity" and which he described as a "tremendous success story from which we and all free Asia can
take heart." Ultimately, of course, this expensive undertaking proved to be a failure and was abandoned. But this
brought me no satisfaction; it was worse than a total waste,
having cost many lives. (From then to my last day in the
United States Senate, Senator McGee and I held diametrically
opposed views on the Vietnam misadventure. These completely opposite interpretations of the same sights and experiences by two senators of the same political party typify
opinions on the Vietnam war and show that the division
started early.)

The views I expressed were not particularly pleasing to my
constituents, but my experiences caused me, thereafter to look
with deep concern upon any move toward military involvement in Southeast Asia. A few months later, I got into hot
water with American Legionnaires in my home state on this
subject by taking the floor at a state legion convention in
Chattanooga to make a vigorous reply to an extremely hawk-

ish speech by the legion's national commander in which he advocated military intervention in Laos.

In 1959, too, I was appointed a delegate to the Nuclear Test Ban Conference in Geneva being held by the United States, the U.S.S.R., and Great Britain. I selected former AEC Commissioner Thomas Murray as my adviser, and made an intensive study of the problem of nuclear-weapon tests in the atmosphere and underground, as well as of the general subject of nuclear armaments. The campaign to stop contamination of the air with radioactive poison from atmospheric nuclear-bomb tests was about as pressing and as popular in 1959 as antipollution is now. And I was astride that white horse, riding hard, with a plan I thought both workable and desirable. I took it to a White House conference with President Eisenhower after a return from the Geneva Conference. All of this received much favorable national coverage.

The recession of the late 1950s became rather more severe than was at first generally realized. This gave me an opportunity to bear down hard on domestic issues both in the Senate and out on the hustings over the country with, I must admit, some partisan gusto. *Time* Magazine of November 3, 1958, carried the following:

> Tennessee's Albert Gore, now safe for another six years in the United States Senate, speaking for a Michigan Congressional candidate: "If the Republican Party were ever re-incarnated into a homing pigeon, no matter from where it were released in the universe, whether from a jet plane or in outer space, it would go directly home to Wall Street without a flutter of the wing."

In speech after speech and with amendment after amendment in the Senate I was fighting to relieve unemployment (then hovering between 5 and 6 per cent of the labor force). Tax reform, as well, was my constant goal and I gained a national identification with this cause.

Senator Robert Kerr of Oklahoma had added a little fuel to my flickering Presidential flame on a visit to Nashville in December 1958, by describing me to the press as "one of the three men that I know to be best qualified for President of the United States." Newsmen pressed him to identify the other two but he declined. (I could have told them the other two were Lyndon Johnson and Bob Kerr, except the order in his mind was Bob, Lyndon, and then Albert.) His praise of me in my home state was generous but I knew that between Johnson and me he would be for Johnson, because from his point of view Johnson was right on the oil tax issues while I was wrong.

Senator Kerr was not without justification in having supreme self-confidence. I think his mind and wit were as quick and sharp as those of any man I ever knew and it was extremely difficult to cope with him in light banter. He might be on the wrong side of an issue but when in debate with him one could only let the dialogue stray from the issue at one's peril.

As for Lyndon Johnson he and I had worked together many times. He always helped me with TVA, and I always helped him with Southwestern power and water issues, but we invariably disagreed on tax policy. I wanted to eliminate special tax privileges, close the big tax loopholes that permit many people to escape their fair share of the tax burden; but the creation and preservation of tax favoritisms had long been a strong arch in Johnson's Texas support and one of the keys to his rise to Senate leadership.

For fourteen years in the House of Representatives I had

been frustrated in my desire to attack the unfairness of federal tax laws. Under the restrictive parliamentary rules of the House procedure, not once did I have an opportunity to offer an amendment to a tax bill, or even to vote for or against one. The House of Representatives was and still is hog-tied by rigid rules which prevent such action. The House Ways and Means Committee, where all tax measures originate, has become the sole arbiter for the House of Representatives as to how, when, and from whom tax money is collected.

Tax bills are invariably brought to the House floor for debate under gag rules that prevent members from offering amendments. Even the one small privilege of a motion to recommit a bill to the committee is reserved to the minority party. (To justify this practice of "gagging" the very men who, the Constitution says, shall originate all revenue bills, the argument is that revenue legislation is so complex that to accept one apparently simple amendment could require wholesale changes in a book-thick bill. I always disagreed with this.)

In the Senate, things were very different. Each senator has whatever opportunity he is willing to take to offer amendments to tax bills and to bring them to a showdown of votes. Being in the Senate, I could fight for fairness for the people from whom I had come, and to fight against favoritism, which I resented and resisted. This opportunity would expand if I could obtain membership on the Senate Finance Committee, which had jurisdiction over tax legislation during its drafting. Here, however, I met the determined opposition of my friend LBJ. His opposition was impossible to overcome because, as Majority Leader, he controlled committee assignments and even appointed members of the Democratic Policy Committee without reference to the Caucus of Democrats. We argued about it; he always wanted me to take some other committee, almost any other. But I waited and gained seniority. Senator Paul Douglas of Illinois, an outstanding economist and an exceptionally able public servant—but an opponent of the 27-per-cent depletion allowance for oil and gas—had likewise tried in vain for membership on this tax-writing committee. He, too, had already gained seniority but still was denied a voice where it counted. Finally, the only way Johnson could keep me from the committee when a vacancy occurred was to take it himself, which he did, and then secretly resigned a few months later to give the place to Senator George Smathers of Florida, who always supported him on tax questions.

The fight about this between Johnson and me got a little rough, so rough that on one occasion he asked his pal Senator Hubert Humphrey to sit in as a witness while he and I exchanged some mildly unpleasant personal compliments on the subject. Then I proceeded to make a public issue of it, calling attention to the reactionary attitude of the finance committee and to Johnson's stubborn opposition to any senator going on the committee unless he was "right on oil." Douglas joined me in this. We kept the issue so hot that both of us finally made it—but once there we found ourselves boxed, being only two out of seventeen.

Not only was the committee a tough nut to crack, but working conditions on it were almost impossible. Still, by working, I was able to reverse its decisions on the floor of the Senate time after time, something that had been unheard of in the Senate for years.

Ironically, one of my first such victories related to the issue of applying a percentage depletion allowance not to ores or raw minerals (or oil) but to finished manufactured products. This loophole had not been intentionally created by Congress but rather by a tax court ruling, and it threatened to become very expensive to the Treasury, probably as much as $600 million a year. President Eisenhower and Secretary of the Treasury Robert Anderson had repeatedly asked Congress to eliminate this unreasonable loophole, but neither the House Ways and Means Committee nor the Senate Finance Committee would do it. Special interests liked it! Not one Republican Senator would so much as offer the amendment on behalf of the Administration in the Senate Finance Committee. I did. But only Senator Douglas and I voted for it.

I prepared to make a do-or-die fight on this on the Senate floor. It was wholly wrong, there was absolutely no justification for it. Indeed, no committee member would even attempt to defend it. They just wouldn't vote to repeal it. I offered my amendment in the course of an afternoon session, and made a long speech in support of it. To my disappointment, very few senators were there to hear me. As I was nearing the end of my speech, it was plain that I had been unable to reach very many of my colleagues, since most of those present were members of the finance committee and I had no chance of persuading them. But the case was so unanswerable that I decided to use a unique strategy to get an audience. I extended my speech, as a sort of an educational campaign. I noticed Lyndon Johnson and Everett Dirksen conferring and looking at the clock, but I kept talking until the dinner hour had arrived and then annouced that I would ask for a roll-call vote after a quorum was present. I knew that when senators abandoned constituents and problems in the office during regular hours to come to the floor to vote, they were apt to rush back again right afterward, whereas when they came to the floor after the dinner hour, when offices were closed, they were inclined to listen to a debate, if it were interesting. Nearly all members of the Senate came to vote, but after my speech. After my amendment was defeated over-whelmingly. I grabbed the floor and began to talk again. They were listening! I spoke longer than I had intended, for I could see and feel the effect of my speech. I announced I would offer my amendment again on Monday, the next legislative day. I noticed Johnson nod to Dirksen and they went to the Republican cloakroom. A few moments later, other Republican and Southern Democratic tax big-wheels went through the same door. I knew then that I had flushed the covey. Encouraged, I announced that I would ask for another roll-call vote on Monday. My amendment passed on Monday by a vote of 87 to 0. Lyndon Johnson, Everett Dirksen, Harry Byrd, Bob Kerr, Wallace Bennett, Russell Long—all the tax titans of the Senate—voted with me!

I had broken the ice. I had defeated the Senate Finance Committee—and by unanimous vote. I was on my way toward working some genuine tax reform. My program was multi-faceted.

—Tighten up excessive deductions for expense accounts and other so-called business expenses of questionable validity.

—Eliminate the dividend credit on corporate stocks.

—Basically modify the formula for depletion allowance on oil, minerals, and other resources.

—Repeal restricted stock-option provisions.

—Repeal or drastically modify the foreign tax-credit provisions.

—Repeal capital gains treatment for lump-sum payments made on pension plans.

—Repeal estate- and gift-tax exemption for certain types of pension payments.

—Provide for withholding at the source of the tax on interest and dividends.

But this kind of program can be politically unrewarding. As columnist Charles Bartlett wrote:

> Few reporters in Washington understand the bills to which [Gore] is objecting, the public has no interest in most of them, and the struggle is between him and the people who want a special tax advantage. In most of his fights, he makes no friends and develops a considerable number of new enemies.
>
> It is certain that Gore would be a far more entrenchable contender for the Democratic nomination in 1960 if it were not for his pre-occupation with the underside of the tax laws.
>
> He is becoming known and feared as a man with little expertise in tax matters but with a powerful sense of smell.

Politics or not, there was a job to be done for tax reform and I was trying to do it. Moreover, I thought there was widespread interest in tax reform and, particularly, resentment at the favoritism and inequities by which many rich people were escaping their share of the burden.

Invitations to speak at party functions poured in from all over the country, even a few in the South, and I was making the welkin ring. What politician is not enthralled by the sound of his own voice, especially when it is orchestrated with a crowd's applause and fired by the hope, however dim, of holding higher office? There may be some who would be immune to this heady wine, but I have have not known them.

It is possible in 1972, after so many bared their ambitions, to look back and smile a bit at the excitement that I felt but which I managed to keep mostly to myself. Perhaps only those few who have taken deep draughts of this wine of kings can really know how impossible it is for ambitious and egocentric young men to judge soberly the enticements of a Presidential campaign. And who, really, would stop them? A sage of my home town once remarked: "Five people can persuade a man to run for public office, but once he has the taste of it and has looked again in the mirror, five hundred cannot get him to withdraw from the race." Ours is a political system and ambition for political service and honor is its life blood.

To say the least of it, or perhaps more accurately, to say the most of it, by early 1959 I had occasional dreams of the Presidency. I was determined to keep myself in circulation and to keep my powder dry, although my pragmatic analysis was that no man from a Southern or border state could win the Democratic nomination—unfair, I thought, but true. Only by a miracle could a Southerner triumph over the long sectional bias against the South—a national attitude—that stemmed first from bitterness over slavery, then the Civil War, and, later, racial discrimination.

My situation had been rather accurately assessed, my better judgment told me, by the columnist William S. White:

> He is a member of a more or less liberal movement in the South. And he probably typifies the kind of politician who will be required in that section if the Democratic Party there is ever to become a positive rather than a largely negative influence within the national organization.
>
> He is among those Southerners, for illustration, who honestly wish to ease the segregation issue. He will go to some length— and run considerable political danger—in the cause of promoting Negro rights and privileges. He is a man, morever, ready and willing to occupy himself seriously with serious issues. . . .
>
> It is probable that he thinks of himself as the sort of politician who will at length lead the South away from its traditional sectionalism. Such an eventuality—and such a man—

might also break the old tradition that a Southerner cannot be elected President.

If Senator Gore does, indeed, ponder these possibilities, it is a perfectly rational ambition. It is, however, no doubt a bit premature. The likelihood of the notion suffers, too, in a less tangible way.

Tennessee in the North is automatically considered a Southern state—and in a way and for purpose of convenience in description it is.

But Tennessee was never all-Southern; not during the Civil War and not since. It was a bitterly divided border state in the last century, and it is politically a border state still. If a Tennessean should return one day to the White House to vindicate the memory of Andrew Johnson of Tennessee in that office, this would not necessarily mean an end to the national apartness of the Deep South.

For such a border-state candidate—Senator Gore specifically in the present discussion—would never be gladly backed by the Deep Southerners. They might take him as a matter of expediency; but he could never really reflect their views.

But the audiences were cheering and eminent commentators were writing things that kept my blood pressure high:

The election this month suggests the people want new faces and voices [wrote Eric Sevareid]. The potential Democratic candidates for President and Vice President, young as most of them may be, are already unexcitingly familiar to professional observers here. And, unless our own antenna is entirely corroded, we detect the beginnings of a shift of attention to Gore of Tennessee.

If the "keep the South in" sentiment of the last two Democratic conventions prevails in 1960, Gore, as a Southerner, would have much the same acceptability to the North, as

Stevenson, a Northerner, had to the South. And his Southern colleagues do not feel the same antipathy toward him that they felt toward Kefauver.

Gore does not have Stevenson's brilliance, but he possesses relative youth—he's fifty—personal attractiveness, and a driving, digging mind that has won the respect of Washington intellectuals; quite a feat for a man whose degree comes from a teachers' college and a YMCA night course in law.

If he does have national ambitions, he's his own worst enemy. He has no publicity sense or machinery. His official biography in the Congressional Directory consists of exactly three lines.

But there is something about him, as there was in a more incandescent way about Stevenson, that is very likely to draw the wavering spotlight in his direction in the months ahead.

I was invited to give the Democratic speech at the prestigious annual Gridiron Dinner in Washington in May 1959, a sure sign, one of my friends said, that "the wise boys see a rising star."

The coast appeared clear for me so far as my own state was concerned. Governor Clement was out of office and out of the picture. My esteemed colleague Senator Kefauver had had his run in both 1952 and 1956, and besides, he wanted re-election to the Senate in 1960. Governor Ellington was proving to be eminently satisfactory to the conservative elements in the state but he did not appear to be a prospect for national preferment, and he had repeatedly expressed gratitude for my quick and firm support of his candidacy when former Governor McCord had threatened his election.

Since Tennessee had given Eisenhower a majority in 1952 and even in 1956 with Kefauver as the Democratic Vice-Presidential nominee, I set out to bring the Democratic hopefuls to my state in an effort to improve their acceptability and thus to improve the chances of winning Tennessee's electoral vote for the Democratic Party. The first to come was Senator John F. Kennedy, in February 1959. He was then my closest friend among the possible contenders. We had been both congressmen and freshmen senators together and had developed a warm personal affinity. Our wives, too, were friends. (This was surprising to some observers, for it had been I who had "thrown" the Vice-Presidential nomination to Senator Kefauver, as I have already written, at a crucial moment in the 1956 Democratic convention. There had been, in fact, a coolness toward me for a while after that, but it proved only temporary, for he knew that my loyalty to a colleague from my home state had to take precedence over a New Englander. He came to believe, also, that had he been nominated in 1956, it may have been the end of his national prospects because, looking back on it, no ticket could have defeated President Eisenhower then and had he been on the losing ticket, its defeat would have been widely attributed to his Catholic religion.)

Mrs. Gore flew from Washington to Nashville in the "Caroline" with Senator Kennedy and his lovely wife, Jacqueline, who was making her first campaign trip with him in the Presidential race. Their reception in Tennessee was by and large a good one; yet I became conscious of a definite coolness toward an Eastern Catholic "liberal" among many party leaders. This was especially noticeable among the right-wing Democrats—the self-proclaimed "Jeffersonians," including Ellington.

The next candidate to come was Senator Lyndon Johnson, with whom a passingly pleasant personal equation had been reestablished. Despite his disavowals, I knew he was a candidate. He was beginning to call himself a "Westerner," trying to escape the Southern hex, though his Texas drawl was even more Southern than my Tennessee twang. He was trying to touch all the bases, a sure sign of a candidatorial interest. His real base, though, was the South—plus the power structure of the Senate. But even with the advantages of the Majority Leadership, there were no substantial signs that he could win the Presidential nomination.

I took Johnson, as I had Kennedy, to Oak Ridge. This was our most liberal and our most sophisticated community as well as our most renowned, owing to the large atomic facilities there. And, besides, I would need the support of my Senate colleague on many questions affecting both the atomic-energy programs and the TVA. Anyway, I took Johnson to an advantageous overlook from which we could view the vast nuclear facilities. For once this gave me an opportunity to claim a sort of superiority for Tennessee: "Lyndon, the plants you see use more electricity than the entire state of Texas."

"Aw, hell," he said, making for the car door.

At Nashville, I noticed a long-lost-friend type of greeting between Johnson and Ellington and heard some good-natured references to "Bob" (Kerr). This was strange because I had introduced Ellington to both Johnson and Kerr only a few months before. So I knew that Lyndon and his pals had been making hay with my conservative governor. In other ways, too, it was apparent that Johnson would have strong support from the conservative wing of the party in my state. His speech —boosting TVA, Roosevelt, Southern Progress, Good Neighbors, etc.—was well attended and well applauded by the Ellington administration clientele.

Senator Hubert Humphrey was the next politico to come to Tennessee. I had difficulty arranging a speaking engagement for him. "Too damn liberal," they would say. Oak

Ridge was again the only place I could schedule him with good local sponsorship. Even there, neither Ellington nor any of his key leaders attended the meeting. Humphrey was aware of a coolness toward him and his performance was not up to par for him. I was disappointed, and he must have been.

Missouri Senator Stuart Symington's name, like mine, was almost invariably included in the speculative political columns. An able man, with a distinguished record of success in private business and as Secretary of the Air Force, Symington's record as a senator had been sound and constructive. But he lacked identification with a popular issue and was not well known. He lacked, too, a political power base, coming neither from a large state nor one possessing a strong regional identification or appeal. But what about the Vice-Presidency? Here his odds were better. I never discussed the matter with him, but I knew him to be astute and pragmatic. My impression was that he never saw an opening that would justify a formalized candidacy. Neither did I. The field of mentionables had narrowed by early 1960 to six—Kennedy, Stevenson, Johnson, the top three; with Humphrey, Symington, and now and then myself as the lightning-rod carriers.

I began to hear of grumbling remarks in my own state by a few conservative leaders that I was "taking too big a hand," that the governor, after all, was the leader of the "Tennessee Democratic Party." (As we have seen before, Southern conservatives tend to identify with the state party and to speak disdainfully of the "National Democratic Party" and of those in national office.)

Stevenson still retained a great deal of support at this time —his eloquent articulation of liberal, intelligent policies throughout the seven years he had been titular head of the party had endeared him to millions of its members, and he so disliked and so distrusted Nixon, the likely Republican nominee, that he was champing at the bit to run again. But the aura of defeat clung to him, and everywhere I went I heard expressions of support for Stevenson—"if he could win." They would prefer him as President but—above all—they wanted a winner.

Two terms with a Republican in the White House were enough. Even the conservative Southern Democrats would take a Democrat by label if he would take an Eisenhower-like go-slow attitude on race matters, and show a dependable sympathy for the vested interests on economic and tax issues. But none of the Democratic candidates was giving much encouragement to them.

So, there was a general uneasiness among my Southern colleagues. They had made Johnson Majority Leader in the Senate, and in the showdowns they had been able to depend upon him for tax favoritisms for their moneyed friends, for deals like the Sugar Act, cotton allotments, and subsidies, and for any sort of pork-barrel project. This type of dealing was right down Johnson's alley. It was his developing "liberalism" on civil rights that had them deeply worried, however. Still, he was their best bet, if not their only one.

With the South secure as his power base, Johnson and his right-hand man, Bobby Baker, became even more high-handed in manipulating the Senate to further his Presidential ambitions. A number of senators had been grumbling about this. William Proxmire of Wisconsin, whose natural tendency was to speak out, was the first publicly to protest, and I was sympathetic to Proxmire's point of view. There should be caucuses of Democratic senators, and the senators themselves should have a voice in determining party policy. The Policy Committee members should be elected by the senators themselves; the Senate should not be a one-man show. There should be no room for argument about all this. It should be a matter of family (Democratic) understanding. So when this issue arose in the Democratic caucus in January 1960, I offered a suggestion for amelioration and compromise. Senator Johnson, presiding with Bobby Baker at his side, recognized me, but after I began, he said (after a quick whispered aside from Bobby Baker), "I did not recognize you for that."

Shocked and angered at this affront, I flushed and shot back:

"Who are you to say for what purpose a senator is recognized, and by what right or presumption do you undertake to say what another senator may speak about?"

I went on to argue that if this was an indication of the Majority Leader's attitude toward other senators then perhaps I was in error in seeking a compromise on the matter.

This was but a minor tiff behind closed doors in a Democratic caucus, but it was prominently reported in the national press and, to my surprise, it had the effect in political circles of drawing liberal fire upon Johnson and Southern conservative fire upon me. Governor Ellington, for instance, publicly remarked, "I kind of like the group Senator Gore is not running with. The conservative group is more in keeping with the thinking of the people of Tennessee." But as I saw it, the only effect of the episode, if any, was to draw more tightly the lines between the conservative and liberal factions and possibly to encourage Johnson to take a more progressive attitude on issues and practices as Majority Leader.

Kennedy was the first to announce his candidacy. By January 1960, he was clearly the fair-haired young man of the Democratic Party outside the South. And his religion was an enormous asset within the party. No Catholic had ever been elected President of the United States, and the prospect that it might happen with Kennedy fired the enthusiasm of many, many Catholics. This alone assured him a crowd of enthusiastic supporters wherever he went—a wonderful campaign aid —and the support of just about all big-city Democratic politicians. Although there was a great deal of talk and press comment about how Kennedy's Catholicism damaged his political fortunes, he, in fact, adroitly used this to his advantage.

By Presidential primary time, Kennedy was so strong in cities outside the South that only Stevenson and Humphrey could seriously think of challenging him in the primaries. Johnson's appeal was either provincial, or so exclusively with portions of the Establishment as to be lacking in rank-and-file appeal. Symington had not caught on. My fuse had lighted a time or two, perhaps, but had sputtered out. Russell Baker put it pretty well in an article in *The New York Times Magazine:*

> In recent weeks we have seen him in a variety of roles, suggesting the versatile statesman. There was "Fighting Albert," leader of the Senate's downtrodden liberals, the "Fiscal Albert," enemy of the tight-money men of the Republican Party. There was "Atomic Gore," with his suspicious eye on the disarmament negotiations at Geneva, and "Honest Al," assistant architect of the "clean-elections" bill (now dying in the House of Representatives). Most recently, there was "International Gore," chiding the Administration for its approach to the Paris summit.
>
> No one contends that this whirl of activity is motivated solely by desire to promote himself onto the national ticket, but it is the kind of thing that helps. Whether it can help Gore in 1960 is the question. For, despite a record of conspicuous service to the party, he has so far proved lacking in one indispensable quality for reaching the political pinnacle—sheer dumb luck.

Stevenson, more and more stuck with the loser image, was avoiding the primaries. This left only Humphrey to make a primary challenge to Kennedy. West Virginia was the big one. If Kennedy could beat Humphrey in this stronghold of Protestantism, hard-hat labor, and Appalachian poverty, then only a convention battle with Johnson stood between him and the nomination. Concentrating his campaign's money, organizing skill, and personal efforts there, Kennedy scored a smashing victory.

Senator Henry Jackson and I flew to the Democratic National Convention in Los Angeles with former Secretary of the Navy Dan A. Kimball in his private plane. Half seriously and half jokingly, Kimball said he wanted to give a ride to the next Vice-President. Jackson and I flipped a coin as to whom it would be. He won (the toss).

At the convention, I found myself immobilized by a Tennessee delegation firmly in the grip of Governor Ellington and firmly committed to his "old-time friend" Johnson, with the unit rule imposed. By then I was a firm Kennedy supporter, believing that he could be elected, confident that he would be a good President, and equally convinced that Johnson could not and should not be elected President. When the final roll call assured Kennedy's nomination, many Southern delegates were crestfallen, and many (among them Governor Ellington) left the convention floor issuing bitter forecasts of political doom for the party. When Kennedy came to acknowledge his nomination, I took Tennessee's standard to the front and stood waving it enthusiastically. Most of my state delegation was nowhere to be seen. The absence of so many Southern delegates spelled trouble in the South generally and especially in the border states. I remember, for instance, a conversation with Senator Kerr, a prominent Baptist, who spoke of Kennedy's dim prospects in Oklahoma because of his Catholicism.

John Kennedy was, if anything, a pragmatic politician. The day of his nomination he and I were in conversation, standing near a window of his room in the Biltmore Hotel, when his brother Bob entered the room and came directly to us. Jack said, "Lyndon." Nothing else. Bob stood motionless for a moment. I'll never forget the look on his face. He stared straight at Jack, whose expression was steady. Without a word Bob walked to a telephone and placed a call.

A few weeks later, Kennedy asked me to head up an anonymous advisory committee of "practical politicians upon whose advice I can depend." I would be glad to do so, I said, but I insisted that he personally select the other members. The next day, he handed me the following names: Clark Clifford, Bill Fulbright, Dick Bolling, Fred Dutton.

All but Congressman Bolling, who met with us only once, were regular in attendance throughout the campaign. We undertook not only a critical analysis and prognosis of the campaign, its strategy and issues, including Nixon's probable and actual tactics, but also responded to *ad hoc* inquiries from the Kennedy campaign plane, sometimes dictating statements to an aide telephoning from the campaign platform itself. In addition, we prepared and submitted suggested speeches on foreign policy (Fulbright), economic issues (me), defense (Clifford), and nuclear armaments (me). The committee always met either in my apartment or in Fulbright's home. We succeeded in remaining anonymous throughout the campaign. These meetings were surely nitty-gritty political sessions, and my admiration for the members grew with each meeting.

I will not undertake to write my detailed observations of the Republican nominating campaign. Suffice it to say that Nixon had an appeal which I was unable to understand. Though it must have been in part my own limitations, I never understood how millions of sensible citizens could bring themselves to vote for him for public office. Deficient in grace or charm, unprepossessing in appearance, plebeian in intellect, and painfully humorless, his appeal was to me incomprehensible. True, he had a certain chauvinistic energy, a cunning shrewdness, an instinct for the narrow prejudice and this may have attracted the rough-and-ready element, the social conservatives, and the economic royalists.

Kennedy, on the other hand, was intelligent, witty, gracious, handsome, and eloquent. A naïve observer might have concluded that there was no basis for genuine contest. Politicians knew better, for Kennedy was also urbane, a Catholic, an Easterner, and a liberal on social and economic issues. This could but mean trouble in a region traditionalist in outlook, fundamentalist in religion, and segregationist in social matters —that is to say, in the South.

So the South became, as it so often is, a major battleground. Richard Nixon spoke in every Southern state, while John Kennedy visited six and made ten speeches in Texas alone.

Race, religion, and partisan loyalties constituted just about the whole campaign. Of course, there was much talk of the missile gap, fiscal irresponsibility, and humor and oratory. Richard Nixon was the heavy, John Kennedy the attractive, warm candidate. Except for the emotional issues of race and religion, the contest should not have been close. But the going was rough for Kennedy, especially in the South.

The black vote—which was steadily enlarging and which had been split between Eisenhower and Stevenson in 1956—

swung heavily behind the Kennedy-Johnson ticket, helping to offset losses of conservative and anti-Catholic votes. Nixon swept the border states of Kentucky, Tennessee, Virginia, and Oklahoma. In these states, like Florida, which also gave Nixon a majority, the normal Republican vote is quite substantial and the Negro population is comparatively small. Thus, a major defection from the Democrats (for whatever reason) means Republican victories.

Kennedy carried the traditional Deep South—Louisiana, Mississippi, Georgia, Louisiana, Alabama, Arkansas, and South Carolina. Yet the size of the popular vote for Nixon, a hard-line Republican, carried vast political portents. For instance, he lost South Carolina by a meager 1 per cent of the votes cast. Texas, too, was close—its majority for the Kennedy-Johnson ticket testified to Kennedy's political wisdom in choosing Johnson as his running mate, since its electoral vote supplied the winning margin over Nixon-Lodge.

It was a sweet victory in which I exulted, though I was sorely disappointed at losing my state. I had been galled by the laissez-faire politics of President Eisenhower, and I enjoyed thinking that by my fights in the Senate I had forged the economic issues on which my friend Kennedy had largely been elected. With a friend in the White House, I was brimming with enthusiasm to get back to work in the Senate.

I must here acknowledge that I never really knew how firmly Kennedy was committed to liberal economics. His votes in the Senate had been solidly Democratic, and his campaign speeches and statements had been satisfactory—naturally so to me since I had some hand in their preparation—and in private conversations his attitudes and leanings were in the public interest. Yet he had an awesome regard or a kind of mystical respect for the financier and the big businessman.

(Still, I sometimes got the impression that the only successful businesman he knew well and respected was his father, Joseph P. Kennedy.)

In view of the country's economic problems and his campaign theme "to get the country moving again," I believed the most important cabinet post would be Treasury. It would be the key to the economic policies of the new Administration. (The 1958–1959 recession had resulted from the big-bank-oriented monetary and fiscal policies of the Eisenhower Administration, whose economic major-domo had been Treasury Secretary George Humphrey.) Loving the Senate as I did, I did not wish to be appointed to the Treasury post myself, as had been rumored in the press, although some economists—Kenneth Galbraith, for instance—had suggested my name to Kennedy. But I surely wanted the right kind of Democrat in that key post. My entire service in the Senate had been during the Eisenhower Administration and I had longed for a Democratic Administration when real tax reform could be accomplished and when the government's monetary policies could be snatched from the financial moguls who profited so enormously from artificially high interest rates and preferential tax treatment. It is the mass of our people—those who must build and buy on credit—who must pay the high interest rates ar.d bear an unfair portion of the tax burden. And repeated cycles of boom and recession only intensify their insecurity. It is their jobs in marginal and unskilled fields that are the first to be wiped out. In the face of what must appear as systematic injustice, who could be surprised that it is the poor and underprivileged who more and more are tempted to violence?

I looked forward with eagerness, therefore, to new and determined Democratic leadership, but my euphoric hope that the day for tax reform had dawned was soon shattered. With disbelief and chagrin, I heard rumors that a Wall Street Republican, C. Douglas Dillon, was to be the new Secretary of the Treasury. I felt that such an appointment would be a tragic mistake, and I set about trying to change Kennedy's mind. In a long letter to him of November 22, 1960, written from my farm at Carthage, Tennessee, I pointed out that:

> Progressive economic and monetary policies have always been distinguishing features of successful Democratic Administrations. Without proper economic policies, no other policies can be successfully implemented. . . . The first requisite is to raise the general level of revenue. Without this, it appears to me that your Administration will be in an economic strait jacket and devoid of the flexibility necessary to use wisely fiscal, tax, and monetary policies in pursuance of proper economic goals.

Since I had heard that a tax reduction was favored by people purportedly close to the President-elect, I firmly warned against starting in that direction. As for monetary policy, I emphasized that a strong President could "require that it be coordinated with fiscal, economic, debt management, foreign, and related policies. . . . It should always be borne in mind that the Federal Reserve System was established to operate the mechanics of the banking system, not to formulate national economic policy." Going on to specify some needed tax reforms, I ended this lengthy letter with the following:

> Why, then, should you consider, even for a fleeting moment, for appointment to the key post of Treasury, one whose chief claim to fame is that he has been a member of a team that has failed its most important test? This applies not only to Mr. Dillon, who is an affable easy-goer, but to other conservative Republicans who have been mentioned. For such an ap-

pointment would be a signal that you had given up the goals of a truly Democratic Administration in domestic affairs, and, consequently, the progress necessary to restore United States position and prestige abroad. It is only by a truly Democratic Administration that we can achieve power equal to today's world challenge.

The appointment of such a person as Secretary of Treasury would mean, for instance, that glaring tax "loopholes" would not be closed; that fiscal policies, monetary policies, and economic policies would not be very different from the present [Eisenhower] Administration. This would not be your intention, to be sure, but would be the likely consequence.

I hoped that the President-elect would attend to my warning. It was I who, more than any other Senator, had forged the economic issues that he had used so tellingly in his successful campaign.

Upon receipt of my letter Senator Kennedy invited me to his Georgetown home, and I flew to Washington for the visit. We settled down to a long and intense talk. He readily acknowledged the need for liberal economic policies but he reminded me that he had received less than 51 per cent of the popular vote which was "something less than an overwhelming mandate."

"But you will be the President," I said, "and that is the difference."

He went on to say that the narrow margin of his election made it inadvisable for him to "shock" the international money marts by his selection for the Treasury post, and he asked me whom I would suggest.

I suggested that he appoint W. Averell Harriman, "a man rich enough to give them confidence," I said.

"But he is too old," Kennedy said.

I let loose at Dillon's record and elaborated on the political and policy meaning of such a choice. Kennedy told me he was going to select Professor Stanley S. Surrey, a liberal Harvard tax-law professor, as an Assistant Secretary, and that Surrey would be in charge of tax policy.

"That won't work," I said. "You'll be busy with a million things and it will turn out to be your Secretary of the Treasury, not his assistant, who will be determining the policies of your Administration, and they will be the wrong policies." I laid it on hard about the traditional and historic policies of Democratic Administrations from Jefferson to Truman, hoping this might deter him:

"You will be inaugurated President while the country is suffering from a serious recession, just as FDR came to power in the Hoover Depression. It didn't take Roosevelt long to learn that retrenchment is not the answer; he set the country on a course of recovery by activist programs, projects, work, and credit policies that provided jobs, opportunities, confidence, and growth, and, the most important factor of all, confidence. Harry Truman . . ."

Kennedy broke in. "There is strong opposition on the Hill to pump priming," he said.

"Yes, indeed," I said, "and among the same people who will be strong for both a big tax cut *and* a big spending cut. Tax reduction is pump priming, too, but the trouble is the pumps are primed for the wrong crowd—those who don't need it." I wanted to get the subject back to Dillon. "Whatever the policy," I asked, "why should Dillon, a rich, Wall Street Republican, who contributed $30,000 to Nixon, be in your Cabinet?"

Kennedy astounded me. He didn't "care about those kind of things," he said, mentioning that one of his advisers, Dr.

Richard Neustadt, had told him that the first requirement for the Treasury post was "acceptability in the financial community." It was all to no avail. His decision had been made. To me, it was a shocking shame that a new Democratic President would deliver the tax and monetary policies of his Administration to the very crowd that had reversed the policies of Roosevelt and Truman with such hurtful results for our people.

Only a few weeks later, at the very first meeting of the Joint Internal Revenue Committee after Kennedy's inauguration, Assistant Secretary Surrey appeared before this hierarchy of Congressional tax writers to discuss Administration tax policies. Senator Byrd—with the support of Senators Kerr, Russell Long, and John Williams, to all of whom Dillon's known predilections were to be preferred over Surrey's Democratic views—felt that it was an "affront to Congress" that one of less rank than "the Secretary" would appear to discuss the tax policies of the new Administration. Congressman Wilbur Mills, chairman of the Ways and Means Committee, as usual concurred with this group, and the meeting adjourned "until the Secretary can appear." There went the plan for Surrey to be tax-policy spokesman for the Kennedy Administration! Like Wilson and Roosevelt before him, young President Kennedy was learning of the power of Southern senators and congressmen. But other lessons awaited him.

Immediately upon the convening of Congress in January 1961, Vice-President Lyndon Johnson undertook to preserve his Southern-oriented power base in the Senate. The newly elected Democratic leader in the Senate, Mike Mansfield, chosen with the support of Johnson, called Johnson to the head table and proposed that the new Vice-President continue to preside over the caucus of Democratic senators. I immediately and vigorously opposed this, making the point that "the distinguished Vice-President is no longer a Democratic senator." It was embarrassing, I said, to have to raise these objections but "the suggestion of our new Majority Leader is highly irregular and entirely improper." Senator Kerr and others spoke in favor of the arrangement. I insisted on a roll-call vote—a procedure awkward for everyone. Even so, eighteen Democratic senators voted with me. (Far more agreed with me.) Though the formal vote was far from sustaining my point that day, I won, nevertheless—for Johnson never again attempted to preside over the caucus. President Kennedy called me the next morning to convey his satisfaction. "A good thing to do," he said. Obviously, he would not wish to have to approach the Senate through Johnson.

In the course of the conversation on the phone, President Kennedy asked me to "come down, keep in touch." Of course, I wanted to. Though I had been friendly with both Roosevelt and Truman, with John F. Kennedy there was a more intimate rapport. So Mrs. Gore, our daughter Nancy, and I were among the early guests of the new President. As an act of favor, Mrs. Kennedy, who said she had been "rummaging in the basement," brought out Lincoln's china and Andrew Jackson's silver service for our first upstairs dinner at the White House. During the friendly and relaxed conversation I recall saying to Kennedy, "The first thing you did with which I disagreed was the reappointment of J. Edgar Hoover."

With quick wit, he responded, "That was the first thing I did."

Throughout those early months, the President was feeling his way along, trying to avoid stepping on sacrosanct eggs. It happened that I had an early morning appointment with him on the morning after the abortive Bay of Pigs invasion. His hair was disheveled, his tie askew, and his eyes sleepy; I had never seen him like that. He seemed relieved to have a friend to talk to, and he told me the fantastic story of the actions of his military advisors, on whose counsels, along with Allen Dulles's of the CIA, he had mistakenly relied.

He was particularly critical of General Lemnitzer, chairman of the Joint Chiefs of Staff. He told me that he had said most emphatically that no American military planes would be allowed to participate in the invasion under any circumstances, and that before he decided to let the venture proceed, he had inquired of General Lemnitzer whether it would be "a feasible military operation without U.S. planes" and that Lemnitzer had assured him it would be. Late in the night of the invasion the military advisers told him the attempt would fail unless U.S. planes were sent to provide cover and support, that a carrier was nearby, and planes could be over the Bay in a very short time. He gave me the impression that he believed the generals had thought he would relent and permit the planes to be used rather than see the venture fail. With colorful language, he said he would never again rely on Lemnitzer's advice.

A short time later, the Latin American subcommittee of the Senate Foreign Relations Committee conducted an investigation of the episode. On the day General Lemnitzer appeared, Chairman Wayne Morse was engaged elsewhere and I served in his place. I asked General Lemnitzer if he had certified the undertaking as "a feasible military operation without U.S. planes." He talked and talked without answering the question. I asked it again and again. Finally, Senator Fulbright leaned forward and said, "General, I was there and heard you say it." Only then did General Lemnitzer admit it.

When the committee adjourned for lunch, I casually remarked to an Associated Press reporter, Ernest Vaccaro, who was a long-time friend, that I thought we needed a new chairman of the Joint Chiefs of Staff. GORE DEMANDS LEMNITZER BE FIRED was the headline on Page 1!

The whole military complex reacted. Congressmen and senators with reserve-officer commissions attacked me right and left for "undermining confidence in the military." Editorial comment across the country was adverse. My defense was General Lemnitzer's own admission, but the records of our hearing were classified as "Secret" and thus unavailable for my use.* I could have quoted what Kennedy had told me, but that was not the right thing to do. So I just took the heat. Meanwhile, pressure was building on President Kennedy to express confidence in his military chieftains. Everyone knew of our friendship and the longer he waited to speak the more the military chafed. Finally, the President called me and said he had to let me down, that he found it necessary to express confidence in the military, that General LeMay, commander of the Air Force, and a delegation of high brass had threatened to resign unless he did so. I realized the painful difficulty of the President's position—what with the whole disastrous fiasco falling on him, and which he fully accepted. So I said, "I'll take it." The President expressed his appreciation and said Secretary of Defense McNamara would call me. Within minutes, McNamara called and threw me a small bone about curtailing some extravagant military hotels in Western Europe about which I had made some criticism.

As if to attract attention to something domestic, the new

---

* There was no justification for secret classification of this testimony. Knowledge of Lemnitzer's blunder would surely be of no aid to Castro. Its classification served only to protect the armed forces from embarrassment, which is the case with most of the secret classification I have seen, and I have seen a lot of it.

Administration lost no time in proposing new legislation in the area of civil rights. Liberals and moderates in the South were greatly encouraged by his stand and gained strength from the moral pressure exerted in the office of the President, and the increasing popularity of Kennedy himself. Kennedy's commitment to Negro rights was refreshing—even sometimes to his foes. "At least," I heard some of them say, "we know where he stands." Nevertheless, it was not long before Kennedy was put to the test. And, predictably, the test came in Mississippi, where the state legislature had made dissent illegal in 1956 by making it unlawful to "encourage . . . nonconformance with the established traditions, customs, and usages of the State of Mississippi."

James P. Meredith, then a twenty-nine-year-old black and a nine-year Air Force veteran, attempted to enroll at the University of Mississippi in the fall of 1962. "Ole Miss," pressured by politicians in Jackson, refused to admit him, but the federal court ordered his enrollment. Ross Barnett, governor of Mississippi, ranted, raved, and postured. It was clear that he could not be trusted to maintain order as he had promised the President and the Attorney General he would do. Five hundred U.S. marshals were ordered to Memphis, and Barnett sent two hundred Mississippi highway patrolmen to Oxford.

What happened then is history. When Meredith was moved onto the campus a mob began to form, and the state troopers suddenly left. The 200 marshals on the Ole Miss campus were unable to handle the situation alone. Barnett blamed a "mixup in orders," and the troopers returned, only to leave again at a critical moment.

Kennedy went on television just as the riot began to peak, to explain his position and to make an appeal for peace in the

South. As he spoke, the mob increased in size and intensity. Deputy Attorney General Nicholas Katzenbach, who had been sent to Oxford by the Kennedys, pleaded for federal troops from his command post inside the Lyceum on the Ole Miss campus. Kennedy was reluctant to take this step, but as reports of loss of life began to come in, he wasted little time. A federalized national-guard unit from Oxford moved onto the campus. As more troops began to arrive, order was restored, and after much low burlesque by Barnett, Meredith began to attend classes. He continued to do so in the company of a U.S. marshal until he received his law degree.

Kennedy's decisive action was widely applauded but it embittered many segregationists. It stood in sharp contrast to Eisenhower's vacillation. Although there were to be other attempts to stem the tide of the civil-rights movement, the incident at Oxford represented a turning point, signaling the end of the era in which the threat of mob violence and state interposition could actually prevent the enforcement of federal court orders.

But Kennedy was soon put to test on still another front.

In the early evening of April 10, 1962, Mrs. Gore and I were attending a reception held by the Tennessee State Society of Washington. Our son, Albert, Jr., fourteen, called me and said the White House had telephoned for me and left word that it was urgent that I call President Kennedy. We rushed home and I placed a call. The President came right on and told me that Roger M. Blough, Chairman of the Board of Directors of United States Steel, had just told him that his company would increase the price of steel. The President was unusually agitated, mad as hops, in fact, and talked that way.

"If this price rise sticks," he said, "my whole stabilization program is through." He recounted how he had asked the steel workers to refrain from demanding a wage increase, how they had settled with the company with unexpected forebearance, etc., how this had had a wholesome effect on the whole economy. "And, now this **** undertakes on his own to undo it all. Can you get some opposition going in the Senate?"

"I think I can," I said. "I will try." He thanked me and asked that I keep in touch.

When I hung up the phone, my son, who had been listening on an extension, came in and said, "Whew! Dad, I didn't know a President talked like that!" I explained that he usually did not, that in this case he was infuriated by what he thought was a deception, and that after he cooled off he would regret his intemperate language. (I am not sure that he ever did.)

I called my staff and reported the President's call and requested them to return to the office for a night of speech-writing. When I left the office a little later to attend the annual White House reception for Congress that evening, my administrative assistant took charge.

The reception gave me a ready-made opportunity to contact my colleagues, which I did one by one, explaining President Kennedy's desire that several speeches be made in the Senate the next day in opposition to the steel price rise. I explained that I would have some ten- or twelve-minute speeches ready the next morning. Many readily agreed to speak. I reported this to President Kennedy. He was pleased and he talked to several senators about the problem and the procedure. He appeared to be more angered than any of us had ever seen him.

I left the party early to return to my office to assist in the speech-writing. After a night's work, we had more than twenty short speeches prepared when the Senate convened at noon, each taking a somewhat different approach to the steel price rise, but each calling for a rollback of prices. About twenty senators, including a few from the South, spoke and this was big news that night and the next day. The steel magnates must have reeled from the surprising onslaught. President Kennedy was highly pleased and encouraged. Meanwhile, he was moving on several other fronts—the Department of Justice, Treasury, Defense Procurement, etc. The full weight of the Presidency and the United States government was used relentlessly to achieve a rollback.

In a matter of days, the price increase was canceled. President Kennedy had demonstrated the power of his office and his willingness and skill in using it had saved his stabilization program, and had gone a long way toward erasure of the Bay of Pigs mistake.

The funeral of Mrs. Franklin Roosevelt on November 10, 1962, also brought me into intimate contact with President Kennedy. In the living room at Hyde Park the President asked me, "What do you think I should do about a tax cut?"

"Forget it," I said.

He turned half way around and then turned back.

"But we must have booming times by 1964," he declared.

"Yes, indeed," I said. "But a tax cut is neither the best nor the surest way to do that, and in the long run it would prove very harmful."

We then fell into a discussion on the relative merits and demerits of stimulating the still sagging economy either by releasing money into the spending stream by a tax cut or by appropriation of funds for priority improvements—spending, in other words. Though he was intent in the discussion and seemed not to notice the line of people waiting to speak to him, I became very conscious of holding up a very distinguished group of people. I excused myself by saying, "I'll send you a memorandum."

After the funeral, the planes carrying groups from both Washington and New York, including Air Force One, were lined up at the West Point airfield for the take-off. Motors were whirring but no plane took off. Of course, the President's plane must take off first. All of us on my plane were peering out the window trying to see why the take-off was delayed.

A military vehicle raced across the field to the plane on which I was aboard with a group of my Senate colleagues for a return to Washington. The door of the plane opened and an officer entered and inquired:

"Is Senator Gore aboard?"

"Yes," I said, standing.

"The President wishes you to ride with him, sir," he said.

"Will my honorable colleagues excuse me?" I inquired with a deep bow from the waist. Their response was a raucous jeer.

Aboard the President's plane, we renewed our conversation on the country's economic conditions and the need for stimulation, the manner of stimulation, the politics of 1964, and the political problems of either a public-works oriented spending program or a tax-reduction and/or tax-reform bill. The President mentioned that Secretary Dillon favored a tax cut.

"That was predictable," I replied, perhaps a bit acridly.

Kennedy hardly smiled, and began talking about the political difficulties of persuading the Congress to support sufficient expenditures, however worthy the purposes, adequately to stimulate the economy to bring full employment. I acknowledged the difficulties and uncertainties but I warned:

"If you go down the tax-cut road, you will not only get the wrong kind of tax bill but an economy wave that will cut deeply into needed programs and seriously restrict not only your flexibility but that of other Administrations that follow. Once taxes are cut, they are not likely to be reimposed. Congress will always be ready to cut taxes, never ready to raise them. It is a beautiful economic theory about moving taxes up and down, but it is only a theory, utterly impractical in our system. It just won't work!"

"I wish you would talk to Walter Heller," he said.

"Well, I'll be glad to. Walter can talk with equal facility on either side."

"Then listen to him on my side," the President said, and laughed.

(I had already talked with Heller at length and I believed from those talks that, if he had his choice, he would prefer to maintain a high level of revenue coupled with a spending program equal to the needs of the economy, but he doubted that such a program was politically possible.)

We then fell into conversation about tax reform and soon found a wide area of agreement on the kind of reform that was needed, but I was convinced that there would be almost no chance of getting such reforms as a part of tax reduction. Only an all-out Presidential fight for tax reform, both from the standpoint of tax equity and the need for additional revenue for urgent economic stimulation, would get the tax bills past the reactionary Ways and Means Committee, chaired by Congressman Wilbur Mills, long footsie with the big oil interests, the American Medical Association, the real-estate lobby and many other special interests, or the equally conservative Senate Finance Committee, whose Chairman Russell

Long of Louisiana is principally noted for wheeling and dealing on his famous "Christmas Tree" bills near the end of a
session of Congress.

Air Force One was circling to land. It was plain to me that
the policy on which the President was bent was a matter of
politics rather than principle. I could not support it. I was
puzzled as to why he had wished to talk with me about it
again.

The fight *was* bitter, and bitterly disappointing. With the
advancing age of Senator Harry Byrd, Senator Robert Kerr of
Oklahoma, a border-state oil magnate, became the Administration leader on tax legislaiton. In fact, he became the most
influential man in the country on tax legislation, undoubtedly the most influential senator on tax matters in our history. Usually the chairman of the House Ways and Means
Committee, where revenue bills originate, is the most influential legislator on tax matters, but Senator Kerr had a canny
way of leading Congressman Mills. Moreover, on tax matters
he became the leader of the Republican Party as well as of the
conservative Democrats. Time after time, I saw the Republicans on the finance committee wait for him to lead and then
support him unanimously. His power over tax questions
spread to still other fields, until the press gave him the title,
"King of the Senate." He used his power with great effect for
what he considered the best interests of his state of Oklahoma.
He and I had a very warm personal equation. We differed on
both tax policy and philosophy (many times I heard him
jocularly remark, "I am against any deal that I'm not in on")
but we knew it and respected it.

Within a few months, a news story in *The New York Times*
on the tax-cut fight carried the following headline:

White House Agrees to Curb Spending
to Gain Support for a Tax Cut

And on November 10, 1963, columnist Charles Bartlett wrote:

> The Administration is being buffeted by a wave of Congressional and public sentiment against government spending that the President and his officials have helped to stimulate. Some Democrats, particularly Senator Albert Gore of Tennessee, predicted that Kennedy, by endorsing economy in order to gain support for tax reductions, would risk stirring an anti-spending movement that could mushroom quickly beyond control.

I must have convinced Bartlett, for he quoted my letter to Kennedy in which I warned that a tax and spending cutback were political handmaidens.

"Gore's point has been," Bartlett further wrote, "that the Democrats must assert the value and validity of Federal expenditure or the balance of public sentiment will be lost to the conservatives and the President's options will be narrowed." This is what I had called an "economic strait jacket" in my letter to Kennedy.

"He senses also," Bartlett continued, "that this hardened mood, with its spending cutbacks, may well generate a repressive climate in which the economy will lose its momentum and hang inertly." Bartlett was expressing my views more eloquently than I had.

One of the issues I had been raising was the preferential tax treatment given to income earned abroad, and the many machinations by which rich Americans used foreign tax havens to avoid paying income and estate taxes.

Though President Kennedy had never been a particular student of tax laws, he was well aware of these inequities and regarded them as most unfair; moreover, they were damaging to the balance of payments. This led him into a confrontation with the Southern Congressional moguls of tax favoritism—Congressmen Wilbur Mills, Thomas Boggs, and Carl Albert; and Senators Harry Byrd, Robert Kerr, Russell Long, and Herman Talmadge.

Unfortunately, tax favoritism is stock in trade with most members of the tax-writing committees of both House and Senate, and many of them are Southerners. Service on the tax-writing committees is, in fact, a severe political liability unless one is prepared to be a tax favoritist, as I learned in many ways. I had a promising opportunity to play just such a self-serving game. Tennessee has several large insurance companies (standing eighth in the nation in this respect), and two of the largest television stations in the state are owned by insurance companies. Yet it fell my lot to lead a fight to close some very large tax loopholes by which insurance corporations were escaping their fair share of the tax burden. This cost me dearly in every political campaign thereafter. The price I could have paid to get other committee members to vote to continue favoritism to "my" insurance companies would have been to vote as they wished for "their" pet clients. That would have included percentage depletion and intangible drilling-cost write-offs for oil, real-estate gimmicks, horse-racing, stock options, and dozens of others. This log-rolling, back-scratching game is precisely why the tax law is so shot full of loopholes. Playing such a game was never my idea of public service and responsibility.

In the broad sense, the tools that the government can employ in achieving maximum economic justice for the citizen include: taxation, expenditure, and money management. Insofar as the work of an individual senator is concerned, the most crucial of these areas is taxation. This is true not only because of its intrinsic importance, but even more so because of the organization of our government and the rules and traditions of the Congress.

In 1963, I asked for an appointment with President Kennedy to talk about South Vietnam. At the time, the Diem regime in Saigon had become extremely cruel in attempting to suppress Buddhist uprisings against the government. Pagodas were being fired upon, Buddhist priests were being held in prison without trial. It was an increasingly authoritarian and increasingly oppressive regime, even, in this instance, practicing extreme religious persecution. I urged upon President Kennedy that this was a good time for him to withdraw all U.S. advisers and military aid from Vietnam, thus escaping from a developing quagmire. He should issue a statement, I suggested, that the United States could not and would not be associated with religious persecution.

He expressed pessimism about the situation in all of Southeast Asia, the Saigon political regime in particular. Our chances of achieving any lasting success there were "very slim," he said. I was particularly impressed when he said, "When China has an arsenal of nuclear weapons, Indochina is in her sphere of influence." Though the President gave no definite response to my recommendation, the very next day one of his closest confidants, and my warm friend, too, Charles Bartlett, who had been with him at the White House in the evening following my conference, came to see me. I considered I had my answer when Bartlett remarked, "After Cuba and with China going Communist under Truman, no Democratic President can pull out of Vietnam." An opportunity to extricate ourselves at that time was lost. Sadly, domestic political considerations thus exerted an inordinate influence on Vietnam policy. This has prevailed throughout the Administrations of four Presidents. And what a price has been paid!

I always had a desire to support President Kennedy's programs. Mostly I did. It gave me much pleasure to support ratification of the Limited Test Ban Treaty, signed August 5, 1963, which President Kennedy considered his finest achievement. I had helped to negotiate it as a delegate to the Conference in Geneva during the Eisenhower Administration and during the early months of the Kennedy Administration, so this was an opportunity to support not only a President whom I admired but a cause in which I deeply believed. Incidentally, Vice-President Johnson had managed, as presiding officer of the Senate, to remove me as a Senate-adviser delegate (in a move which the *Chattanooga Times* called "Johnson's Revenge"), but this did not alter the cause or my support of it. I continued to believe that a mutual cessation of atmospheric nuclear-weapons tests by the great nuclear powers was imperative not only as a beginning of arms control but to prevent the most deadly pollution of the world's atmosphere with radioactive poisoning.

By stopping atmospheric atomic tests, dangers to the health of all nations and that of unborn generations would be radically averted. In the 1950s and early 1960s potentially the most dangerous augmentation of pollution was coming not from industrial wastes but from radioactive fallout, and would be decades before the effects of bombardment from strontium-90, the deadly bone-destroyer, would no longer be harmful. Iodine-131 had already appeared dangerously in the milk supply.

The treaty, limited and incomplete as it was, would have a healthy impact on recruitment of other members into the nuclear groups or on the expansion—to use the terminology of our casual strategists—of "the nuclear club." And the treaty would prepare the way for later negotiations to reduce atomic testing even further. I agreed with President Kennedy that psychologically it would be an important opening wedge in our effort to "get the genie back into the bottle."

No one could doubt that our relationships with the Soviet Union were more amicable then than a decade before— though neither was there any doubt that suspicion and distrust between the two nations still existed, the differences between their philosophies of government and society forming a basis for continued conflict. These differences had made agreements between the two countries unbelievably complex, and each party, understandably, tried to write guarantees for its own safety into any agreement. Some of those guarantees— which were certainly understandable, given the intense mistrust and hatred of the past—left it possible for each to conduct comprehensive and continuing underground tests, to maintain nuclear-laboratory facilities, to maintain the resources and facilities necessary for prompt resumption of atmospheric tests, and to improve the capability of detecting treaty violations. Caution for our own security had dictated these reservations for us, and vice versa for the Russians.

I was profoundly convinced that improved relations and negotiations with the Soviet Union would be in grave danger of being undermined if we failed to reach an agreement or if the Senate failed to ratify the treaty. I worked, therefore, for both.

Since those two fateful days, August 6 and 9, 1945, when American planes dropped atomic bombs on Hiroshima and Nagasaki, the United States and the Soviet Union had engaged in potentially the most suicidal military struggle ever known to man. They had piled nuclear armaments on top of nuclear armaments, and had spent more than a trillion dollars each in trying to get the better of the other. The weapons created in this mad race were many hundreds of times more destructive than those which in 1945 caused more devastation in a shorter length of time than the world had ever previously experienced. And the two powers seemed to have delighted in counting up their kilotons and megatons each night after the world had gone to bed, chalking up a victory sign at the birth of each new and more destructive weapon. The entire course of events for the innocent bystanders, that is, the people of the globe, assumed the dimensions of some vast cosmic nightmare in which humanity found itself again and again being hurled into a chasm of destruction.

But time passes, passions subside, and hatreds dissipate. The two rival giants, emerging from nuclear adolescence into something approximating maturity and parity, concluded an agreement. And despite continued opposition in the Senate (more than half of which was from Southern Senators), the Limited Test Ban Treaty was ratified. My small part in its negotiation and ratification was a high point for me. I felt as if a cloud had been lifted from the world.

Then a different cloud loomed over our country. I was standing just off the Senate floor when the Associated Press teletype machine, about ten feet away, carried the flash message that President Kennedy had been shot in Dallas. No one, not even in heartbroken despair, could see the extent of the shadow cast by this tragedy. In shock and sadness, I promptly joined my wife in the quietness of our home, where we could sorrow together all alone.

Albert Gore, Sr.,
Carthage, Tennessee,
1920

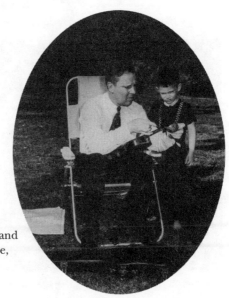

Albert Gore, Sr., and
Al Gore, Carthage,
Tennessee, 1953

The Gore family, winter 1952
Moss Photo

Summer at the family farm, Carthage, Tennessee, 1952

Wedding day of Al and Tipper Gore, Washington, D.C.,
May 29, 1970

The Gore family during the 1970 senate campaign of Albert Gore, Sr.

Family friend Tip O'Neil with Albert Gore, Sr., and Mrs. Pauline Gore
Nancy Rhoda

Al Gore and his father working together in Tennessee during the
congressional campaign, 1976

Election night, 1976
Nancy Rhoda

Senator Gore, Sr., and his son resting at the farm during the congressional campaign, 1976
Nancy Rhoda

Al Gore's senate announcement, Carthage, Tennessee, 1984
Bill Thorup

Al Gore and Albert Gore, Sr., on the family farm during the senate campaign, Carthage, Tennessee, 1984

Senator Gore, author of the Interstate Highway Bill, Carthage, Tennessee, 1996

Albert Gore, Sr., on the campaign trail,
New York City, 1992

Win and Waste

TWO P.M., NOVEMBER 23, 1963—"I am nothing today, but to-morrow I may be everything," said John Adams when he was Vice-President. The famous remark stuck in my mind as I walked from window to window in our living room. Maybe it was because my feelings about Lyndon Johnson being President were so mixed up with heartache over Kennedy's death. My heart thudded, my thoughts raced. *President* Johnson! Lady Bird was a fine woman, would be a fine First Lady. But Lyndon—friend one day, cajoling and accommodating, for the next, kicking and knifing. Still, the Presidency has a way of making the man, I thought, and that was something to tie to! He came from good, common stock. He could be President of the whole people, as Truman had been. Johnson, Johnson . . . alternately my friend and foe *so many times*. I *must* get this out of my mind. The Presidency would humble him; yet there were two Johnsons, each bigger than life, one good and one bad. The *good* Johnson would be President. I must help him when I could. Would he want me to? Yes, I thought so. Many times before he wanted me when the fights were tough.

What strange and discomforting paradoxes! Twentieth-century South finally had a President—a Southerner, born and bred—I liked that. First a Populist, then so long allied with the most reactionary, big-money interests of Texas, now the leader of the Democratic Party. Well, I must accept things as they were. Johnson was President, Jack Kennedy was dead, what was done was done. Like millions of others, I had to look ahead.

During the days after John Kennedy's funeral, I marveled at how skillfully Johnson took charge. I knew he was accustomed to power, yet he seemed to take hold of the reins of office and government with extraordinary smoothness, almost as if by instinct. His first task was to re-establish confidence, to give a sense of direction, a sense of repose, and a sense of security to millions of shaken, distraught Americans as well as to a grieving world. The remarkable intensity and adroitness of his efforts impressed me. And one was grateful for his humility, the seeming total absence of his customary ebullience.

On November 27, 1963, Johnson addressed a Joint Session of Congress. President Kennedy had said at his Inauguration, "Let us begin." President Johnson said, "Let us continue." And I applauded.

My first opportunity to speak with the new President was a few weeks later, on December 17, when he invited me to accompany him to New York, where he addressed the General Assembly of the United Nations. His speech was good, emphasizing disarmament and the necessity for East-West cooperation. On the return trip, Johnson asked my views about the pending tax bill. I minced no words in responding, "It is a bad bill and it should not be passed."

"Now, *how* can I turn my back on Kennedy's program?" he inquired, his tone of voice indicating that he regarded such action as impossible.

"I know it'd be difficult, Mr. President," I replied, "but even if it were an equitable bill, taxes should not now be cut. There are too many unmet needs." He seemed to be listening, and I went on. "By expenditure you can direct the money to points of need. You would have far more flexibility, far more control of it, and there would be more and quicker stimulation. A tax cut is just as much an expenditure of revenue as an appropriation. It would strip the Treasury of money that is needed for many, many things, and that would restrict the government's ability and flexibility to meet new needs."

"But," Johnson countered, "when I said to the Congress 'Let us continue,' you led the applause." By then, others on the plane were listening, Johnson always enjoyed having a group around as he talked, especially when he was ribbing a colleague. Also, he had an intense personal reaction to an opponent or critic (to him they were the same, and it remained one of his abiding weaknesses that he could not or would not make the distinction between them). So he put on an exaggerated little act and demonstrated how I had applauded. "And now," he concluded, looking around but gesturing toward me, "he won't support my tax bill." When the laughter was over, I answered the best I could, "I reserve the right to applaud a good speech, Mr. President, without committing myself to vote for a bad tax bill."

Then the conversation drifted to international trade, something we largely agreed upon, and he had some nice things to say about how he had always supported my trade moves; I thanked him. Once again, Lyndon Johnson and I were at once agreeing and disagreeing.

Upon my return home, I made notes of this conversation and contemplated this complicated man, who was now at the apex of power which he had coveted for so long. We had several things in common: a Populist heritage, descent from small landed gentry in scrabbly hill country—he in east Texas, I in the Appalachian foothills. Both had scrambled for education, and both had taught as youngsters. Both came under the spell of FDR and entered politics early. Both were Southerners, at least in part, and we had both been favorites and confidants of Sam Rayburn. Both had a fierce competitive instinct and an unfortunate tendency to personal reaction. And, of course, both of us loved our service in the Congress, in politics, and in power. There were some differences, too. One was that I had grown stronger in Populist leanings and had become an inveterate enemy of special privilege, while Johnson had become bedfellow of big money, oil, and military brass. Though in philosophy a New Dealer, he had managed to keep closer political ties with Southern senators than I.

By the time Congress reconvened in January 1964, Johnson had succeeded in restoring confidence to the country in a very, very remarkable way. It had long been said of him that he was a "take charge" man, and he had surely taken charge of the government. The very first item high on his calendar was the budget and taxes. The economy needed a boost, and Johnson endorsed the tax-cut route to boost it. He even severely cut funds for needed programs in order to persuade Senator Harry Byrd and other Southern conservatives to support the tax cut. Imagine finding it difficult to persuade conservatives to cut taxes! But a "balanced budget" was a cardinal political theme with them, especially Senator Byrd, a patriarch of the Southern conservatives. This meant that such programs as aid to education, hospital construction, urban renewal, housing, etc., many of them more direly needed in the South than in any other region, would be short-changed. But the conservative Southern Democrats had swung so far to the right that they were really indistinguishable on domestic issues from the most reactionary Republicans, with whom they had forged a firm working alliance.

Ever clever in maneuver, Johnson had also persuaded the AFL-CIO to support his proposed tax-reduction scheme, even though an unfair proportion of its benefits would go to high-income brackets. (This was difficult for me to rationalize except on the basis of a political deal that involved other matters.) With both Southern conservatives and labor lined up to support it, a fight against it was futile, but I felt too strongly about it to acquiesce. After all, there really was no point in serving in Congress unless one were willing to fight for what one thought was right. So I launched a fierce fight against Johnson's tax-reduction bill, though I was up for election that year.

During committee hearings, I brought from Secretary Dillon an acknowledgment that a taxpayer in a very high income bracket would receive an 84-per-cent reduction in his taxes from the new bill, while a taxpayer with an annual income of $6000 would receive only a 5-per-cent reduction. Imagine that being proposed by a Democratic Administration! This simply did not square with any yardstick of social justice or of governmental policy I could endorse. An exchange I had in committee hearings with Henry Ford II, co-chairman of the President's blue-ribbon group of businessmen supporting the tax bill and chairman of the board of the Ford Motor Company, served to illustrate my point. I noted that a Ford employee having $4000 of taxable income a year would receive a tax reduction of less than $3.00 per week by the bill, while a $300,000-a-year executive at Ford would get a tax cut of more than $50,000 per year. (I chose my example carefully because I had seen the Ford company's annual report, which showed Henry Ford with an income from the company of more than $300,000 per year.)

"Do you think that's fair?" I inquired of Ford.

He answered, "If a man has worked his way up in the organization, the reductions will be greater than for a fellow with lower pay."

I waited a moment for this to sink in at the press table, where there were low chuckles.

"What would be the average rent of a working family that lives in Washington or Detroit?" I asked.

"This is nothing I would know about," Ford answered. "I guess it would vary tremendously."

"Those of us who represent the people must have some knowledge of these things," I said, "Take-home pay is something that working people understand."

The bill proposed to give a family of four with an $8000 annual income an increase in take-home pay of less than 5 per cent, whereas a taxpayer in the $100,000 bracket would receive a 100-per-cent increase in his after-tax income.

"There are always inequities in things and it's too bad, but that's the way things are," Ford said.

Stuart Saunders, chairman of the Pennsylvania Railroad and a stanch friend of Senator Byrd, was appearing jointly with Ford and sat beside him. Uncomfortably fidgeting during this blabbering, Saunders tried several times to intervene and take over the testimony, but Ford wanted to talk. As I studied him, the thought occurred to me that except for the ingenuity and the fortune of one of his grandfathers this man might be a check-out clerk at a supermarket, or perhaps the manager of a small store after he had "worked his way up." Yet because of his gargantuan inheritance from one of America's richest fortunes, permissible by our faulty tax laws, there he sat as chairman of one of the world's largest industrial combines, a frequent guest at the White House, prating on as if his financial position somehow endowed him with a wisdom he must impart to Congress. Many politicians, too, equated money with brains and esteem.

So, I argued out of both conviction and moral commitment that further tax favors for the affluent was wrong and that the principal stimulus of the proposed tax cut would be to the very people and to the very sectors of our economy where stimulation was least needed. The result would be greater corporate profits, larger cash reserves, more investment savings, and more automation, and that this was not needed since records in all of these categories were then at all-time highs. Instead of a shortage of productive capacity, there was vast idle capacity and a large surplus of consumer goods for want of purchasing power. The proposed tax cut would but worsen instead of correct this imbalance. What was needed, I argued at length, was stimulation of consumer demand and employment. Not only did this appear logical and right, but, it would help release money for the 108 public-facility projects then awaiting funding in my state; at least this would partially offset the criticism for opposing a tax cut. Nothing wrong in political benefit for supporting a correct measure! There were always enough lumps for one's errors and misfortunes.

"Why is it," I asked my colleagues, "that a Democratic Administration, having promised tax reform, submits this bill which contains very little of worthwhile reform, but a great deal of tax benefits to the vested interests and to the high-income brackets?" There was, of course, no answer, for every senator knew the answer: Johnson was seeking election by means of a double-barreled appeal—tax favors for the affluent with job stimulation for the poor as a partial result, a trickle-down tactic as old as Herbert Hoover, but, to my keen disappointment, proposed by Kennedy and then pushed by Johnson. It was infuriating to me that this aberration would be advanced as "new economics." The only thing "new" about it was that a Democratic Administration would propose such a deviation from traditional democratic policy. I cited the writings of Andrew Mellon, Secretary of the Treasury in the Administrations of Harding, Coolidge, and Hoover, in which he used language almost identical with that used by Secretary Dillon and the ambivalent Fair Deal-Great Society economist-rationalizer Walter Heller. Mellon wrote, "A decrease in taxes causes an inspiration to trade and commerce which increases the prosperity of the country so that the revenues of the Government, even on a lower basis of tax, are increased." Mellon's "new economics" of the 1920s had been put into practice, of course, and had helped to concentrate wealth in a few and to bring on the great collapse of 1929. Yet in 1964, these same dogmas of privilege were the centerpiece of the Great Society. How could I fail to fight?

But any sort of tax reduction is easy to pass, especially in an election year. My fight against it was politically costly. It alienated many Tennessee conservatives, not so much because of my opposition to tax reduction per se, the soundness of which many also questioned, but because of my emphasis on the social inequities involved. It was about this time that pejorative references to me as a "Populist" began. Even so, I exulted in the battle, for I considered the inequities of tax law to be a crying injustice of our society, and I thought my party should be dedicated to true tax reform.

Despite this fight, Johnson telephoned me twice about his choice for a replacement for Dillon as Secretary of the Treasury. First he discussed Donald Cook, president of a New York private utility. I had met Mr. Cook, and I had heard several people whom I respected discuss him commendably. So I reacted favorably toward him. Later Johnson called and said, "I have decided to appoint Henry Fowler as Secretary of the Treasury."

"You have made a **** poor choice," I replied.

"Now why do you say that?" Johnson asked.

"Because he has already shown that he is on the wrong side." The conversation ended shortly.

I later learned that Byrd and some other conservatives had been called to the White House for a confidential conference about the appointment before it was made, which showed whose advice Johnson considered most important on tax matters. After a talk with Fowler, they became his enthusiastic supporters. (He pleased them pink with his tax performance throughout his term.) This episode and the tax-bill debate illustrate Johnson's constant ploy to the conservatives through tax policy, the deep commitment of Southern conservatives to undemocratic fiscal and tax policies, and my own growing disagreement with fellow Southerners about both.

Yet, Johnson was a spender, too. His pet program in domestic affairs, the War on Poverty, had wide appeal, but it needed some promotion at the start. Thus it was that on a beautiful early spring day in 1964, Johnson took one of those "nonpolitical" Presidential trips (at taxpayers' expense, of course, for which all recent Presidents have been notorious) to visit the poverty-stricken Appalachian area. He invited me and several other senators and congressmen from the states on his itinerary to go along on the Presidential plane. The first stop was at a college campus in Ohio. The grass was fiercely spring green, the trees in fresh leaf, and the early flowers in bloom. The girls were mostly dressed in pastel colors, with a pleasant, soft breeze moving their hair; boys were in short-sleeved, many-colored shirts. It was a beautiful scene—and no sign of poverty. Poverty doubtlessly existed in nearby slums, but none was in evidence before us. Johnson tilted with the unseen enemy and slew it with words of great vigor.

We then enplaned for a flight to Lexington, Kentucky. During the flight, there was some good-natured kidding of Johnson about the evident lack of poverty. He kidded back quite charmingly (though he could usually dish it out better than he could take it). Then, of course, the blue-grass country around the University of Kentucky was if anything even more beautiful than Ohio had been. "When will we see some poverty?" a reporter asked again. I don't remember Johnson's reply, but by the time we reached Knoxville he was certainly on the lookout for something less than affluence. His speech was scheduled in the new municipal auditorium, some twelve miles from the airport. As the Presidential car turned the corner from Market Street onto Vine Avenue, there stood before us a dilapidated frame house with weather-beaten siding, rusty tin roof, and a front porch with some planks missing from the floor. A man, two women, and five or six children huddled together and waved to the big black Presidential limousine with its overkill of escorting motorcycles.

"Stop here," the President said.

Slowing but not stopping, the driver said; "Sir, I'm under

instructions not to stop in this area."

"I said stop," Johnson snapped, and stop we did. He hurried to the porch and shook hands with the whole family, asking the man questions about his income, number of children, etc. Cameras flashed and whirred in a sort of photographers' field day. A friendly policeman let me go past him to join in the melee. "That fella's the biggest bootlegger in town," he confided in a whisper.

The President's speech at Knoxville was well received, and he was generous to me, referring to issues that were important in Tennessee—TVA, REA, interstate highways, urban renewal, aid to education—which both of us had supported. Unmistakably, Johnson was a candidate, and he was touching the bases skillfully.

Despite my considerable reservations, I had to admit that, except for taxes, the unfolding of Johnson's domestic legislative program was a model of liberal political craftsmanship. Proposals for social security, civil rights, education—the whole gamut of liberal causes—came regularly from the White House. The over-all effect of this energetic onslaught was to make virtually all Southern senators—including me, I must admit—feel that Johnson was going too far. I felt this way about his 1964 civil-rights bill in particular because of its extreme grant of power to unelected, often faceless executive officials to write law in the form of guidelines and then to force compliance by withholding, or threatening to withhold, federal funds from whole counties or states. I waged a fight to strike these grants of power from the bill. Though unsuccessful in this matter, I was instrumental in securing the adoption of an amendment designed to forestall requirement of massive transcommunity bus transportation of public-school pupils.

Though I did not share in it, deep bitterness toward Johnson began to prevail generally among Southern politicians because of these liberal domestic programs. Frequently denounced as a "turncoat" to get elected, he became an object of scorn in Southern conservative circles. But he was still President, the leader of the Democratic Party, and the author and giver of tax favors, patronage appointments, and project approvals; Johnson was prone to award these on a purely political basis. Formal breakaways, then, were scarce except in the Deep, Deep South.

As Johnson swung to the left, the Republican Party swung to the right, with Senator Barry Goldwater as its leader. Actually, Goldwater had gained much of his momentum as a prospective challenger to John Kennedy, whose religion and Eastern orientation encouraged the first version of the Southern Strategy. Maps and political dopesterism that showed how Goldwater could be elected by combining the South and the Republican "heartland" of the Middle West had appeared as early as 1962. This strategy gained such momentum in the South and such credibility in other conservative circles that not even the succession of Johnson—whose birthplace, accent, and manners gave him a much wider appeal in the South than Kennedy could naturally enjoy—was sufficient to stop it. This rise of the Republican right wing in the South grew with such force that for the first time both Georgia and Tennessee sent all-white delegations to the Republican national convention in 1964.

Goldwater, perhaps erroneously but willingly, became stamped as the segregationist candidate. Strom Thurmond announced his switch to the "Goldwater Republican Party." In Alabama, Republican leader John Grenier openly urged his party to form an alliance with white Democrats in the Black Belt, where the people couldn't be "jarred loose from the Democrats" he said, without somebody they thought was a segregationist." On military and "national defense" questions, too, Goldwater took such aggressive or get-tough positions—"defoliation" of the jungle in Vietnam was one notable strategy he favored—that he became a militaristic, if not the "war" candidate to many people. This, too, pleased the conservatives in the South, and they gave Goldwater their solid support—enough to assure his nomination for President.

One week before the 1964 Democratic National Convention, the Senate Finance Committee met to consider a social-security bill. I helped to secure adoption of an amendment to increase the monthly check of each social-security beneficiary by $7.00. Attuned to my own election contest that year, in a state with more than 400,000 social-security beneficiaries, I was pleased to receive some political credit for it and I hoped it would help offset my opposition to the tax cut. But a heated controversy over Medicare turned the social-security bill into a severe political liability. There had been endless skirmishing over Medicare for several years without adoption of any proposal. I believed the time for decisive action was at hand, and it was logical that a federal health-care program should start with the elderly and should be a part of the social-security program (experiences with the social-security program would be helpful). But opponents of Medicare, especially the American Medical Association and its allies in Congress, the chief of whom was Mills, sought to kill it by proposing an increase in social-security taxes and benefits. Kerr and Mills led this fight. I believed very strongly that no increase in monthly social-security benefits would give to the elderly the security and serenity they deserved in their declining years. Only health and hospital care would suffice. Without this, old people had either to "take hat in hand" in search of welfare, or to go without medical care.

Under Mills's leadership, the House passed a bill to raise social-security cash benefits in such a way that payroll taxes would be raised to the "magic" level of 10 per cent, beyond which, it had long been widely believed (and I shared this belief), payroll taxes could not be increased since this form of taxation was regressive and would bear heavily upon young workers who are concerned with their immediate expenses and who may not be inclined to look ahead to old age and its entirely different problems.

There were cloakroom rumors that an understanding had been reached even between Johnson, the AMA, and certain well-placed senators and congressmen that no major fight for Medicare would be made in 1964. The AMA, a prime source of campaign contributions to anti-Medicare candidates, had been extremely active in support of the Kerr-Mills proposal. I was disturbed since the Administration was strangely silent on Medicare, and because Senator Clinton Anderson, the perennial author of the Medicare bill, was not in Washington to propose it as an amendment to the social-security bill, as he had been expected to do. When he did not return to propose the amendment, I offered it in the Senate Finance Committee, where it was voted down by a vote of 11 to 6 on August 17, 1964, just as the Democratic Platform Committee was gathering in Atlantic City. I announced I would propose Medicare as an amendment to the social-security bill when it was called up for action on the floor of the Senate, scheduled immediately after the return of Congress following the convention in Atlantic City.

When I arrived at the convention, I learned to my amazement that the draft of the Democratic platform, which had been written at the White House under the watchful eye of Johnson, had only a milk-toast provision about Medicare. I was furious, thinking this may have confirmed the rumors of a deal, and I began to plan a floor fight at the convention for a platform plank that would give strong approval of Medicare. Very shortly, I met Hubert Humphrey, to whom I expressed my surprise and exasperation. "I intend to take the microphone and read what Harry Truman said about Medicare," I said, "and what the last three Democratic platforms have said about Medicare. And then I'm going to read this **** piece of namby-pamby, and then ask the delegates, ask them if this is a convention of Democrats or of the American Medical Association."

"Oh, my gosh!" Humphrey said, rapidly scribbling notes. Although he was Johnson's man at the convention, as he had long been in the Senate, we were friends and I favored him for the Vice-Presidential nomination, and I was confident that he would be Johnson's choice (even though Johnson was playing a public guessing game, dropping hints here and there that Eugene McCarthy, or Thomas Dodd, or somebody else might be selected). When Humphrey hurried off with his memorandum in hand, I was confident the message would be in the White House in a matter of minutes.

The one thing Johnson did not want at the convention was a nasty fight with the liberals. The emotionalism in the affection for the martyred President Kennedy was too potent among the delegates to risk this, with Bob Kennedy waiting in the wings. The next draft of the platform contained a strong endorsement of Medicare through social security: "We will continue to fight until we have succeeded in including hospital care for older Americans in the social-security program. . . ."

Following his nomination, Johnson began pushing for adoption of my Medicare amendment in the Senate. We conferred on strategy and votes, and I was pleased to be working with him again. He was truly a master legislative tactician, and I admired his skill. But the opposition was determined. Southern senators and congressmen, led by Russell Long of Louisiana and Wilbur Mills of Arkansas. Republicans stood almost solidly against it.

When my amendment was adopted by a vote of 49 to 44, this helped the Democrats nationally but built further conservative opposition to Johnson in the South, where he was already in deep trouble on the race issue. It hurt me in Tennessee, too. Only one congressman from my state supported me and only two of my Senate colleagues from the South— Ralph Yarborough of Texas and Olin Johnston of South Carolina—joined me in the vote. Except for us, the Southern Democratic senators were a solid phalanx in coalition with Republicans against Medicare. (Only five Republicans voted for it.) Though I respected their views, as always, I was convinced that it was I, not the majority of Southern senators, who represented the true best interest of the people of the South. The people of no other region needed Medicare quite so badly.

The fight was far from over. A *New York Times* editorial observed: "The measure now goes to the Senate-House conference, where it must survive the one-man blockade erected against Medicare by Chairman Wilbur D. Mills of the House Ways and Means Committee." As forecasted Mills proved to be unalterably opposed to Medicare. Though the conference met for days, neither House nor Senate conferees would budge. With Johnson strongly supporting Medicare and the election campaign already under way, Congress was understandably impatient for adjournment. The pressure for an agreement mounted, especially for an increase in Social Security benefits, just before election. This was a tried and true Mills-Long tactic. The choices were threefold:

1) An increase in social-security benefits without Medicare. This was the goal of Congressman Mills. It certainly had an immediate appeal to the millions of people who depended on their small social-security checks.

2) A social-security increase *and* Medicare—decent medical care and hospitalization without the stigma of charity. This was my goal and my fellow Senate conferees were committed to this by Senate action.

3) A deadlock, which would kill both Medicare and the social-security increase.

Mills would not even discuss a compromise. During one conference session, Mills wondered aloud, "Who will take the responsibility for killing the social-security increase for the old people who need it so badly? I do not wish to accept such responsibility." He gazed not at me but toward the top of the door beyond me when he made the remark. So I assumed a similar pose, gazing toward the opposite door, and said, "I wonder who will take the responsibility for denying needy old people a program of decent hospitalization and medical care? I do not wish to do so."

This is how the conference ended—hopelessly deadlocked. The blame, or credit, for killing Medicare fell upon Mills, and at that time in the South there was far more political credit than blame. On the other hand, the onus of killing an increase in social-security benefits fell squarely upon me, and this was a heavy load to carry in Tennessee. My Republican opponent, a Goldwater conservative, and the Republican press pounced upon the issue. I hoped it would be clear that my fight had saved Medicare and that in the end this would assure both Medicare *and* increased social-security benefits early in 1965. But many social-security beneficiaries did not view it that way, no doubt thinking that a bird in hand was worth two in the bush. I learned once again that explanation is a most unrewarding exercise in politics. My opponent made hay with the issue, strongly aided by many physicians, and I lost the votes of thousands of the very old people I had fought to serve. Some blacks, too, refused to vote for me because of my views on the 1964 Civil Rights Bill, the only civil-rights bill I had not supported. These circumstances, plus Goldwater's ineptitude, especially his proposal to sell the TVA, caused me to run behind Johnson in the election returns.

Even so, my re-election was by a comfortable margin, well ahead of my ticket mate, Ross Bass, who was elected to the unexpired term of Estes Kefauver.

In 1964, Governor George Wallace of Alabama briefly tried out for a spoiler role, attempting to cash in on white backlash against the Democrats' civil-rights efforts and scoring well (although losing) against LBJ stand-ins in the primaries in Wisconsin (33.8 per cent), Indiana (29.8 per cent), and Maryland (42.8 per cent). In early June he announced his candidacy at the head of a third party, but the nomination of Goldwater by the Republican Party pre-empted his natural constituency, so on July 19 he formally withdrew.

Goldwater ran a stupid campaign, allowing himself to become known as an extremist on the war and on race, a reactionary who wanted to make social security "voluntary" (which everyone knew would destroy it), to sell the TVA, and generally to turn the clock back. Nevertheless he took the five Deep South states in addition to Arizona. Still, Johnson actually beat him in the South *as a whole,* as the following table illustrates:

	Deep South No. of Votes	Per cent	Rim South No. of Votes	Per cent	Total South No. of Votes	Per cent
JOHNSON	1,388,698	37.9	4,919,064	56.9	6,307,744	51.3
GOLDWATER	2,270,470	62.1	3,722,914	43.1	5,993,384	48.7
TOTAL:	3,659,168		8,641,978		12,301,146	

In other words, Goldwater won substantially in the Deep South, but there are so many more voters in the rim or peripheral South that Johnson carried the area as a whole.

Although Goldwater did better in the South than Nixon had (actually, about as well as Eisenhower had), his 1964 base was very different and not too promising. He did less well in the old mountain GOP strongholds and, more importantly, less well in the booming cities. In Southern urban counties with cities of more than 50,000 population, Goldwater did worse by several percentage points than either Nixon or Ike. Goldwater's strength, then, was in the Black Belt. In Southern counties containing 40 per cent or more Negro population, he vastly outstripped (almost 60 per cent) either Nixon (33 per cent) or Ike (30 per cent in 1956 and 36 per cent in 1952). This Deep South strategy was obviously a disaster for the Republicans, but it helped pave the way for George Wallace in 1968 and 1972.

Soon after Johnson's triumphant 1964 election, even before Congress convened, I learned of Administration plans to send combat troops to Vietnam. Though I did not foresee the extent of the impending tragedy, I surely was strongly op-

posed to the move, and I urged a negotiated settlement to
the war in a speech before a Southern business convention in
Miami in late December. My speech was not well received—a
few people walked out—and it attracted very little attention.
Yet a few days later, when I proposed a negotiated settlement
in Washington after the Congress convened, it made national
news—and got me a telephone conversation with Johnson
the next morning. The pleasantest thing he was disposed to
say was, "You *looked* good on TV." Clearly my statement had
been displeasing to him, and shortly afterward he began inviting congressmen and senators in groups to the White House
to be briefed on his policy in Vietnam.

At these sessions, the President would lead off the discussion and then would call on Secretary of State Dean Rusk,
Secretary of Defense McNamara, and various members of the
armed forces. Each in turn would denounce any hint of a negotiated settlement: it would give aid and comfort to the
enemy (how often I heard that!), create divisiveness at home,
etc., etc. On this subject the President was hypersensitive to
criticism and reacted in his usual intense personal way when
it occurred: disagreement represented disloyalty and, since we
were at war, dissent was unpatriotic. With other issues, one
might fight against Johnson one day and work with him the
next, but Vietnam was different.

On one occasion I tried personally to dissuade him from
the policy of sending combat troops to Vietnam. He briefly
reviewed for me the whole situation as he saw it, stressed how
at a meeting with Eisenhower in 1954 he had opposed sending paratroopers to aid the French at Dienbienphu—while
Nixon, he carefully emphasized, Secretary Dulles, and others
had favored it; how Eisenhower had refused to send troops
but had sent aid and advisers; how Kennedy had sent more

aid and more advisers. The situation in Vietnam was extremely grim, he concluded. "I must either send troops or withdraw our advisers, and I'll be **** if I am going to be the first President to run." I did not think that was the issue, nor did I think this the right context for decision.

Since the "peace" candidate had been elected, the issue of war had been temporarily defused and the attention of Congress and the public was focused on other matters, including Medicare, which had also been a principal issue in Johnson's unprecedented victory. The Medicare bill was now expected to pass quickly, yet months were still required to overcome the bitter-end opposition in the Senate led by Russell Long. Progress was easier in the House because Mills recognizing its inevitable passage executed one of his many pragmatic switches by announcing his support of it. The bill finally passed the Senate on July 9, 1965, by a vote of 68 to 21. Seven Southern Democrats (Byrd, Eastland, Ervin, Holland, Robertson and Stennis, plus Ellender, who was paired against it), joined fourteen Republicans in last-ditch opposition.

President Johnson, in a very nice gesture to Truman, flew to Independence, Missouri, to sign Medicare into law. Despite my outspoken criticism of the Vietnam war, I, along with other members of the Finance and Ways and Means Committees, was invited to go on the Presidential plane. I accepted, this being a notable day for which I had long fought and in which I took much pride. President Johnson gave a speech extolling the accomplishment. Before speaking, he called the "Medicare champions" to the stage—President Truman, Mills and Long—to receive the highest plaudits for leading the "successful battle for enactment of Medicare." Near the end of the ceremony, I received one of the several ceremonial pens with which the President had signed the bill into law. I thanked the President with meaningful profusion: "I will preserve it for posterity—framed."

My relationship with President Johnson, who was already having to practice parsimony on domestic expenditures because of the war, worsened with each criticism I made about his Vietnam policy. As criticism of the Vietnam war mounted, he pushed one liberal social proposal after another, as if to demonstrate that the country could afford both war and domestic reform to divest attention from the developing tragedy in Southeast Asia. One of his most progressive proposals was the Elementary and Secondary Education Act of 1965. I enthusiastically supported this, as did nearly all other Democrats except those from the South, where the need for aid to education was direst in the nation.

Johnson's unwillingness to face the economic facts of an undeclared war soon began to take its toll. High interest rates, for example, cut deeply into a budget strained by the insatiable demands of the Vietnam front. There was bitter irony in this since as congressman and senator, Johnson had been opposed to high interest rates. Both of us had enthusiastically supported the long-term, low-interest-rate housing and home-finance policies of the Roosevelt and Truman Administrations, and had attended many a late-afternoon or night session with the Rayburn team in Congress, where I had often heard Johnson extol Populist policies. Yet interest rates were now running wild, not only choking his program and burdening his budget, but working great hardships on borrowers and consumers. I criticized this vigorously. It must have gotten under his skin, for he accosted me about it at the White House one night after a reception line had broken up. Several of us were standing together in a small group listening to him talk when suddenly he turned to me and said, "Albert, I am a low-interest-rate man, too."

"I know," I said, "but your Administration isn't."

I was glad the President had raised the subject because it was then generally reported in the financial pages that he would soon reappoint William McChesney Martin, one of the architects of the high-interest-rate policy as chairman of the Federal Reserve Bank Board, and I wanted to express my opposition to him. Martin was not only the inveterate champion of tight-money policies, but the very personification of these policies. He was, of course, strongly supported by the banking and insurance interests, groups Johnson sought to please.

The President did not immediately respond, so I quickly added, "I hope you are not going to reappoint Martin. He has long been a tool of the big banks."

Johnson then recounted that before going to the hospital for surgery he had reached an agreement with Martin that interest rates would not be changed during his illness and convalescence, but that Martin had violated the agreement. He told this story in such a manner as to leave the impression that he had been dealt with unfairly, had been put upon.

"Then, don't reappoint him," I pressed. Johnson hesitated, pursed his lips, looked irritated, and turned to speak with someone else about a different matter. I wondered if I had pressed my point too hard and maybe a bit rudely. After all, he was President. But why not? He had just proclaimed himself in favor of low interest rates while planning to appoint a person who would execute precisely the opposite policy.

Frequently, sometimes daily, I returned to the attack on "Johnson high-interest rates." On August 17, 1966, for instance, while Vice-President Humphrey was presiding, Rus-

sell Long and I had a field day. Though my speeches in the
Senate were usually somber and, I fear, dull, I was in a mis-
chievous mood that day. As a U.S. Senator Humphrey had
been a champion of liberal monetary policies, and I proceeded to have some fun at his expense. Powell Lindsay,
a reporter for the Scripps-Howard newspapers, described it as
follows.

Gore's almost daily attacks on "Johnson interest rates"—the
high cost of money which the Administration has been either
unwilling or unable to do anything about—had gone largely
unnoticed by most of the nation until last Tuesday. Then two
things happened: Vice President Hubert Humphrey, an un-
happy warrior these days, had the misfortune to be presiding
in the Senate when Gore began his speech; and Senator Russell
Long, the canny majority whip who backs Gore to the hilt in
the fight against tight money, looked up to the press galleries
and accused the nation's press of suppressing Gore's statements.

Bingo! Gore's speech was all over the wire services that afternoon.

Gore had barely begun to speak when he spotted the Vice
President chatting with another Senator at the presiding officer's chair. "I shall await the attention of the presiding officer,"
Gore said, with no small bite in his voice, "because I think he
might be the one who could take the message to the right
place," meaning to President Johnson.

"The presiding officer is listening," said the startled Humphrey.

Then Gore really teed off. Who benefits from high interest
rates? he asked. Not the American people, not the small businessman, not the consumer. And not, he added pointedly, the
Democratic Party. "Franklin Roosevelt would turn over in his
grave if he could hear this speech," Gore declared. "Franklin
Roosevelt ran the money changers out of the temple and

financed a war at reasonable interest rates. Harry Truman did the same thing. Now the money changers are back in the temple and we have the highest interest rates since the Administration of Warren G. Harding, 45 years ago."

Long began to feel sorry for the Vice President, who himself is an easy-money man. "May I suggest to the Senator," he said to Gore, "that he ought to chastise someone other than the Vice President. . . ." The Vice President could stand it no longer. He scribbled out a note and showed it to Gore a few moments later. It read: "The VP doesn't set interest rates. You are making a good fight!"

Associated Press saw the note later. The White House saw the AP story, which revealed a Vice President encouraging an attack on the Administration. Washington eyebrows shot skyward.

Gore's second splash . . . came Wednesday and concerned the huge tax break the Internal Revenue Service is apparently going to give Continental Oil in its purchase of the vast Consolidated Coal Co.

This was destined to be one of those lonely battles against powerful and entrenched interests for which the Senator gets so little credit. It is a highly complex matter, difficult for many to understand, and his efforts were doomed to failure, anyway. All it did was to make some silent Senators squirm.

The Continental Oil deal was the beginning of the movement by the big oil companies to acquire most of America's coal production and reserves thus gaining a quasi monopoly of fossil fuels—largely with tax-free money. The far-reaching consequences of this may not have been foreseen by the general public, but higher utility rates were soon to follow in the wake of the tax ruling that invited and subsidized the monopoly.

Lindsay later wrote:

"In spite of Albert Gore, we got what we wanted," laughed a Continental Oil Co. spokesman.

The oil official was talking about an IRS ruling which the Tennessee Senator says "should shock the conscience of all who understand it."

Senator Gore said that the ruling will permit Continental to buy out Consolidated Coal Co. and virtually write off the cost on the huge oil company's income tax.

The IRS revealed yesterday that it had given its permission for Continental to execute the intricate scheme of acquiring the vast coal property, and the oil company followed shortly thereafter with a statement that it had found the ruling to be "satisfactory."

Continental will in effect "mortgage" its acquisition for $460 million and charge this off on its income tax over the next fifteen years, Senator Gore said. In a floor speech following the announcement of the ruling yesterday, Senator Gore linked this "tax favoritism" with what he calls the Administration-condoned high bank-interest rates. . . .

Over a year ago, Senator Gore introduced legislation that would require the IRS to publicize such private tax rulings that affect the Government's tax revenues by $100,000 or more.

"The Treasury Department said they'd support my bill," the Senator said yesterday. But a Treasury Department spokesman, asked about the Department's position on Senator Gore's bill, replied Wednesday, "We have nothing to say at this time."

A spokesman for Continental Oil, in announcing the company's satisfaction with the IRS ruling, declined to elaborate on its provisions or on Senator Gore's charges of tax favoritism. "He sure did give us the devil," the oil company official said.

The transaction also will increase the already tight money market, Senator Gore said, by withdrawing $460 million from the banking stream into this transaction. Consolidated Coal Company, Pittsburgh is liquidating, and this money, along with the company's other liquid assets, will be divided among the company's stockholders.

Continental Oil Company said that the deal will be closed September 15 after stockholder approval—a foregone conclusion—is secured on August 30.

I never knew whether such private arrangements as these resulted from Johnson's penchant for wheeling and dealing or from his urge to shore up support in the business community to help offset the rising opposition elsewhere to his Vietnam war policies; maybe both, since he loved to wheel and deal and he surely became obsessed with holding popular approval of his Vietnam policies. Nonetheless, disillusionment with those policies was growing, particularly in the Senate and notably on the Senate Foreign Relations Committee. At first, the opposition was generally characterized by critical questions and admonitions in closed-door sessions of the committee, but feelings were so intense that sentiment for an open challenge to Johnson's policies mounted. Classified information in the hands of the committee as well as public information raised the most serious questions both as to the credibility of the Administration's public expressions and, even more importantly, the postulates upon which a war was being waged. This information came from four principal sources:

First, the Central Intelligence Agency. Throughout the horrible episode, I found that the assessments and estimates provided by the CIA to be the most reliable available. I know there have been many questions about the CIA and many criticisms of its covert operations. Many covert operations are not actions of which the country can be proud, and I do not wish to be understood as defending them. I do not. But one thing needs to be clearly borne in mind—the

CIA is not a policy-making agency; it executes policy directed by the President and the National Security Council. In the intelligence information and assessments it gave to the Senate Foreign Relations Committee, the CIA displayed integrity and responsibility.

The second source of information upon which the committee came to rely with confidence was its own staff, headed by Dr. Carl Marcy. Under his direction, and inspired by Senator William Fulbright, the Committee Chairman, staff task forces of two or three men went to Vietnam time after time and returned with more reliable analyses than the committee could obtain from the White House or the Pentagon. (This was later borne out by publication of the Pentagon papers.)

The servicemen either wrote letters to committee members while in Vietnam or communicated to them privately upon their return. Scholars, observers, and newsmen on assignments in Vietnam were very helpful. These constituted the third source of information.

What should have been reliable sources of information—the Pentagon and the Department of State—practiced deception upon the Congress and the people. So did Johnson, Rusk, and McNamara personally. Yet by diligence some facts were ferreted from these sources.

A majority of the Senate Foreign Relations Committee became convinced that the Congress and the people were being misled; that the war was, at best, a misadventure, rapidly being escalated into disaster. (Southerners on the committee were sharply divided on Vietnam. Fulbright and I were opponents of the Administration's policies while Sparkman, Long, and Smathers were supporters.) Members of the committee conveyed their growing concern to Johnson and to officials of his Administration, but to no avail. Johnson publicly ridiculed the war critics—"nervous Nellies"—and repeatedly equated dissent with giving aid to the enemy. (Spokesmen for the Nixon Administration continued this tactic into the summer of 1972.)

The committee finally decided to hold public hearings. In an opening statement on January 28, 1966, Fulbright said:

> The Committee is meeting this morning to consider S. 2793 which would authorize an additional $415 million in foreign economic aid for the current fiscal year. A related question not formerly before the Committee is the manner in which military assistance to Vietnam will be authorized in the future. The Secretary of Defense has proposed that the financing of South Vietnamese and Korean forces in Vietnam be transferred from the military-assistance program to their fund for requested military appropriations.

Despite this deadening beginning, the committee proceeded to conduct a full-scale televised public hearing on Vietnam policies. And a remark I made during committee hearings on February 10, when George F. Kennan was appearing as a witness, was interpreted as defining the real purpose of the investigation. The committee, I said, "hasn't suddenly burst forth with concern and interest," but this concern had been "repeatedly expressed in Executive Sessions" to Administration officials, but "unfortunately, we seem not to have made a dent. Therefore, what we are seeking to do now is to go over the head of the President to the American people. There is nothing particularly un-American about going over the head of someone. After all, Congress has been the victim of this . . . by many Presidents. Indeed, the State of the Union message is no longer to Congress but in the prime hours of the evening by way of television to the American people. So Congress, this Committee, is trying to reach the American people. We think it is necessary."

The hearings had a major impact upon the nation both pro and con. After these hearings, Vietnam became an even more divisive issue and Johnson could no longer claim a consensus in support of the war. The actions of the committee were severely criticised, too. Criticism was especially harsh in my state. Not one congressman from Tennessee joined me in opposition to the war, and some were personally critical of my actions, including William E. Brock III, Ray Blanton, and Dan Kuykendall. During my frequent visits to my state, now and then a former supporter would even refuse to shake hands with me because of it. Many people sincerely believed that I was giving aid and comfort to the enemy by my criticisms, as these Tennessee congressmen charged, many good citizens considered my actions unpatriotic. Though respecting their rights to their views, and being deeply troubled about them, I believed, on the other hand, that patriotism, conscience, and duty required me to speak out strongly against the greatest tragedy of our times.

This was the political climate in 1966, when the Republican-Dixiecrat coalition first succeeded in electing a Republican to state-wide office in Tennessee. Previously, the coalition's victories in state-wide politics had come through the nomination and election of conservative Democrats, a customary pattern in the heyday of "Boss" Crump's domination of state politics. This was the pattern of Ellington's election to the governorship, as we have seen.

But in 1966, an all-out attempt was made to control both the Democratic primary and the general election. Ellington ran again for governor and Clement ran again for senator. (They belonged to the same faction and had alternated—"leapfrogged"—as governor for many years.) Ellington was opposed in the primary by John J. Hooker, Jr., a progressive young attorney from Nashville. Clement's opponent was Senator Ross Bass, the liberal who two years earlier had defeated Clement for the senatorial nomination and had then defeated the Republican nominee Howard H. Baker, Jr., for Kefauver's unexpired term. The 1966 rematch between Bass and Clement was for the Democratic nomination for a full six-year term. Clement then finishing his third inconsecutive term as governor still smarted over his primary 1964 defeat by Bass. Though his years as governor had taken their toll of him, he rallied for a strong primary fight determined to avenge the only defeat he had ever suffered for public office.

Howard Baker, meanwhile, was ineffectually opposed by Ken Roberts of Nashville in the Republican primary—a contest that did not generate very much public interest. Republicans and their conservative Democrat allies were satisfied with the idea of another Ellington term as governor. So, no one sought the Republican nomination for governor. (Of course, in case Ellington should not win the nomination, the party could later select a nominee by convention, and it was widely understood that they would do so unless Ellington won, since Hooker's platform and performance were too progressive for them.)

With no Republican primary contest for governor and with only scattered interest in the senatorial primary, Republicans "crossed over" into the Democratic primary by the thousands to nominate Ellington and Clement. When the returns were in, it was clear that the Democratic Republican votes had given nominations to both Clement and Ellington. Clement was nominated over Bass by 384,322 to 366,079, Ellington over Hooker by 413,950 to 360,105, with many pre-

dominantly Republican precincts casting big majorities for
Ellington and Clement. The telltale total vote in the Republican primary was only 148,660.

Ordinarily, either party is more concerned with capturing
the governor's office than a senate seat. The incoming governor for a four-year term is always the most powerful man in
the state: patronage, contracts, election-machinery control,
and many other political matters are centered in his office.
But in 1966, the Republican Party centered its attention on
the Senate seat. They were, as I have said, satisfied with Ellington. Many Republicans openly said they crossed over to
vote for Clement in the Democratic primary because they
thought he would be easier than Bass for Baker to defeat.

Clearly, Clement was in deep trouble, but the consensus
was that the Democratic ticket—Ellington and Clement—
would nevertheless win.

The November campaign was scarcely under way though
when rumors of friction between Ellington and Clement became widespread. Indeed, there were informed whispers that
Ellington and Baker had met and worked out an agreement
to dump Clement. (I was later told by a widely recognized east
Tennessee business leader, Hugh McDade of Maryville, that
he had arranged a meeting between the two men at a mountain retreat owned by Alcoa and that Baker and Ellington
did in fact reach a working agreement to avoid hurting
each other.) In any event, teamwork between Ellington and
Clement was ineffectual, if not totally lacking, and Baker defeated Clement by 483,063 to 383,843, becoming Tennessee's
first popularly elected Republican senator. (Clement actually
received 479 *fewer* votes in the general election than he had
gotten in the primary. Many precincts which he had carried

overwhelmingly in the primary went overwhelmingly against him in the election—portending future problems for the two-party system in Tennessee.)

Bitterness toward Ellington was deep and lasting in the Clement camp. Clement's state campaign manager, Lon Varnell, told me: "There was a deal on, no doubt about it. If there was ever a man who let the Democratic Party down, it was Buford Ellington." In any case, Ellington was governor for four years, a conservative supporter of Johnson and of the Vietnam war. Moreover, he was a "constant and severe critic of the National Democratic Party" after Johnson's retirement.

Nationally the economic, political, and moral cost of the war on the domestic concerns of American citizens forced ever-sharper curtailment of funds for the social programs Congress had enacted under Johnson's leadership. Funds were withheld, projects postponed, and vaunted reform were reduced to little more than sloganeering, or enactment of enabling legislation to wither without implementing funds. Yet, still determined to prove he could wage a constantly escalating war and at the same time establish a record as a great social reformer, Johnson pushed for more far-reaching domestic legislation. An unprecedented bill for college education, for instance, became law with his support (though funding of the program had to wait). Then, one of the landmark civil-rights acts— the Open Housing Bill—became law in 1968. This was highly unpopular with the real-estate interests everywhere, but especially in the South, where white homeowners who had moved to new suburban developments feared racial "block busting" and possible loss in values, or simply did not want a black or any other kind of poor family in their neighborhoods. Many

of these people were my personal, social, and political friends.
And home-building and home-financing programs had long
been a prime interest to me. I took much pride in the work I
had done to promote the American dream of home owner-
ship, but I did not believe that dream should be limited by
race. Yet it was. I talked with many blacks who told me of the
humiliation, insult, and frustration they endured in their futile efforts to buy or to build homes. And I talked with blacks
who had become so disenchanted with integration that they
now advocated separatism—a position that seemed to be gaining favor with militants. I considered it morally wrong and
unconstitutional to place or to permit racial restrictions on
the locations where an American citizen might live or own
property. Removal and prohibition of such restrictions, it
seemed to me, was a much better way to achieve true integration than to rely on such disruptive expedients as improvident
transportation of school children beyond their communities
to overcome unbalanced racial conditions which could or
should be alleviated more effectively and fairly by other
means. (I had anticipated the fierce opposition to massive,
cross-town transportation of public-school pupils to achieve
racial integration. This resistance undoubtedly stems in part
from opposition to racial integration, but this is by no means
the sole reason. Much of it arises from a belief that the travel
is an inconvenience and a hazard to the children. Then there
is an element of simple rebellion at this degree of governmental intrusion into daily life.) I thought this step toward
fair housing policy was both possible and right, and that it
could have a great democratizing influence. Its enactment was
one of Johnson's many splendid domestic legislative accomplishments.

But no domestic program, however worthy or appealing,

no public-relations effort, no deception, no strong-arm pressure, nothing could now quiet the growing furor over the horror of Vietnam. One of the most irrational events of our history, the war cast a dark shadow over America's future. We had sent more than 2 million young Americans to participate in what had been accurately defined as "the wrong war at the wrong place at the wrong time," and, in the end, it had influenced the Vietnamese only to fight each other *and us* all the more fanatically. Massive destruction and suffering had left a lasting legacy of hatred. Allegedly seeking civilian solutions, but in fact allowing the decisions to be made by the military, the government had found itself propelling the American people into an undeclared war that became increasingly more violent and insoluble. We had lost friends around the world. Yet, paradoxically, the more we escalated, the more inextricably we became bogged down and the more we suffered from political division at home, frustrating the nation's pursuit of its own historic goals and eroding the moral base of its leadership. Along with many others I intensified efforts to change the Administration's irrational and contradictory policies, to challenge the erratic shifts of strategy, and to expose the misconstructions and deceptions. A deep conviction that the first priority was an end to a horrible, needless, immoral war drove us on. Moreover, there was deep fear that another escalation would gravely risk war with China. So there was a well-planned drive to keep Johnson under unrelenting pressure, and I considered my part in the movement to be my highest patriotic duty.

Johnson, in turn—with a determination, a bitterness, a resourcefulness, and, finally, a false chauvinism seldom if ever displayed by an American President—strove to hold on to popular, political, and press support for his Vietnam policies.

Resorting to extreme measures, his manners became ugly as he attempted to discredit critics of the war, manage the news, distort the facts, and deceive the Congress and the public. More and more, the *other* Johnson became visible, at his unappealing worst, squandering his still-considerable political credit. In a tragedy of vast proportions, he was frustrating the popular need for reassurance and legitimacy in the Presidency, and no straining for consensus would close the credibility gap.

Opposition to the war became a deep moral cause for millions of people while other millions (many of them in the South) fervently supported it and clamored for victory. The country was torn asunder as it had never been except in our own civil war.

None of us who served in the government through this tragic time can ever erase the scars they incurred. Least of all Johnson, whose announced decision on March 31, 1968, that he would not run for re-election came as both a total surprise and great relief to many of us. Our most productive President, in terms of the legislation he supported for social betterment, had been consumed by the flaming passions of an immoral, destructive war.

CHAPTER VI

The Showdown

THE TRADITIONAL FUN and sport of American politics deserted the country in 1968. It was a time when false patriotism was prevalent, a time when frustration, bigotry, recrimination, fear, and littleness of spirit and mind spread across the land like waters from a flash flood.

Richard Nixon, thriving in a climate of war and racism, took up where Goldwater had left off and gathered about himself a team with remarkable talents for exploiting these sulfuric attitudes. Kevin Phillips, a key Nixon analyst, put it bluntly, "The whole secret of politics [is] knowing who hates whom." Nelson Rockefeller, from the Eastern seaboard (which Goldwater had proposed be cut off and let float out to sea), was Nixon's only serious opponent for the Republican nomination. He could be shut off at the gate by one good Southern deal. Moreover, this might do the Democrats in, too, for with the support of some of the traditionally Democratic Southern states, the Republican heartland might be sufficient for election to the Presidency at long last.

Eureka! The deal was consummated in Miami on Tuesday morning of the Republican National Convention between Richard Nixon, Strom Thurmond, and a group of Southern delegates who were supporters of Thurmond's views. Fortunately, for the sake of history, we do not have to guess about the deliberations because a Miami newspaper tape recorded and published the whole dialogue. Stick by stick, wire by wire, we can see the structuring of the Republican Party's strategy. Of Nixon's performance at the conference Gary Wills writes in his book *Nixon Agonistes* that "he was never trickier."

Nixon's Southern Strategy was based upon a cleverly mixed appeal to three traditional Southern prejudices (or values): 1) racism, 2) a leaning toward hawkish militarism, and 3) Southern sectionalism. No Southern delegate at the conference could mistake Mr. Nixon's meaning when, in reference to the 1957 Civil Rights Bill, he said, "I felt then—and I feel now—that conditions are different in different parts of the country . . . [and] ought to be handled at the state level rather than the Federal level." This would particularly appeal to Thurmond, who takes great pride in holding the record for the longest filibustering speech against civil rights and "federal interference" (24 hours and 19 minutes).

As if this were not sufficient, Nixon passed the word—his personal word—that he wanted Supreme Court justices who would not "try to make the law" by their decisions. (This was what the "Southern Manifesto" had accused the Supreme

Court of doing in *Brown* v. *Board of Education*.) "I want men on the Supreme Court," he assured Thurmond and his delegation, "who are strict constructionists, men that interpret the law and don't try to make the law."

That drove the point home, particularly to Thurmond, who says, "The Constitution means today exactly what it meant in 1787." The point was: Nixon made "perfectly clear" that he would appoint judges who would oppose change. He said:

> I know there are a lot of smart judges, believe me—and probably a lot smarter than I am—but I don't think there is any court in this country, and judge in this country, either local or on the Supreme Court—any court, including the Supreme Court of the United States—that is qualified to be a local school district and to make the decision as your local school board.

Race questions, then, "ought to be handled at the state level rather than the federal level," and Nixon, if President, would appoint judges who would not change things ("make the law") by Court decisions. Mr. Nixon, the delegates would say (because they heard him say it), did not want Supreme Court judges who would upset the established practices of the South. "Strict constructionists" meant judges who would not change or "make the law" by their decisions. The message was quickly spread to all Southern delegates—indeed, to all Southerners—Nixon is against changing our Southern way of life.

But that was not all. Nixon "made it perfectly clear," also, that he shared the traditional Southern leaning toward aggressive use of force against social malcontents at home. He zeroed in on troublemakers ("agitators," Thurmond called them) when he said he would "open a new front—against the narcotic peddlers, the numbers' boys, and the peddlers of filth." There were no defenders of this ilk.

This Tuesday morning conference was apparently not an appropriate place to discuss either the dangers and costs of a nuclear-arms race or the threat of nuclear war. It only had to do with the selection of a nominee for President of the United States. A reordering of national priorities might concern some Americans, but this did not seem to bother the Republican high command that morning. An examination of an enlightened foreign policy, programs for peace, arms control, or for the needs of the people in education, full employment, better housing, or adequate health care evidently seemed out of place. One thing Nixon did say, "We are going to restore our strength in the missile program." His favored scheme, the deployment of an antiballistic-missile program, was a pet project of the industrial-military complex. Of course it had Thurmond's full support. (After an earlier meeting with Thurmond at which Nixon had advocated deployment of the ABM weapon system, Harry Dent, Thurmond's former assistant, reportedly remarked, "That grabbed Strom like nothing else.")

If the Republican National Convention was a charade that catered to the basest of our hates and prejudices, the Democratic National Convention in Chicago was a complete political disaster—a tragedy for our whole process of self-government. President Johnson, out of the race but trying to run the convention, was in close communication with the convention from Texas by a battery of telephones, insisting that no compromise be made with critics of his Vietnam-war policies. Many delegates, including myself, felt so strongly about the war we simply could not give up the fight. Nor, I guess could he. The debate was a bitter one, echoing the deep division within the party—as within the country.

And whom did the conservatives from the South support for the nomination? None other than their old pet peeve, Hubert Humphrey! Not because they loved him; they remembered his civil-rights record. Not because they still loved Lyndon Johnson; they had expressed themselves on that score by voting for Goldwater in 1964. But Humphrey was a hawk on Vietnam. There was really no other reason. The peace forces suffered a great handicap. They had no strong candidate. Senator Eugene McCarthy had performed a signal service to the country and party by exposing the weakness of Johnson's political position, but he lacked positive appeal and had little organizational strength. Senator George McGovern was a latecomer whose only support, other than on the anti-Vietnam issue (on which McCarthy had all but pre-empted him), was the hope of many delegates for a holding position which would open the way for a "draft" of Senator Edward Kennedy. They believed real enthusiasm for Kennedy only awaited a rally.

I was well aware of the trouble I was creating for myself. Every American politician with an understanding of our system knows that he has two general imperatives: 1) to serve his country, and 2) to hold the confidence and support of the people who elected him. Often these tasks interfere with one another. Fighting for the right course of action when it is contrary to traditional mores can disrupt the harmony of the entire process. Yet in matters so important as peace or war or the integrity of our courts, no politician has the right to permit consideration of his own political interest to divert him from an enlightened, conscientious course of action. True, a senator can ill afford to forget he is a politician, but, above all else, he must always remember he is a senator. Unless he can meet this test he should never have been elected in the first place.

Cordell Hull once said he felt that "any congressman worth his salt should be able to furnish leadership in his district and at the same time perform a much broader duty to the nation as a whole. This duty manifestly devolves upon him and is in addition to that towards his immediate constituents." It devolves even more so on a senator, who not only represents a whole state but is one-hundredth of the most powerful legislative group in the world, serving the whole country. He represents his state nationally, but his vote and voice represent a segment of national responsibility.

This dual role of representing the people of Tennessee and the nation had not often troubled me. I believed that in almost every case, if not in every case, what benefited the nation as a whole would benefit Tennessee and its citizens, and that a parochial or narrowly regional loyalty would stifle progress. The great English parliamentarian, Edmund Burke, observed:

> It ought to be the happiness and glory of a representative to live in strictest union, the closest correspondence, and the most unreserved communication with his constituents. Their wishes ought to have great weight with him; their opinion high respect; their business unremitted attention. It is his duty to sacrifice his repose, his pleasures, his satisfaction, to theirs; and above all, ever, and in all cases, to prefer their interests to his own.
>
> Your representative owes you, not his industry only, but his judgment; and he betrays instead of serving you if he sacrifices it to your opinion.

I regarded it as a travesty on democracy that with three candidates for President in 1968, the people had no way to vote against the greatest tragedy of our time. Humphrey was bound to Johnson's war policy and dared not vary from it. Wallace was as hawkish and Waspish as they come. Nixon, who favored military intervention in Vietnam as early as 1954, had been a constant supporter of Johnson's escalation of the war. (His only criticism, in fact, had been that Johnson was not doing enough fast enough. In 1967, for instance, he opposed the proposal to halt the bombing of North Vietnam because, he said, it would "simply have the effect of prolonging the war by encouraging the enemy.") "A strategy for the future," he said, "must be devised that will increase the military, economic, and diplomatic pressure to end the war and will guarantee peace without surrender throughout Asia." That was precisely what Johnson said he was doing, but Nixon thought the pressure should be escalated! (He is still doing just that, as this is written in July 1972.)

Wallace's only hope of success was to prevent anyone else from winning the election. In this way, he frankly said, the Presidential choice would be thrown into the House of Representatives. Some took this lightly, but such a result was not so impossible as many thought. The potentially serious threat of the Wallace movement was exactly that. Its promise of permanency was not very substantial, however, because it sought to turn the clock backward, catering to the prejudices of the past without attempting to adjust to the realism of the times. Only a sick and decadent society could tolerate such a movement permanently.

In the South, a decisive battleground for the Presidency in 1968, a fierce contest quickly developed. Though Humphrey had been the favorite of Southern delegates for the Democratic nomination, he was far from being the favorite of the Southern electorate. He could neither escape from his own past nor from Johnson's embrace. Nixon, on the other hand, plied his Southern Strategy with marked cleverness. His statements on racial issues before 1968 had been ambivalent as to principle, but in 1968 he came down hard as an anti-black, thus challenging Wallace, the all-wool-and-a-yard-wide white supremacist, for the support of the social reactionaries. Wallace, it should be remembered, however, was a Populist on tax and economic issues. As governor of Alabama, he had favored New Deal-type economic programs, provided they did not promote integration. Humphrey had been a true-blue liberal on social issues, but as Johnson's man he made his peace with the big oil and other special interests on tax questions. Nixon, of course, had favored every tax gimmick for the vested interests that had ever come down the pike. He was reactionary on social issues and laissez-faire on economic issues. Neither of the candidates gave a sense of fulfillment to a majority of the people. It was a period of antipathy and animosity.

In this climate, Nixon's Southern Strategy paid off in all the border states (except in Maryland—ironically—where, with Spiro T. Agnew's help, the Republicans managed to lose to the Democrats). Humphrey carried only one other Southern state, Texas; Wallace carried only four Deep South states. The remainder of the South gave Nixon 79 electoral votes, more than his final winning majority.

In Tennessee the campaign was fierce and bitter, with Democrats fighting an uphill battle all the way. Though I had opposed Humphrey for the Democratic nomination, believing that only a Democrat who was free of Johnson's domination could win, he was clearly superior, in my view, to

Nixon or Wallace. So I supported the Humphrey-Muskie ticket and accepted all invitations to speak for it; Governor Ellington and his group had responsibility for organizing and running the campaign. In the end, Humphrey received only 28 per cent of the vote, with Wallace getting 34 per cent, and Nixon 38 per cent—a disaster for the Democratic Party in my state.

The cause of the Republican victories in the South lies, I believe, in the backlash from racial issues and in conservatives' long dissatisfaction with the economic policies of Democratic Administrations. Whatever the reason, 1968 witnessed an end to the Solid South. Many think the South is in the midst of a long-term trend toward Republican dominance. Other observers question and challenge this. However that may be, after 1968 most of the South had a two-party system.

Although Republican Presidential strength and Congressional gains had been important in building up the GOP in the South, even more important was the ability to win positions in state governments. Howard Baker of Tennessee, upon his election to the United States Senate in 1966, said that although his victory was an important boost to the Republican Party, the real test of strength for the Tennessee GOP would be its ability to gain influence at the state-government level. The state had supported a Democratic candidate for President only once (1964) since 1948, when "Boss" Crump bolted to the Dixiecrats. The state government, however, had remained in the hands of men who were at least nominally Democrats. In 1968, though, the Republican Party gained control of the lower house of the Tennessee General Assembly, bringing to Tennessee the strongest two-party system in the South. Yet the main prize—the governor's chair—had eluded Republican candidates.

Various strategies had been tried by Republican leaders for winning gubernatorial races in the South. Most of them met failure. Winthrop Rockefeller in Arkansas, who was successful at it, made a determined effort to gain the support of the liberal elements of the electorate. This strategy sought a coalition of interests not unlike the earlier Populist one, but it ran against the tide of growing Nixonite strength. Rockefeller won with this strategy in 1966, against an arch-segregationist, Jim Johnson; and in 1968, he went contrary to the Republican Southern Strategy again and won against his conservative Democratic opponent, Marion Crank.

Kevin Phillips, Nixon's famed Southern Strategist, held that the Democratic Party in the South would eventually become the party of the blacks. George Wallace's third party would simply be a way station toward eventual GOP dominance. The outer South would become Republican first, but would surely be followed by the Deep South. Phillips continued, "Patterns vary in individual elections, but on a cyclical basis, the party of white Tennessee is going to be the party of white Mississippi." The 1968 election results (except Rockefeller's) tended to sustain this thesis, but Phillips's optimism about a Republican majority in the South was based on *Presidential* elections. Whether the same strategy of catering to economic conservatives and social reactionaries would work toward building the GOP at the state level was still unproven. The success of his strategy on the state level depended on the Democratic candidate having a liberal image, in which case the voters, he held, would choose a conservative Republican—assuming, of course, that with a choice between a liberal Democrat and a Republican, conservative Democrats (Republocrats, they are frequently called) would vote for the Republican.

The obstacles facing any Democratic candidate in Tennessee in 1970 were both obvious and formidable. The social and political trends ran deep. Only by a hard campaign on basic issues could I hope to win re-election. This meant that intensive personal campaigning could not wait until 1970. It would have to begin early, with all that this entailed for both me and my family. It required a family decision, and we thrashed it out at Christmas, 1968.

During my first and second terms in the Senate, I had never made any conscious, analytical decision to run again; there was just never any doubt about it. But 1970 did require consideration, lots of it. There was no question about my desire to continue in the Senate. The few senators who step aside by choice are usually motivated by considerations of health, a distaste for the work (there are very, very few of these), or a conviction that defeat is likely, if not unavoidable. My health was good; there was no doubt in my mind that I would be physically able to wage a vigorous campaign; as for the work, the Senate was my life, and I exulted in it. The opportunity to seek to influence my country's course of action from the vantage point of the Senate was something I had worked hard for, and I enjoyed it to the hilt.

Nevertheless, I seriously considered retirement, not so much because of apprehension over the election outcome, though as a realist I recognized the uncertainty involved, but more because of the ordeal that would have to be borne by me and my family.

Many have written about it, but few who have not experienced it really understand the physical and mental effort and the degree of disruption of personal lives that are inescapable in a prolonged campaign (or, for that matter, during non-campaign years for one who is in public office). Through seven campaigns for the House and three for the Senate I had had my wife's unstinting, uncomplaining, indispensable help. In later years our children, Nancy and Albert, Jr., had also been dedicated campaign workers. For thirty-two years my wife and later my children had endured it, and it seemed to me the decision was as much theirs as mine to make.

Though my family was not enthusiastic about my making another long campaign, in the final analysis they left the decision to me. They were acutely conscious of the adverse political trends, and of the degree of alienation I had suffered because of Vietnam and liberal economic and social policies. We discussed these frankly. In the end, the deciding factor was precisely the issues at stake. Not one other Democrat in my state who was likely to have a chance at the nomination was saying one word against the Vietnam war. No one could effectively take up my fight for tax reform for years to come. Arms control, a limitation on military expenditures, a reordering of national priorities, improvements in education, a hundred and one projects and programs I had started would not, or might not, be pushed if I stepped out. Worse still, my replacement would almost surely be in sharp disagreement with my record and with my philosophy. The two most likely Republican candidates were Goldwater-type reactionaries. The only prospective Democratic candidates, should I not run, were of the Republocrat variety. Perhaps this was simple vanity—one must have a considerable degree of vanity to survive the stresses of political life—but I thought I was the only Democrat who had a chance to win.

My decision, perhaps the inevitable one, was to run and to make the hardest fight I could. I knew the odds were against me, and I knew my opposition to the Vietnam war was unpopular, that my pro-civil-rights record was resented, and that my fights for tax reform had offended many interests. But I knew also that I had represented the best interests of the mass of people, that I could speak their language, and I believed I could go to the people and win.

There would be no point in making a hard two-year fight unless one was fighting for something important. So I determined that mine would be a campaign as clear-cut as possible between right and wrong, as I saw them, between enlightenment or ignorance, between a forward or a backward look, between tolerance or prejudice, between a broad or a narrow view. The campaign should be directed toward a worthy goal; it was to be a model and an example, not just a means to an end. Instead of demagoguing about them, I would honor the young, listen to their words, and speak to them—of understanding, confidence, and hope. I would follow a course of political morality and be ready to give up the honor and the office if the people decided that I should. I knew our system was far from perfect, but I wanted to give the people a clear choice. I believed they would make the *right* decision.

One of the charges frequently leveled against me which I understood although I never considered justified was that I had lost contact with the people and that I returned to Tennessee only in an election year. As a matter of fact, we had not only maintained our home in Tennessee throughout my Senate service but I had made more visits to Tennessee from Washington than any other senator from my state in history. (For years I had averaged almost one trip a week.) But Tennessee is a large area—when one is in Bristol, one is nearer to Canada than to Memphis—and there are ninety-five counties.

Even though I felt the charge unjustified, I decided to lay it to rest by obtaining maximum public exposure in Tennessee during 1969. The only way to do it was by press and television. I followed a rigorous schedule, and made myself easily available for regular press, radio, and television interviews. Each week I would leave Washington Friday afternoon and arrive in Nashville to be interviewed for the evening newscasts of two stations. On Saturday, a plane for Knoxville and Chattanooga for similar interviews for use in newscasts; then on to Memphis for Sunday interviews, and Monday at my Memphis office. My exposure on the newscasts would last perhaps only a minute or so, and the questions were invariably on the most controverial subjects, but it was prime time—and it was free except for the travel expense (by no means inconsiderable).

It is hard to measure how effective this activity was in terms of votes. After thirty years in Congress, my name was well known. Name recognition was not one of my problems. But I was able to communicate with hundreds of thousands of Tennesseans. I was getting my views across and I felt the responses in many ways. For one thing, there was instant recognition by people I met on the street—cabdrivers, hotel clerks, waiters, and other working men and women. This was particularly heartening to me because these were the people whose interest I had earnestly tried to represent.

There were other effects, too. I recall receiving a postcard almost weekly from a nonadmirer with a Mississippi address —he may have lived just across the line in Tennessee. Each time he implored me to please get off television. Once he almost promised to vote for me if I would desist. Republican officeholders took notice, too. Some of them began to inquire about television-studio interviews. Of course, the stations told them they would be accorded the same treatment. None followed the schedule I did, however.

Through the winter that followed Nixon's inauguration there was no discernible change in the Administration's policy on the Vietnam war. Search-and-destroy missions and other costly tactics of attrition were continued. Though Nixon had repeatedly said, "I have a plan," Congress and the country waited and waited for some definitive statement from the new President. Meanwhile, our losses were high.

It was not until May 14 that Nixon made his first policy statement on Vietnam to the people. I had been advised in advance that it would be a "peace" speech. Even so, I was surprised by it. He flatly ruled out a "purely military solution on the battlefield"—which seemed to me to leave a peaceful settlement through negotiation and compromise as the only viable alternative. He advanced a number of steps which I had long advocated: 1) creation of an international body agreeable to both sides to supervise troop withdrawals and cease fires; 2) "all parties [to] agree to observe the Geneva Accords of 1954 regarding South Vietnam and Cambodia, and the Laos Accords of 1962"; and 3) "mutual withdrawal of non-South Vietnamese forces from South Vietnam and free choice for the people of South Vietnam." (In support of this latter point the President condemned, in three different places in his speech, "a one-sided withdrawal"—a fact of considerable importance which I shall take up later.) And he went on to say, "Almost without exception the leaders of non-Communist Asia have told me that they would consider a one-sided American withdrawal from Vietnam to be a threat to the security of their own nations."

He did not rule out a coalition government. It had been my view for a long while that a compromise government and neutrality status for the former French colonies was the most feasible form of settlement in consonance with the terms of the Geneva Accords. In this regard, the President said, "We have no objection to reunification, if that turns out to be what the people of North Vietnam and the people of South Vietnam want; we ask only that the decision reflect the free choice of the people concerned."

From the speech, I concluded that the President had decided, as Eisenhower had with the Korean war, to use the mandate of his election to extricate the United States from Vietnam as quickly and as best he could. I commended the speech in the Senate. Several of my fellow anti-Vietnam-war Senate colleagues were leery of the speech, calling it but a public-relations "change of pace." One senator warned that it was wholly inconsistent with the military strategy the President had followed. But Senator Frank Church, who had been telephoned before the speech by Henry A. Kissinger, special assistant to the President, agreed with my interpretation of the speech and he too praised it. This benign interpretation was encouraged by Kissinger in a number of remarks and telephone calls he made to other senators on the Foreign Relations Committee. Many editorials applauded the speech as a move toward peace.

But as the scheduled meeting at Midway with President Thieu approached, all the factious fury of the Saigon regime was echoed here at home. The hawks screamed about giving in to "the Communists." Then Nixon gave another speech —on June 4, at the Air Force Academy—that struck a chord quite different from that of his speech of May 14, and which in fact added up to a ringing defense of the military. "It is open season on the armed forces. . . . Patriotism is considered by some to be a backward, unfashionable fetish of the uneducated and unsophisticated. . . . We shall reaffirm our aspiration to greatness or we shall choose instead to withdraw into ourselves. . . ." For this, he must have used a different speechwriter!

Then, at Midway, Nixon found himself stymied, as Johnson so frequently had. Hemmed in by political, militaristic, hawkish pressures at home, by a wily "ally" abroad, and by insistent military advisers from both places, Nixon trimmed his sails. Or else he had not meant what he said on May 14. Without formally announcing the abandonment of his peace plan, he charted a different course—"phased withdrawal." This meant prolongation of the war, of course. The psychological sop he offered the American people was a gradual "unilateral withdrawal"—which he had thrice denounced in his speech of only a month before. This scheme, launched with the Madison Avenue title "Vietnamization," proved to be an attractive package for the home market, but the contents had yet to be appraised and tested.

I warned that a "phased withdrawal" would involve keeping U.S. military forces in South Vietnam for a long time to prop up the Saigon military regime until it *could* and *would* maintain itself in power. It was simply a semantic cover for prolonging the war. I urged, instead, a negotiated settlement, which I believed then possible for a newly elected President to achieve.

> It is my view that we should utilize our overwhelming presence in Vietnam to persuade the establishment of a broadly based government that would include the diverse factors, sects, and factions to serve as a means of concluding a peaceful settlement and to provide some hope for the ultimate survival of democratic processes and freedom in South Vietnam. . . .
>
> Every American who is returned home from Vietnam gladdens our heart, the more the better. But the peace program that is in the vital interest of the United States and in the

interest of world-wide peace, and one which I believe the American people earnestly desire, is one which will permit all U.S. troops, not just a few at a time over a long withdrawal period, to be disengaged and returned to the peaceful and fruitful pursuits of a normal life.

But no argument would avail. A "negotiated settlement" had lost its priority with the President, displaced by the urgency of keeping the hawks content at home and keeping the Thieu-Ky regime in power in Saigon. "Vietnamization" was merely a plan to continue the war and to maintain in power a putative democratic republic controlled by satraps approved by the United States government.

Soon after the President's return from Midway, a number of visitors quoted him as saying that he would not be the first President to negotiate a U.S. defeat. Yet no one had suggested "defeat" for the United States. Nixon himself had taken the war out of the rhetorical context of "victory" or "defeat" in his speech of May 14 by saying that he ruled out "a purely military solution on the battlefield." It reminded me of Johnson's statement that he would not be "the first President to run." The meaning was the same.

The announcement of incremental withdrawals of American troops, even though small in number, won widespread popularity. Leading Democrats—Hubert Humphrey, for instance—praised "Vietnamization," though they had not been given any idea whatsoever as to its schedule. Even Mike Mansfield, Senate Democratic Leader, and George Aiken of Vermont called it "a step in the right direction." Strangely, even the win-the-war-at-any-price advocates endorsed it. Questions as to whether it was a carefully considered strategy for peace or a political maneuver to placate the public while continuing the war seemed off-key. All those asking such "impudent" questions came under the lash of Vice-President Agnew, who suggested that Americans should "divide on authentic lines."

Nixon's *complete* about-face from his negotiated peace position of May 14 was not publicly accomplished until his television speech to the nation on November 3, 1969. He then reiterated all the discredited Johnson arguments for American involvement in Vietnam, but affirmed again that he was going to "get us out" of it anyway. Assuming that "Vietnamization" might gradually get us out of the war *some day* it was difficult to understand *why* Mr. Nixon, believing the war was justified and in our national interest, would still withdraw from it unilaterally. This was a war, he said, for the defense of freedom, for the prevention of world conquest by Communist powers, and for proving America's loyalty to commitments—so much in our own self-interest, he assured the country, that he was going to "get us out" of it.

In this same speech, he made his touching plea that the "silent majority" support his contradictory policy. I was filled with revulsion at the thought that an American political leader should conceive of our citizenry as a silent majority. The President used the phrase to flatter complacency and to promote the fantasy of a Gary Cooper America—one short on words and ideas but strong on guts. What the phrase really identified, it seemed to me, was an American denied any real participation in specific issues, an American given—and hopefully satisfied with—lulling reassurance instead of hard facts and logic.

Kissinger sought ways to bolster support of Administration policy. At a meeting with him and several senators in the home of Senator Fulbright, I urged that the President negotiate a coalition government in Saigon and end the war. Kissinger replied that Nixon felt he must maintain "political cohesion" at home. (By February 1972, Kissinger was communicating the same thought publicly. On the day after, the President revealed a long series of secret negotiations with the North Vietnamese. Kissinger said that "composing the domestic disharmony is a very major objective of our entire policy.") By whatever name, politics smells the same.

My continuing objections and speeches against the war were, of course, in violation of a cardinal rule of senatorial politics: be bland the last two years before election. I had fully intended to be bland, "quiet and easy," for all of 1969 and 1970! But how could I remain bland when I knew that thousands of boys were dying and our country's moral position was being eroded for no good cause whatsoever? I could not. A person, believing as I did, who could or would stay quiet with such provocation should not be in the Senate anyway.

And then another issue arose on which I could not be *bland* or quiet. This was the proposed deployment of antiballistic missiles (ABM), which was referred to the Arms Control Subcommittee of which I was chairman. I was convinced that this costly, and at best useless, undertaking would be likely to further the nuclear-arms race and impede agreement with the Soviet Union on strategic-arms limitations. Some small steps toward peace had been taken, and both the United States and Russia had expressed an interest in negotiations for a strategic-arms-limitation agreement. (On a trip to Russia in December 1968, Senator Claiborne Pell and I had a long conference with Soviet Chairman Aleksei Kosygin, who spoke forcefully of Russia's willingness to initiate such a conference.) I was profoundly convinced that such future negotiations would be delayed, if not torpedoed, by deployment of an ABM system.

Instead of being bland about this, I recommended that the Arms Control Subcommittee take the issue to the people in public hearings. The result of that nationally televised debate was an unprecedented public involvement in a technical issue. Nixon won his go-ahead by a tie vote.

Many of my constituents thought my fight against the ABM deployment was associated with my opposition to the Vietnam war. Indeed, arms control, gun control, reduction of military appropriations, and questioning either the Vietnam war or repressive violence by police against dissenting students seemed to be lumped into one package by a large segment of people. Both Nixon and Agnew appealed to this large group, and my state harbored a great many who shared their sentiments. This may have been demonstrated when I was loudly booed at a football game at the University of Tennessee in Knoxville in the fall of 1969. I would just as soon have missed that game, but I recalled that Kefauver had been just as roundly booed by just such a football crowd before receiving his largest majority in the state.

Another reason for the booing may have been that many of the affluent there would not receive the big tax cuts Nixon had proposed for upper income brackets because I had led a successful fight to kill his proposal by substituting my own— to increase the personal exemption of each taxpayer and each dependent.

The personal-exemption provision in the tax code, and its neglect since World War II, illustrated as clearly as anything I knew the cavalier treatment of the general taxpayer by Congress and successive Administrations over the years. It also reflected the consequences of a lack of organized pressure for tax reform on the part of the public.

A personal-income-tax system should have two main features. First, a sufficient amount of income should be exempt from taxation so that the taxpayer and his family can enjoy a decent basic living allowance. Second, a graduated tax scale should be applied against all income above the exempt amounts. Tax rates should begin at a very low level—1 or 2 per cent on the lowest taxable amounts—and rise gradually to high rates on large amounts of income.

Because I regarded the personal tax exemption as a key to tax equity, I had made repeated efforts to get the figure increased. The reason most often advanced for rejecting the increase was loss of revenue. Conservative senators and Administration spokesmen would invariably intone pious laments and would hasten to point out that a loss of revenue could not be afforded *at this time.* Unfortunately, it always seemed to be *this* time.

In 1969, the political climate was right for my fight. Nixon had proposed what he called a tax-reform bill but which actually provided the most benefits to those with high incomes. I was determined not to let him give his benefits to those with high incomes and call it "tax reform." It was reform in the wrong direction. Thus, when the bill came to the Senate from the House of Representatives, I undertook to awaken in my Senate colleagues a concern for the "little man," and to fan into flame the residual populism which lies deep in the hearts of all real Democrats, even the conservative ones.

My earliest recollection of events that shaped my political, social, and economic philosophy are of conversations I had with my father when I was a boy, sitting around the fire or on the front porch after supper. Reading his newspaper by the light of the kerosene lamp, he would frequently stop to discuss some new development. We would often speak of William Jennings Bryan, whose earlier achievements as "the

Great Commoner" he still cherished. The Bryan to whom my father referred was not the ineffectual Secretary of State under Wilson, nor the pitiful old man of the "monkey trial," but the dynamic young Cross of Gold orator—the "prairie Populist" who voiced the aspirations of many common men in his day.

As one who deeply believed there was much merit in this Populist heritage, it had always seemed to me perfectly logical that government should play an active role in the nation's business affairs, and I had never lost faith in the government's ability to guarantee economic justice to all its people. I had never sympathized with the attitude of those economic royalists who prated about the impropriety of positive governmental action in the economic arena. I was determined, on the other hand, that the government take precisely such action, and a decently fair tax bill was a good place to start.

With the help of the Democratic leadership of the Senate, but over the opposition of the Senate Finance Committee and its chairman, Russell Long, I completely rewrote the Administration's tax bill on the floor of the Senate. I considered the raising of the personal exemption in 1969 my greatest triumph in tax legislation, yet I could not take wholehearted joy from it because 1969 really was not the time to reduce taxes. As I pointed out during debate on my amendments, "This amendment offers a fundamental choice to the Senate . . . between types of tax reductions. It may well be that the bill should contain no tax reductions, and I think I might prefer no tax reductions to the type proposed in the Committee bill." But that was not the choice. The choice was between a big tax cut for the few or a fair tax bill for all. My amendment was adopted by the Senate, but those who benefited were not in the U.T. football stadium. The most important aspect of this achievement was that at long last we had halted, at least temporarily, the trend toward the destruction of progressiveness in our federal income-tax system. We had broken the log jam with the personal exemption. The sacrosanct exemption of $600, which had acquired such permanence since 1948, was finally increased by my amendment.

Though my victory had been complete in the Senate, I still faced a battle in conference with the House of Representatives which had passed the Administration's bill. Congress has never come to grips with the archaic ways and often dictatorial powers of conference committees. It is here, in secret meetings often not even announced until the last minute, that a few men sit down and undo in one hour months of painstaking effort made by several standing committees and the full membership of both houses. It is here, after the tumult and shouting and public debate have faded and after the headlines have shifted to a new subject, that substantive legislation can suffer remarkable mutation.

After the conference committee's "report," or agreed action, is taken, the two houses must then vote on it up or down, in toto, without amendment. There is usually scant explanation or debate before the vote to accept or reject. The conference deliberations are not published, and the reports are often all but unintelligible to the public and to the Congress alike. And, perhaps most important, there is usually a finality about conference-committee decisions. Any senator or congressman who opposes only a specific provision is faced with two choices: to accept the provision to which he objects, or to try to defeat the entire bill, a move which would cost weeks or months of work. Often, the most important legislation comes up right before recess or holiday, which makes a successful fight against the conference report even more unlikely. For these reasons, the reports, even when they distort the intent of either house, are rarely challenged.

The conference committee on the tax bill, made up of seven senators and nine representatives, had been appointed by the President of the Senate and the Speaker of the House, respectively. (In practice, the chairmen and ranking minority members of the standing committees handling a given piece of legislation actually name the conferees. Almost invariably, they name themselves.) The committee was brought together to compose, "settle" in congressional cloakroom jargon, the hundred or so differences between the versions of the Tax Reform Act of 1969 as it had passed each house of Congress.

The conference committee met in secret on a cold December night in 1969. By 2:30 A.M., it reached a decision to increase personal income-tax exemptions from $600 to $750 (in stages), a beneficial step and a victory for me. But part of the decision also ultimately gave an enormous tax reduction to the relatively few with very large "earned" incomes (salaries, bonuses, commissions, as opposed to "dividend" or "interest" income). The head of General Motors, and others with similar earned incomes, may gain as much as $90,000 per year from this reduction. And the reduction was available only to those in the upper brackets and denied to everyone below them.

This reduced tax on large earned income was only an extra dividend added to the already staggering benefits the rich had received in recent years. It is generally believed, I think, that we have a graduated income tax based on ability to pay. But since 1964, the tax rates have become much less graduated, and each successive "reform" tends to give even more money back to the wealthy. Prior to 1964, the tax rates were graduated from 20 per cent on low incomes to 91 per cent on top incomes—a spread of 71 points. In the Tax Reduction Act of

2 2 6 LET THE GLORY OUT

that year, the top tax rate was reduced from 91 per cent to 70 per cent of income—a 21-percentage-point tax cut on high incomes.

Then, in 1969, the House passed the Nixon Administration bill which again lowered the top tax rate, this time from 70 per cent to 65 per cent, with no reduction whatsoever in the rates applicable at the bottom. And, in addition, the bill proposed to cut the top rate on "earned income"—salaries, fees, commissions, etc.—from 70 per cent to 50 per cent. This provision was added by the Nixon Administration with the support of Congressman Wilbur Mills, the committee chairman, at a midnight session of the House Ways and Means Committee just before the bill was approved and reported to the full House. I took single-shot aim at this unfair provision and built such a case against it that the Senate Finance Committee, of which I was a member, adopted unanimously an amendment to strike this provision from the bill. The amendment was even offered by the committee chairman, Russell Long, a member of the Southern club and whose favorite ploy has been to dish out tax favoritism. (I always thought he grabbed the issue and offered the amendment himself in order to keep me from winning another victory.) He said to the Senate:

> In establishing the new tax rates, the committee deleted from the bill a House provision limiting to 50 per cent the maximum marginal rate applicable to an individual's earned income. This action was taken because the committee believed that a 50-per-cent top marginal rate, though beneficial for work incentives, would provide unduly large tax reductions to those with substantial earned income.

The most important difference between the House and Senate tax bills, which must be resolved in conference, was the amendment I had offered and won on the floor of the Senate to strike out the Nixon-proposed rate changes and substitute instead an increase in personal exemption from $600 to $800; another difference, of course, was the big cut in taxes on high incomes which the House had passed but which the Senate had rejected unanimously.

On the first point, we agreed on a compromise that eliminated the rate changes and adopted a gradual increase in personal exemption from $600 to $750. On the second, the argument became quite heated, despite the fact that no one could advance any better justification for the provision than restating a point made by Edwin S. Cohen, Assistant Secretary of the Treasury, before the Senate Finance Committee, "We do get to the point where with respect to services . . . inordinately high rates may cause a person to spend more time trying to figure out some of the incentives in the law than he does concentrating on his work." In other words, the best way to guarantee the efficiency of corporate or professional leaders, to relieve their minds of the burdensome task of getting around the taxes, would be just to remove a large part of the tax on their high income. This argument could be carried further by saying that the best way to insure maximum productivity of the nation's highly paid managers would be to charge them no taxes at all, freeing their imagination from material things and elevating them to the disinterested plane of public service. The debate continued fiercely until finally Mills, a pillar in the Southern tax-favors club, suggested a compromise: that the 50-per-cent earned-income figure be set as a maximum "effective rate" (an average of all taxable income) rather than the "marginal rate" (applicable to the last dollar of income). This was a much, much smaller reduction. I accepted his offer as a compromise.

Mills then announced at 2:30 A.M. that the committee would adjourn for the night but would meet again at noon to sign the conference report, which the staff would meanwhile prepare. As we began to depart, I could not help overhearing a whispered conference between Senator Wallace Bennett, a ranking Republican on the Senate Finance Committee, and Cohen.

At 10 A.M. Democratic caucus that morning, Senator Long whispered something to me about giving the "Administration something" in order "to avoid a veto," and he made some imprecise reference to the 50-per-cent ceiling on high-bracket earnings. I was thus forewarned that a deal had been made. Sure enough, on the reconvening of the committee at noon to "sign the conference report," usually only a formality, Mills quickly reopened the earned-income-tax-rate question and looked toward Long who, despite his statement on the floor of the Senate in support of his own amendment to knock the provision out of the bill, went on the offensive in support of the Nixon Administration position and belabored me for my obstinacy. Bennett, who had also voted to strike it out, joined Long, as did others. This was a clear breach of our earlier agreement—a double-cross by Mills—but it availed me nothing to make this charge, which I did angrily, for I was hopelessly outnumbered. The committee quickly voted in favor of giving corporate officials, doctors, lawyers, and other high-income taxpayers an absolute top marginal tax rate of 50 per cent of their so-called earned income—a costly favoritism available only to a small high-income group.

The conference report was presented to the Senate and House on December 22, 1969, and adopted by both houses the very same day. It was impossible for me to hold up a multi-billion-dollar tax bill two days before Christmas. There was never a separate vote on the earned income provision by either Senate or House. Neither the general public nor a majority of Congress was aware of its passage. This is an example of how one new loophole for the well-off was opened in the tax law, already so complicated and riddled with favoritism that most people do not understand it. (The same Wilbur Mills, who has either authored or approved every loophole in the tax law, grabbed the flag of "tax reform" in his effort to gain the Vice-Presidential nomination in 1972.)

Though my tax fights helped me with some people, they embittered many others, especially the Administration and their high-income supporters. Agnew branded me as a "radic-lib." All this attention removed any doubt about the battle I was facing in Tennessee. The full resources of the Nixon Administration and the National Republican Party, both financial and political, would be arrayed against me. But there was another side of the coin. National attention would be focused on my campaign, and perhaps I, too, might receive more in the way of financial contributions than had ever been available to me before.

I had never been very successful in raising campaign money. To me, soliciting campaign funds is distasteful and I had no stomach for it. Less than $100,000 had been spent in my behalf in any one of my previous Senate campaigns. In the finance committee and in the Senate I had opposed special-interest legislation. So there never was any point in my expecting support from the people and the special interests with big funds to contribute. Their contributions would go to my opponent. I knew I had to depend on small contributions from many people, and a nationally symbolic campaign promised to help me in that regard.

When Congress adjourned in late December, it delayed the

convening of the 1970 session until the last week of January. This gave me three weeks of free time, and I decided to spend it making a sort of barnstorming tour through some of the less populous counties of Tennessee. My reasoning was that I might find it difficult to get back to some of them during the campaign, and if I later missed any of them, they would not have been left out altogether. My staff thought I should have spent the time otherwise: selecting a campaign manager and a finance chairman, starting on the task of building a campaign organization, and raising money. Perhaps so, but there were other things to consider. At the time it looked as though I might not have serious opposition in the primary in August. I thought it very important to avoid a primary fight if possible. There were rumors and reports about possible candidates to oppose me, but nothing substantial developed. So I chose to stay among the people.

Moreover, the race for the Democratic nomination for governor, then already under way, was a hotly contested campaign. It was evident that this would be a spirited, perhaps bitter, campaign, and I did not want to risk getting caught in the political cross fire by setting up a county-by-county organization. I wished to maintain a low profile in order to be in a position to run *with* the nominee for governor, *whoever* he might be. As I saw it, the November contest would be Democrats against Republicans, with the Democratic nominee for governor and I conducting a joint campaign.

Throughout the late winter and spring of 1970, I continued making trips to Tennessee and at the same time continuing to take the lead on important issues in Washington, as if to burn the candle at both ends. I began having "nonpartisan" receptions in traditionally Republican east Tennessee. Since Republicans outnumbered Democrats so heavily in the eastern part of the state, it seemed to me that subdued partisanship would be in order. (I am indebted to my Senate colleague Bill Proxmire for the mechanics of the arrangements. He had used a similar technique in his campaign.) These events were usually held in the high-school gymnasium in the county seat of the smaller upper eastern counties, with the high-school band, the Boy Scouts, and other groups on hand. First, we would obtain the names of perhaps 100 ladies in the town. Each of them was called from Washington and invited to serve as a "hostess" and to suggest the names of people to be invited. The response was good, and it wasn't hard at all to get 30 to 40 hostesses. Printed invitation were prepared and mailed to all those suggested by our hostesses—and also to everybody else in town whose name appeared in the telephone directory. Pauline and I enjoyed these affairs and I think they were helpful, especially because of her warm gracefulness. Speech-making at these socials was kept at a minimum, but I always made some nonpartisan remarks and then answered questions. One sure subject, nearly always the first, was about the Vietnam war.

On April 20, 1970, the President made a placatory television speech in which he spoke with "confidence" that ". . . we finally have in sight the just peace. . . ." Only ten nights later, he dramatically said over the same networks that our situation was so precarious that he had widened the war by ordering ground "attacks" in Cambodia. This caused a severely critical outcry in which I joined, both in Washington and in Tennessee. Nixon gave precisely the same arguments for this escalation as Johnson had given for his. The Senate Foreign Relations Committee, in an action which I helped initiate, formally requested a meeting with the President. Unable politically to refuse the request, Nixon avoided a confrontation by inviting the thirty-five-member House Foreign Affairs Committee, a thoroughly hawkish group, along with the Senate committee. This large group met with the President in the State Dining Room of the White House on April 30.

The President opened the meeting with a formal statement. I found the exposition of his position just as muddled as his two contradictory speeches had been. His only explanation was that the enemy had taken "actions in Cambodia" that had created a "Cambodian crisis," which meant, the President said, that either we must stop the gradual withdrawals he had announced and get out now, or "go to the heart of the problem"—and destroy the sanctuaries. I wondered just how this situation had changed between April 20 and April 30. Nixon gave his answer to this, at least for me, when he said that the military had wanted "to hit them for years. This gives Vietnamization a better chance," he added but did not explain why or how.

The President assured us that the operation would be limited in both time and extent, and that the invasion would not go deeper than "thirty-five kilometers without the approval of Congress."

The first senator to speak up, according to my notes, was Senator Jacob K. Javits of New York. He propounded a weighty question about the Constitutional equation between the executive and legislative branches with respect to war-making powers. The President replied in legalistic terms which, I noted to myself, were not a "strict construction."

Senator Fulbright asked if, in the President's view, China would "accept defeat of North Vietnam." (We had been informed that this would cause China to enter the war.) The President replied that we were "not attempting defeat upon

North Vietnam," and that he was open to settlement "on the basis of present power balance" in South Vietnam. Senator Fulbright inquired, too, if the President thought the strategic-arms limitation talks under way in Vienna would be "adversely affected." The President declared that the SALT talks would not be seriously affected, that the Russians and we had a mutual interest in achieving a limitation of armaments, etc. In the course of his reply, he said, "We expect the Soviets to protest this just as we protested their invasion of Czechoslovakia." To me, this was a disturbing analogy, but then I did not foresee his visits to Russia and China in 1972.

When my turn came I inquired: "Mr. President, you have told us that you will not invade deeper than thirty-five kilometers into Cambodia without the approval of Congress. What is the difference, in principle, between invading thirty-five kilometers and fifty kilometers? The important event was the crossing of the boundary of a sovereign nation with an invading Army, which you ordered without authority from or even consultation with Congress. Yet you tell us now you will not go beyond thirty-five kilometers without the approval of Congress. What is the principle and where is the logic?"

The President tersely replied, "Because this is not a sovereign territory. It had become completely dominated by the enemy," and he sharply turned, pointing to another person on the other side of the room. Though he had not answered my question at all and I wished further to explore the rationale of both the action and the limits, I was cut off and not again recognized. This was far from the kind of "consultation" the Senate Foreign Relations Committee had desired and requested. It had in mind the advice-and-consent provision of the Constitution.

Nixon was still following the familiar path of seeking

"peace" through a "wider war," "saving lives" by increasing the casualty rate, pursuing a mirage in Vietnam by a policy that eroded his own as well as our national credibility, and tragically prolonging the war by making negotiations for peace more difficult. The deaths of thousands of American boys, and hundreds of thousands of North and South Vietnamese civilians as well as soldiers, seemed to be regarded as though they died in some distant make-believe drama to be viewed from a safe, remote vantage point by the military and political spectators.

Each and every bill making appropriations for the war had had my support. For I drew a clear distinction between support of our troops in Vietnam, on one hand, and approval of the war policies on the other. Most of the fighting men were there not by choice but in duty to their country and by order of military authority. They deserved the best weapons, munitions, equipment, medical supplies, and food to execute their orders with the least possible danger to themselves. Though this position was subject to logical challenge, up to 1970 almost every antiwar member of the House and Senate shared it.

Congress unquestionably had the Constitutional power to stop the war by withholding appropriations. This would have been an unusual, an extreme, use of Constitutional powers by the legislative to restrain the actions of the Chief Executive. Yet no less extreme, of course, than the Presidential usurpation of the war-making power in the case of the Cambodian invasion. More and more senators considered such a course of action. For my part, I was unwilling to do so. (I later had serious doubts about this position.)

Following the Cambodian invasion, a wave of mass protests broke out over the country, especially among the young.

Though I opposed violence, I sympathized with those young men who had sacrificed so much, those in service, or those who might soon be drafted and who found themselves in a state of uncertainty and travail. From the time these young men who faced the draft were three or four years old, they had known only a climate of increasing military violence and, as a consequence, increasing civilian despair. An endless war did not make for an atmosphere in which young people could remain content and well-disposed to the institutions of their society. To continue the war when it was honorably possible —as I believed it had surely been—to negotiate a peaceful settlement, was heartlessness toward the youth who had to suffer for the errors of their elders.

Two million boys had answered their country's call to a war not of their own making, and they had served heroically. No other generation of Americans had been sought for such a sacrifice, not merely of their lives but of their very intelligence itself, a sacrifice which demanded their possible death in a war which defied understanding. How could there be understanding when the Nixon Administration had reached the point of not even bothering to justify its action by rational argument? The government of the United States was entrapped in the domestic political appeal of its own contrived rationalizations—"self-determination," "free elections," "anticommunism," "resisting Communist aggression," "our honor," etc.—while the killing, and the demoralization of our society and even of the armed forces themselves dragged on and on. Why? In order to maintain "political cohesion" at home, or to "compose domestic disharmony."

Meanwhile, general planning for my campaign was under way, but with the severe handicap of uncertainty as to the amount of funds that would be available. There were no pledges of the kind of money we needed for the sophisticated media-type of campaign everyone seemed to think was necessary. I knew I would be outspent 5 to 1, and probably more.

Organizationally, there are several ways to structure a campaign. At the top of the scale or the bottom, depending on your point of view. One may engage a professional firm to take complete charge of a campaign, to program it, to merchandise the candidate with Madison Avenue techniques. There are many such firms, and my staff talked to several representatives who called. My Republican opponent had already engaged Treleaven Associates, the firm that had handled Nixon's campaign for the Presidency. But there never was any chance that I would or could take this route, even if I wished to. The fee such firms charge required funds that were not available to me. Anyway, I would not have been comfortable in a campaign that did not place heavy emphasis on personal campaigning or that I did not control.

A second way of campaigning is the system whereby the nonprofessional campaign staff deals directly with professional agencies that offer their services—sort of like being your own contractor in building a house and dealing directly with the subcontractors. There are many kinds of subcontractors—poll takers, ad agencies, computer letter-writing firms, television producers, computer firms doing precinct analysis, and many others. My staff also talked to representatives of all kinds of firms in this category, somewhat wistfully. Letters can be written by computers, for example, by the hundreds of thousands (with slight changes being made, depending on the geographic location or predetermined political philosophy or avocation of the recipient). At first, it seems inexpensive, too, at about 14¢ a letter, but when you add it up, a million letters means $140 to $145 thousand dollars. We didn't have that kind of money, nor did we expect to get it. When one's resources are limited one must establish priorities, and the decision was made to forego professional assistance—with one exception. We engaged Guggenheim Productions, Inc., to prepare material for television and radio.

Charles Guggenheim does not come cheaply, but he is a master craftsman. Everyone agreed that television was a must in a modern campaign, and there was no question but that the opposition would saturate the airwaves. It seemed important to have quality material for the limited time we expected to be able to pay for. I had never previously used a professionally produced television commercial in a campaign, but having decided to do so, I went for the best.

Guggenheim simply filmed me in all kinds of situations, none of which were staged or "produced." He and his technicians came to Tennessee in early June to arrange to film some events at which I was scheduled to appear; he set up other events—a patio party in a suburb, a group of workers at a plant gate, and so on—and came to Carthage to film my family and me at home and around my home town (catching me at a game of checkers, entirely unplanned). There was never any script or cue cards, or even suggestions as to what was to occur. He just filmed what happened. In about three days, he shot thousands of feet of film and took it all back to Washington. I had little idea of what would come out of it. From this mass of material he culled several thirty-second and sixty-second spots and one five-minute film. It was generally recognized that the material he produced was among the best used during the 1970 campaign year. All my TV spots were affirmative. That is, they were pro-Gore. None attacked anyone.

Some newspapermen labeled the 1970 Tennessee senatorial campaign as a match between Guggenheim and Treleaven. That was not so. Guggenheim did not *in any sense* direct my campaign. His role was limited to the production of radio and television material and general advice about the timing of its release.

My votes against the confirmation of Clement F. Haynsworth, Jr., and G. Harrold Carswell for the Supreme Court before the Democratic primary hurt me badly in Tennessee. Both were from the South, and my opposition to them raised once again that old canard that I was disloyal to my region. Yet it did seem to me that the quality of the nominee was more important than where he was born, although of course, all other things being equal, I would have a natural preference for one from my native region. In fact, I joined Howard Baker in recommending the appointment of Federal District Judge William Miller of Nashville.

I decided to oppose Haynsworth because he had violated the code of ethics in deciding cases in which he had a personal financial interest. From the standpoint of principle, this was an easy decision but politically it was very rough. It brought down on me the wrath of the Dixiecrat element, the very group I needed to placate.

The Supreme Court had long been a source of controversy to many Tennesseans as to Southerners generally. It was the Court which had made the decision that "forced" integration upon the people of the South, and had ruled that prayers could *no longer* be "forced" upon children in public schools. The sentiment for racial separatism and for religious orthodoxy had been an integral part of our culture. What many desired was a Court that would be in agreement with these social mores.

When Nixon nominated another Southerner, Carswell, I was elated. I had been fearful that he would not nominate another Southerner, and this would cause my vote against Haynsworth to be even more hurtful. Now this gave me an opportunity to vote for a Southerner, freeing myself of the regional disloyalty charge. My enjoyment was short-lived, though, because Carswell was soon unraveled in broad daylight, and it was plain for all to see that he was unfit for the Court. This placed me in the anguishing position of having to choose between voting for the confirmation of a justice of the Supreme Court whom I considered unfit or of voting for him for no other reason than to serve my own personal political interest. I made the mistake of delaying an announcement of my decision, for the longer the investigation lasted the worse Carswell appeared and the stronger Southern sentiment for him became. I kept hoping that some break would come—maybe Carswell would withdraw his name, maybe Nixon would withdraw his nomination, maybe the Judiciary Committee would refuse to report his nomination to the Senate. But nothing like that happened, and the pressure to vote for his confirmation became terrific. Then a dusty old newspaper file was discovered which showed Carswell's 1948 campaign vow to "yield to no man" in his "firm, vigorous belief in the principles of white supremacy." Then there were more records showing that in 1956 the nominee—then U.S. Attorney for the area—had helped incorporate a private club that got around desegregation of the city's municipal golf facilities. The pattern of racial bias hardened.

I realized full well my political life might be riding on a "no" vote. It had become the litmus test of loyalty or disloyalty to the South, of white supremacy or civil rights for blacks with no room left for moderation or reason. When my name was called I voted a firm "No," and I felt good inside.

Letters and telegrams from my state surely verified my assessment of the political potency of the issue. This was illustrated, too, by a news dispatch from Memphis which reported that on the day following the Senate vote, a straw poll was taken at a meeting of a plumbers' union which showed an astoundingly overwhelming disapproval of me and my vote.

Nixon sharpened the issue still further by his charge that the two judges had been bludgeoned because they were Southerners. "It is not possible to get confirmation for a judge on the Supreme Court of any man who believes in the strict interpretation of the Constitution, as I do," he said. "I understand," he added, "the bitter feelings of millions of Americans who live in the South about the act of regional discrimination that took place in the Senate yesterday. They have my assurance that the day will come when men like Judges Haynsworth and Carswell will sit on the High Court."

If the President's political motives had been suspect before, they were now stripped bare. His aides had denied the existence of an anti-black Southern strategy, yet here was venomous verification. He was, indeed, playing racial politics with his choices for the Court.

I had voted against them *despite* their Southern heritage. I considered Nixon's slur on the Senate as untrue, and I felt outraged by it. Neither could I accept his implication of Senate hypocrisy about no Southerner getting confirmed. I knew there were many outstanding Southern jurists and lawyers who could readily be approved by the Senate, if he would but nominate one of them.

With this vote and my Vietnam record to answer for, it was not entirely surprising that an opponent quickly announced against me in the Democrat primary. It was Governor Ellington's press secretary, Hudley Crockett. Though my low profile primary stance had to be abandoned, I did everything possible to avoid bitterness in the primary because a divisive primary would be very hurtful. I refrained from any reference to him by name.

I named James F. ("Tim") Schaeffer, a Memphis attorney, as my campaign manager. An able, active Democrat, he did not have state-wide political contacts, but Bill Allen, my efficient administrative assistant, could provide that. And Memphis, Schaeffer's home, with 20 per cent of the potential vote, was the single most important center in the election. Gus Kuhn, Jr., a Nashville businessman, was named finance chairman. A state committee was named, and campaign headquarters were opened in Nashville.

Throughout the primary, my eye and my aim was on November. Some of my advisers contended that I was taking the primary too lightly and that I was underestimating my opponent's strength. I don't think I did, but I did underestimate the depth and bitterness of the feeling among some Tennesseans about my Senate record. I was surprised, too, at the extent of hostility on the part of members of the Ellington Administration. But even if I had considered the matter otherwise, I would have played the game the same way. The real danger was in November, so I campaigned hard against my November challenger, ignoring my Democratic primary opponent who, coincidentally (perhaps) was making precisely the same criticisms of me that my Republican opponent was making. It was almost as though the same person were writing speeches for both: Gore was not a loyal Southerner, had opposed Southerners on the Court, had forgotten Tennessee, had given aid and comfort to the enemy, was anti-South, and had lined up with the (vague and somehow evil) Northeastern liberal establishment, etc. I learned about a chance meeting between them during the primary campaign, and there was some good-natured kidding about the similarity of their "issues" against me.

On July 15, the *Nashville Banner*, a Republican newspaper, carried the following headline and news story:

BROCK, CROCKETT VOICE SUPPORT OF PRESIDENT

Two U.S. (Senate) candidates of opposing parties campaigned in Shelbyville Tuesday and expressed similar views on several subjects. Both candidates expressed agreement with the Vietnam conflict. Both also attributed college campus disorders to a general lack of discipline.

Early in the primary race, on a Sunday in June, a meeting of my campaign committee was held in my home in Carthage. This was the day Guggenheim was completing his work, and he filmed my son and me riding horses. This had not been planned at all. It more or less just happened. I was astride my white horse, a Tennessee walker, and Al rode a bay mare. (It turned out to be one of our best television spots, too good to have been planned, and we promptly renamed my horse "Traveler.") Anyway, we entered the room as the meeting was about to break up. I introduced Guggenheim to those assembled. "Charles, tell them what it's going to take to win this election," I said. Guggenheim answered, "A lot of manure." This broke up what had been a serious meeting.

Nothing particularly significant happened during the primary, except the concert of the Brock and Crockett campaigns which were directed at the Wallace voters of 1968 and Republican crossovers. There were no shrewd strategy meetings, no major goofs (though I made several minor ones), no dramatic turning point. It was just the usual kind of daily smear attack against me, almost like a broken record, which sought to alienate the people from me. I made no reference to Crockett but kept campaigning with my Republican opponent clearly in my sights.

In Tennessee, a candidate is still expected to tour the state as in days gone by, although people, by and large, no longer come out to hear him speak. It's not a very good idea to have a "speaking" with a small crowd, so courthouse speeches have largely been abandoned in favor of informal handshaking, visits to the local newspaper, and a short talk on the local radio. I always went to the radio stations and usually, instead of just making a speech, I would have an informal discussion with my local campaign manager and often include other local citizens, just whoever happened to be around at the time.

My margin of victory in the primary was disappointingly small—a 31,000 majority in a light vote. I intend no adverse reflection on my erstwhile opponent by saying that many, perhaps a clear majority, of the votes he received were from Republicans who crossed over into the Democratic primary to take a whack at me. "Get Gore in the primary, why wait till November," wrote a Crockett-Brock supporter in a letter to the editor appearing in the Memphis *Commercial Appeal* of June 3.

The total vote in the Republican gubernatorial primary, though contested between five contenders, was only 232,000, while more than twice that many, 570,000, voted in the Democratic primary. In the senatorial primary, only 224,000 votes were cast in the Republican primary, while more than twice that number voted in the Democratic primary. In some counties in middle and west Tennessee there was a large Republican vote in the Democratic primary—against me. For instance: In Coffee County, where Nixon got 3337 votes in

1968, only 477 people bothered to vote in the Republican primary; in Obion, where Nixon got 2420 in 1968, there were only 262 Republican primary voters. Overton, Lauderdale, and Henry counties, which together gave Nixon 4206 votes in 1968, produced only 820 persons to vote in the Republican primary.

Republicans in Tennessee have developed, over years of practice during "Boss" Crump's domination of state politics, a habit of voting in the Democratic primary. There is no party registration, and challenges are almost unheard of. Until recent years, Republicans did not bother to hold state primaries of their own and the Democratic primary was the only game in town. But in 1970 there was a spirited contest for the Republican nomination for governor, and I hoped this would keep Republicans in their own primary. The vote totals showed, however, that a lot of them—perhaps more than half of Crockett's vote—couldn't resist the chance to take two cracks at me. "Why wait 'til November?" one said.

(On September 10, the *Nashville Tennessean* carried a small news story under the headline: CROCKETT BACK ON STAFF OF ELLINGTON.)

Though I had tried hard to hold the damage of the primary to a minimum, it had hurt me badly, especially because of my opponent's appeal to racism and provincialism. Yet during the primary, I had established what was to be the central theme of my campaign. I proposed to take to the people of Tennessee the contrast between my Republican opponent's record and mine on numerous issues important to them, to appeal to their interests and to their intelligence instead of their hates, fears, and prejudices. Moreover, I demonstrated that on key issues the majority of Tennessee's

Congressional delegation had supported my position rather than his; that in fact on many questions he had voted all alone, out in right field, against measures supported by all the rest of the delegation. To drive home his negative record, I called him "Mr. No-No." This approach not only illustrated our contrasting positions, but it was an answer to the charge that I had not represented Tennessee. "Who, then, has really represented Tennessee?" I was to ask rhetorically many times during the campaign, after pointing to votes in which he stood all alone. I did enough of this in the primary to get many people to think twice about the consequences of my threatened defeat. My supporters worked very hard during the primary to prevent a flight of voters to the opposition camp.

After the primary, detailed plans for the campaign could not be made until we could determine just how and to what degree my campaign would be meshed with the one for governor. John Jay Hooker, Jr., had won the gubernatorial nomination in a campaign characterized by bitter personal attacks. He had narrowly lost the previous primary in 1966 to Ellington, but had handled himself quite well after that defeat, supporting Ellington strongly in November and generally paving the way for another try. Meanwhile, he had attained fantastic business success—making millions—primarily in fast food franchising, and was, until late 1969, considered practically a shoo-in for election. Hooker encouraged the notion that the state needed a successful businessman for governor. This had strong appeal until his business empire began to collapse in 1969. By primary time it was in shambles, several bankruptcies having already occurred with more threatened. This became a big question in his campaign. Moreover, Hooker and the publisher of the *Nashville Banner,* James G.

Stahlman, became embroiled in a series of extremely bitter personal exchanges. These developments in the primary clouded his prospects too.

Nevertheless, I concluded that success in November would require a united Democratic effort. There were still more Democrats in Tennessee than Republicans. Decidedly so if those who were wavering could be kept in the fold. The size of the primary vote demonstrated this. A campaign in which Hooker and I went our own separate ways, each disregarding the other, would, I feared, be fatal to both. There were areas where Hooker, as head of the party organization (implicit in the nomination for governor), could be enormously helpful to me—in west Tennessee, for example, where there had been a marked trend toward conservatism and Republicanism for years, propelled by racism and business-oriented opposition to Democratic economic policies. In many of these counties, courthouse organizations were still strong and local officials were predominantly Democrats. They could see the handwriting on the wall. A Republican sweep at the state-wide level would lead to a Republican legislature and perhaps inevitably to courthouses across the state filled with Republicans. To these people and to the traditionalists, the party appeal was strong. In other areas, the Oak Ridge-Knoxville area and throughout middle Tennessee, for example, I was demonstrably stronger than Hooker. We needed to share our strengths, run a unified campaign, appeal to party unity, and establish a victory band-wagon psychology. Hooker and I met beside the pool at his beautiful home in a Nashville suburb late in the night after our primary victories. With only my son present, I outlined my views on campaign plans. Hooker agreed and we shook hands on it—we would run a unified "one-for-all-and-all-for-one" campaign.

Several strategy sessions between Hooker and his staff on one hand, and me and key members of my campaign staff on the other, followed during the last half of August. I was anxious to go all the way with a completely unified campaign, as we had agreed, with a single headquarters, a single campaign manager, a genuine ticket campaign, traveling and speaking together—the whole works. I believed both of us could win in this manner, and I urged this repeatedly at these meetings, pointing out advantages for both of us. Hooker still appeared to agree, but his campaign leaders did not, and he was either unable or unwilling to direct it. In their view, Hooker was far stronger, with a much more effective organization (they had been building it since 1966). They felt, plainly, that I would be a load to carry, and they simply didn't want to be tied too closely to me. My assurances that I would pull my part of the load did not convince them. They were more impressed by the polls, which showed me far behind my opponent and showed, too, a strong hawkish majority on Vietnam and a heavy pro-Carswell sentiment.

Moreover, some of the more conservative or Dixiecrat elements of the party would support him but not me. Some of Hooker's financial backers who disliked my record, we were told, had threatened to withhold their money if the campaigns were unified. Hooker's brother-in-law and treasurer of his campaign, Gilbert Merritt, though my friend, plainly said, "We cannot finance a unity campaign. Some of our best contributors say they will not contribute."

Unable to unify, we sort of drifted into an informal understanding by which there would be mutual support and coordination whenever local conditions were favorable. But in practice this did not mean very much. This inability to unify at the top-command level soon became common knowledge all over the state and tended to undermine our whole Democratic party appeal.

Party unity was sadly lacking in other important respects. Hooker's principal primary opponent, Stanley Snodgrass, did not come forward with the public endorsement that losing primary candidates had customarily given the nominee in Tennessee. Instead, he only endorsed the "Democratic Party," pointedly failing to mention either Hooker or me. This was very hurtful to Hooker and also to me. So I went to see Snodgrass. We had lunch in the City Club atop the Third National Bank Building in Nashville. A long-term friend and supporter, I had no doubt that he would vote for me, but this was not enough. I told him it would be extremely helpful to the party and to me—and to him in the long run—if he would forthrightly endorse both Hooker and me, and I urged him to do so. He did not turn me down flatly, but did say, with a meaningful nod toward the newspaper publishing plant, that he had "obligations down the way." (The *Nashville Banner*, which had strongly supported Snodgrass for the Democratic nomination, was not far away and I thought he referred to it, though he was not vocally explicit.) Finally Snodgrass publicly made some generous personal and nonpolitical remarks about Mrs. Gore and me; he never endorsed either Hooker or me.

The State Democratic Executive Committee, which had been a governor's club for years, swung into action behind Hooker, but it showed very little interest in me. In fact, neither its chairman, Jimmy Peeler, nor its treasurer, Joe Carr, favored a unified campaign. This is not to say they opposed me—I'm confident they voted for me—but not one single dollar of party funds was available for my campaign! Moreover, the State Democratic Headquarters was a frequent meeting place for those who put "first things first"—the race for governor.

I telephoned my own primary opponent and asked him for an appointment. We met at the Holiday Inn near Vanderbilt University. After some light chatter about the hot weather during the campaign, I solicited his support, saying, "Your party needs you, and as the Democratic nominee I need your endorsement and support." He said he had no desire "to play the role of a kingmaker." I wasn't sure just what he meant by that, so let it pass. After some more references to weather and traffic, I again asked for his active support in a "show-down battle with a reactionary Republican." He then brought up the subject of Vietnam. With a tightened throat I said I had written about this fully in my book, *The Eye of the Storm,* which I proposed to send by courier to his home immediately. He said he would be glad to receive it.

Hardly knowing what else to say, I remarked on the vigor of his primary campaign. He said he had expected to do much better in the Third Congressional District, and added that he had agreed to speak to a party rally at Cleveland, Tennessee, in about two weeks. "Good," I said. "I hope you will endorse the Democratic nominees." He again said, "I do not want to play the role of kingmaker," which I could only interpret as meaning he did not wish to help me win. We took our leave as pleasantly as possible.

My daughter, Nancy, was invited to speak in my behalf at that same rally at Cleveland. Upon her return I anxiously inquired about the speech of my erstwhile opponent. "You would be better off if he had said nothing, and so would he," she said.

Ellington was the principal speaker at a luncheon meeting

sponsored by the Democratic Executive Committee where he proclaimed himself a "Democrat," conspicuously stopping short of an endorsement of either Hooker or me. This too signaled deep trouble with conservative elements within the party.

Later, in the heat of the campaign, a Memphis television station (WMC–TV) broadcast an interview with Ellington from Jackson, Mississippi, during a conference there of Southern governors. Though he may not have intended to be hurtful, and he surely was not responsible for the comments and intonations of the newscaster, it was widely interpreted as hostility toward me and it was never rebutted in any way. It seriously hurt in west Tennessee, where I needed help. Here is a portion of the interview and the observations of the right-wing newscaster Norman Brewer:

BREWER: Buford Ellington is leaving politics in Tennessee, at least for a time, and that undoubtedly contributed to the candor he displayed in an interview here today. . . . And, finally, Ellington let go with a not-too-indirect slap at his party's senatorial nominee, incumbent Senator Albert Gore. The question concerned his [Ellington's] recent attack on the U.S. Defense Department and Capitol Hill doves over the National Guard.

GOVERNOR ELLINGTON: Now, I made this statement in a speech in Tennessee last week. . . . Well, I'm strongly opposed to that, because we need our National Guard now in every state. Take the National Guard away from Tennessee . . . look what could happen again . . . in Nashville, in Chattanooga, even the smaller cities. Now they don't have the police power, and they can't maintain the police power to take care of a situation like this. They have a right to look to the State for help, and as long as I'm here, and as long as the National Guard is there, city officials know they can get help from the state level. We've proven that, and we are going to continue to do it. But if you pull the National Guard out, and put them into the active Army of the service and we have no National Guard, law and order wouldn't prevail in Tennessee for thirty days.

BREWER: Is this a concession to doves on Capitol Hill?

GOVERNOR ELLINGTON: Well, of course, it will be denied, but figure it out for yourself. Why would this change come about unless it was to appease the so-called doves, or those that are against the war or against the draft?

BREWER: Governor, does that position put you a little bit at odds with Senator Gore who is running for re-election this year? [I had not said one word about the National Guard or the draft issue.]

GOVERNOR ELLINGTON: Well, I don't know who it puts me at odds with. But I am going to say what I think is best for Tennessee and for the Tennessee people. Uh . . . I could care less who I disagree with, or who I agree with, as long as I know and I think I am right in doing the best thing for the people of my state.

(Near the end of the campaign, I telephoned Ellington and requested he grant permission for some nearby state employees to attend a 10 A.M. coffee break that my group was sponsoring in front of the old Andrew Jackson Hotel, where Pauline and I first met when she was working there at night to pay her way through Vanderbilt University Law School, and I was attending classes of the YMCA night law school. He readily granted my request and later sent a telegram of personal congratulations upon the success of our marriage. During the conversation he expressed the view that I would win but said, "I can't help Hooker." I was not sure whether he meant that Hooker was beyond help, a lost cause, or whether he could not support him.)

The odds against me were overwhelming. To win, it would

be necessary to weld a majority from thoughtful independent or nonpartisan citizens, the loyal Democrats (Humphrey's 28 per cent), and the Wallace voters (34 per cent), many having racist sentiments. Impossible as it appeared, I believed I could do it, for I knew the Wallace voters were, as I said, "mostly working people whose genuine interests I have diligently represented." I campaigned hard on economic issues, drawing sharp contrasts between Brock's reactionary votes and my record of concern and action for the average citizen, and the poor. And some normally Republican voters offered their support.

The very first thing I had to do was to restore some spirit among my own supporters. The narrowness of my primary vote and the lack of party unity discouraged many of them and demoralized others. My principal help in this regard came from women supporters. The small margin of victory in the primary frightened many women who appreciated the stands I had taken. The very issues—the Vietnam war, gun control, support of civil-rights measures, priorities, Haynsworth and Carswell, etc., etc.—that put me in disfavor with Republocrats were ones that women were deeply concerned about. Across the state, women leaders were spreading the word: "We can't let them do this to Senator Gore." "We can't afford to lose him." "We didn't do enough in the primary— we must do more now." Women came independently to the conclusion that the only way women could really help re-elect me was to have their own organization. The suggestion for this was made in response to a rising tide of determination edged with frustration. Many women truly wanted to "do more for Gore."

And that was the generating force of Volunteer Women for Gore, an organization headed by the talented and indefatigable Mrs. Carleen Waller, which grew to 19,000 volunteers, who worked hard and long hours as if their lives depended on it. They mounted a tremendous letter-writing campaign, each writer emphasizing the facet that was of most significance to her and to the people she was sending the letter to—some marvelous letters—and they went into every county in the state. Local radio stations were widely used. While they sent out suggestions for material to use on the radio spots, many wrote their own and all paid for them locally. Intelligent and creative ads in many county newspapers, some signed by dozens of women, supported and clarified my record issue by issue. The women helped set up local organizations (we had a chairman in every county), had meetings in their homes, spoke, reviewed my book, did door-to-door canvassing, toured courthouses and downtown areas, distributed thousands of pieces of literature at special events (county fairs, Hill Billy Day, etc.), talked on the radio. This outpouring of effort from women across the state was a phenomenon that was a source of great pride and of encouragement, a tonic to my own spirit. Other loyal supporters, including students, were galvanized by the difficulties. They were issue-oriented and filled with conviction, as I was.

Back in Washington, Mike Mansfield, the Majority Leader of the Senate, had instituted a rather novel procedure. The Senate was bogged down in a lengthy debate on the $19.2-billion 1971 Defense Procurement Bill. Other bills, which included such controversial issues as the Volunteer Army and the McGovern-Hatfield amendment to end the war, were piling up. Agreement was reached for the Senate to debate the bill during the daytime, then lay it aside in the later afternoon, and take up other bills for action. So, with my steam up, I began a commuting schedule, campaigning in Tennessee by day and being a senator in Washington by night. I would take an afternoon plane to Washington, be there for evening voting sessions, and catch an early morning plane for Tennessee, where I tried to arrange each day to be in one of the metropolitan areas (where television was available). In Washington too I would speak on some issues, thus taking advantage of the Senate as a forum, with the wire services and representatives of Tennessee newspapers keeping my name in the news. Meanwhile, there was much to be done to get ready for the full-scale campaign in mid-September.

Adjustments had to be made in my campaign organization across the state, and some counties remained to be organized. In a few counties in the west of the state where the Mississippi delta culture still dominates, underlying racism and general reactionary sentiment were so strong that it was difficult to find a recognized community leader who was willing to be openly active as my campaign manager. I had tried to avoid making this bad situation any worse during the primary. Rather than push too hard then, I had decided to wait until the general election in the hope that by then a unified party campaign organization could be built around the official party organization which would assist me in communicating my cause in this traditionally solidly Democratic area, except that it had voted overwhelmingly for Wallace.

But the Hooker local leaders in this area generally wanted nothing to do with my campaign, and this handicapped me. In fact, in some counties the Hooker leaders didn't seem even to want the Snodgrass supporters to participate and in some cases rebuffed them. These local leaders wanted to be sure that no one shared their seat at the patronage table after the victory in November. I warned Hooker that his chances of victory were being endangered by this.

In some other sections of the state, greater unity was achieved. In several small counties a single campaign headquarters was opened, with Gore and Hooker leaders jointly directing the campaign along with a representative of the Congressional candidate. Wherever we achieved this arrangement, things worked more smoothly and more effectively. In still other counties, there were separate campaign committees but close cooperation. In all counties, my managers were instructed to unify to the maximum degree possible, even though they believed it would hurt me. In Memphis, for instance, the home town of Hooker's opponent, my group cooperated right down the line with Hooker's workers.

Except in rural west Tennessee, most of these organizational difficulties had been cleared up by election day, largely as a result of information contained in polls commissioned by Hooker which showed me making rapid gains. Even in west Tennessee, local Hooker leaders were remarking, almost in wonderment, that "Gore is gaining strength." After that we were able to achieve some degree of cooperation in most counties. Everywhere a lot of valuable time was lost in getting a real party effort going at the local level—where organization really counts.

Money, as always, was a dominant factor in many decisions. Billboards, for example, were ruled out. The agency handling my advertising drew up a plan for what it considered a minimum "showing" on a state-wide basis but the price tag was $100,000. My staff didn't even bother to tell me about it until later. No use. My opponent had billboards, it seemed, on almost every corner.

We planned a television-radio time purchase of $150,000— 40 per cent allocated to middle Tennessee (the Nashville market), 30 per cent to west Tennessee (largely Memphis), and the remaining 30 per cent split between Chattanooga, Knoxville, and Tri-Cities. The heavy emphasis on middle Tennessee was in recognition of the fact that it was absolutely essential that traditionally Democratic middle Tennessee provide substantial majorities. And the 1968 Wallace vote had been very strong in this area. Memphis was very important, too, but a lot of a Memphis buy is wasted because one has to pay to reach so many viewers in Mississippi and Arkansas who can't vote in Tennessee. East Tennessee is a large market, but irretrievably Republican. So, we tried to put our limited money where we thought it would do the most good. The agency was instructed to plan a time-buy on the basis described, but to be prepared to cut back by establishing priorities in each market. And indeed, when the time arrived to deliver the check, the buy had to be slashed about 30 per cent. The money simply was not there. The buy was thinned out in a way to permit beefing it up if funds later became available. Fortunately, some did; and in the last two weeks we were able to increase our television and radio almost up to the original level, although some of the choice times that had been available earlier were then unavailable.

Gus Kuhn tried all kinds of ways to raise funds. Organized labor helped substantially, as had been expected. Friends in Tennessee responded generously, in large number if not in large amounts. A newspaper ad soliciting funds was tried with the expectation that it would at least break even. It barely did. We tried one computer letter to all teachers in the state. A former teacher, I had supported every bill for aid to education. My opponent had opposed every such bill. Yet the letter barely paid for itself.

I was the beneficiary of fund-raising drives launched by national organizations supporting a number of senatorial candidates, such as the Council for a Livable World and the National Committee for an Effective Congress. These contributions came mostly in small checks from individuals. From council supporters the checks averaged about $37 but totaled $70,000. The Committee for an Effective Congress raised another $20,000. We undertook a substantial amount of direct-mail solicitation and this was rewarding.

I was most grateful when the entire Democratic leadership of the Senate—Senators Mansfield, Kennedy, Robert C. Byrd, Muskie, Ernest F. Hollings, Harold E. Hughes, and Daniel K. Inouye—sponsored a fund-raising event in my behalf at the lovely home of Senator Edward Kennedy in McLean, Virginia. About $25,000 was raised in this effort and it certainly came in handy. More importantly, it helped to dramatize the national character of my issue-oriented campaign. And the Democratic Senatorial Campaign Committee provided support to me as it did to other Democratic candidates. The amount did not approach the $50,000–$60,000 which a national news magazine said had been allocated to me, but I think I received my share of the limited funds available. The total result was thousands of small, individual contributions. In toto, I learned later, between $500,000 and $600,000 had been raised for my primary and general-election campaigns taken together.

This was about six times the largest amount ever spent before in my behalf, but still it was dwarfed by the amount spent by my opposition. The amount of money available *for* my opponent, or *against* me, seemed to be unlimited, and its sources were by no means limited to the United States. In addition to the usual sources and methods of fund-raising for candidates aligned with vested interests, the White House had a fund-raising program that reached out to interests in foreign countries. Had I not cut some of the tax preferences for income earned abroad? I had and, what was more, I intended to close other foreign tax-haven loopholes. I released information on this, and the following story was written in the *Chattanooga Times* by Fred Travis:

> Senator Albert Gore charged Wednesday that a group of international financiers met Wednesday night in London to raise campaign funds for Representative Bill Brock of Chattanooga, the senator's Republican opponent.
>
> Gore, Democratic nominee for a fourth term in the Senate, released a copy of a letter headed "European Republican Committee (UK)" which he said had been intercepted and forwarded to him by the Democratic National Committee.
>
> It presented plans for a fund-raising dinner at Claridge's, a world-famous London hotel, at which Herbert G. Klein, President Nixon's director of communications, was to be the main speaker.
>
> V. W. Warren Pearl, who signed the letter as chairman of the committee, described Klein as "the best possible man to tell us what we all ought to know about current American political issues.
>
> The letter mentioned specifically use of money raised at the dinner to help Brock in his campaign against Gore, saying:
>
> "Proceeds of the dinner, plus contributions received, will be forwarded to the 'European Republican Fund' in Washington for allocation to the campaigns of Republican candidates. This year the fund will be allocated among the senatorial races including, in particular, the campaign of Republican Congressman Brock in Tennessee to unseat Senator Gore.
>
> "You are urged to encourage your friends—including your British friends—to join us. It promises to be a most rewarding evening," the letter added.

Though we were unable to hire a large professional staff or to finance "coordinators" to range over the state, we had volunteer workers by the thousands—women, men, students, children. Never before had I had such citizen participation in a campaign. This was attributable to the stands which my opponent and I had taken. Our disagreement was almost complete. Indeed, he made the public statement that he disagreed with my positions on "everything." This was not exactly true, of course, but almost.

In the spring of 1970, following the Cambodian "incursion," students in universities throughout America became actively interested in my campaign. This encouraged me in a way, but I was wary of it too. They might come to Tennessee in droves to campaign for me, and this could be dangerous. Student demonstrations against the war had unfortunately created an antistudent attitude. Grateful as I was for their interest, we discouraged plans for many out-of-state students to come to Tennessee for door-to-door campaigning. Tennessee students were also interested, and it was important that their efforts be properly channeled. Dr. David Price, a young political-science professor at Yale, whose native home was Erwin, Tennessee, volunteered to spend his summer working for me. I gladly accepted him, and he took general charge of the effort to organize the activities of students and young people generally.

We decided early that there would be no separate "Youth for Gore" organization with a state-wide director and a separate youth-oriented program of activity. Rather, we sought to bring the young people into the regular campaign organization at the local level. Student groups were instructed to work with, through, and under the local campaign structure. In this way, we could use their talents and enthusiasm while minimizing the possibilities of public abrasion. Over-all, the young people, including several from outside the state, were enormously helpful, and I was deeply grateful to them. As in all such efforts, the plan worked better in some areas than in others. In Nashville and Memphis, students, both Tennessean and non-Tennessean, provided the manpower for precinct canvassing efforts that paid off. The distribution of campaign literature, promotional work for rallies, and many other campaign chores were handled largely by young people.

One of the strongest assets I had in the campaign from the very beginning, as I have said, was the *Gore Women*. I had three of them in my immediate family—Pauline and our daughter, Nancy, both veteran campaigners; and the new addition, our daughter-in-law, Mary Elizabeth ("Tipper"). All hit the road for appearances at teas and other events arranged by the women's group. In addition, they represented me at Democratic rallies and generally campaigned all over the state. Almost every day there were four Gores making campaign speeches in Tennessee.

My son was in the Army, temporarily stationed at Fort Rucker, Alabama. He would come home for the weekend whenever he could get leave, and he spent his pre-Vietnam leave with us the last two weeks of the campaign. Frank Hunger, Nancy's husband, virtually abandoned his law practice in Greenville, Mississippi, for several weeks, working mostly in the "hard country" of west Tennessee. I was immensely proud of both of them.

Vice-President Agnew announced that he would fulfill his promise to come to Tennessee to campaign against me by appearing in Memphis on September 22. It was also announced that earlier in the same day he would participate in a ground-breaking ceremony for the construction of an Internal Revenue Service building in Memphis. At that time, Agnew was popular in Tennessee, especially in west Tennessee. Moreover, he had a practice of baiting hecklers and then blaming the rowdiness on his political opposition. His prospective visit, then, posed a double danger to me. So I took a calculated risk. I announced that, as senior senator from Tennessee, I would meet him at the airport and welcome him to the state. Some of my advisers were uneasy about this ploy. They pointed to the number of times that Agnew's appearances around the country had met with angry, denunciatory demonstrations on the part of young people. They feared that such a demonstration might occur in Memphis, and, if I were there in the midst of it, this would further polarize the feelings of those who took a hard line on such matters and whose votes I was seeking on the basis of my record on economic issues. "Precisely," I said. "Those are the very reasons I am going to be there. Agnew would like nothing as much as a big ruckus, the rowdier the better. I'm going to prevent it." I publicly requested all my friends to give a polite, respectful welcome which the Office of Vice-President of the United States deserved, and said I proposed to do everything I could to see that there was no untoward event to mar Agnew's appearance in Tennessee.

My campaign organization in Memphis was instructed to seek to learn of any possible plan for a demonstration and to squelch it if at all possible. (We did, in fact, learn of a plan by a group which already had their placards made and managed to persuade the leaders of the plan to abandon it.) A few did not get the word and there were still one or two signs in evidence at the airport, but there was no rowdiness whatever. I felt rewarded.

I attended the ground-breaking ceremony too. This was not a partisan project but a public building project financed by the federal government, which I had supported. I had received no invitation; I didn't need any. I went anyway, as if it were my affair. In a way, it was—certainly more than Agnew's.

All went well, both at the airport and at the ground-breaking. The publicity associated with my presence was favorable. The stakes were high that day and I had won the round.

That night, Agnew was exhorting the paying Republicans to vote against me, calling me the "Southern regional chairman of the eastern establishment" . . . a "radic-lib." Such an image, Agnew knew, would put me on the wrong side of the social issue, for Tennesseans associate civil rights, dissent, and permissiveness with the East and with the National Democratic Party. While Agnew was traveling the low road, I was busily autographing copies of my new book at a Memphis bookstore. I could think of no more appropriate way to contrast myself with his buffoonery.

The Associated Press reported on one thesis in my book (quickly used by my opposition)—the urgency of improving relations with China:

> Senator Albert Gore urges full diplomatic, cultural, and trade relations with Red China in his newly published book, *The Eye of the Storm.*
>
> "The United States has been led astray by its obsession with communism," Gore writes, and calls for "radically readjusting our relationship with Communist China."
>
> The Tennessee Democrat says the United States should recognize the Peking regime as the legitimate government of China "as clearly, unqualifiedly, and openly as possible.

"And we should add that we are ready to exchange diplomatic representation with China and to negotiate mutually advantageous trade agreements.

"Instead of opposing Red China's admission to the United Nations," Gore writes, the United States should "urge China to qualify for membership in the family of nations and we should assist her in achieving this qualification."

If my campaign had an "opening," it was at Chattanooga, on September 29. My Chattanooga speech at a $10.00-a-plate fund-raiser, was billed as a campaign kickoff, deep in opposition territory, my opponent's home town. (I carried it in November!)

I had campaigned in almost all of Tennessee's ninety-five counties during the primary and was ready to do so again. My headquarters was instructed to arrange my schedule so as to have me in or near one of the cities every day, if at all possible at a time that would permit live television coverage of my campaigning for use on evening newcasts. A minute or two on a news program is worth half a dozen spot commercials— and doesn't cost anything. Throughout the campaign, I continually emphasized the record on issues of interest to Tennessee. A record of fifty key votes was compiled, showing how I voted, how my opponent voted, and how the remainder of the Tennessee delegation had voted. It was reproduced for distribution as campaign literature, and also was the basis for newspaper ads. It was by far the best seller of the campaign literature we produced. This leaflet illustrated that my opponent had voted against almost every farm bill presented since he had been in Congress, had consistently opposed education and health programs, had voted against most of the appropriations bills providing funds for veterans' benefits, and had opposed programs for economic development, all of which I had consistently supported, as had a majority of the Tennessee delegation. Also, I believed an overwhelming percentage of the people of Tennessee had favored them.

I carefully reviewed, county by county, the public-works projects—sewer and water projects, hospitals, industrial parks, and the like—that had been financed, in part, with federal funds that I had supported. My opponent had opposed the great majority of the legislation authorizing these programs and the appropriations to fund them. This leaflet on projects, distributed to my county campaign leaders and to the local news media, became the basis for locally produced ads and literature. When local managers and committees pointed to the actual bricks and mortar I had fought for and my opponent had opposed, it was quite effective, particularly in rural communities. I was appealing to the interests of the people while my opposition appealed to their prejudices.

Above all, my campaign, like all my previous ones, emphasized personal campaigning by me and my family. We took the issues and my record directly to the people. The prejudice against a "liberal" was so thick that, as I used to hear my mother say, you could cut it with a knife. But the people had favored most of the liberal issues—TVA, social security, full employment, farm-price support, tax reform, minimum wages, public works, low interest rates, control of monopolies, educational aid, community development. Name a New Deal program and most voters reacted favorably, but to call a politician a liberal was to condemn him with prejudice. We talked issues. The severe antagonism against the liberal *label* was my greatest political handicap, so my task was to take the truth to the people. We did. We did. We did. Day and night, night and day, talking sense.

The people who had voted for Wallace in 1968 began to

swing back to me. (I had to have about 65 per cent of them to win, and most of them had voted against me in the primary.) It would be hard to find a tougher political row to hoe than for a liberal, anti-Vietnam, pro-civil-rights Democrat to get 65 per cent of the Wallace votes, but I continued to believe I could do it, and I was making headway. I was confident I could do it if I could get them in my audience for a few minutes, not that I was a Billy Graham orator, but that truth and right and conviction were my allies.

One main reason I had wanted a campaign of unity with Hooker was that a joint appearance of Democratic nominees would attract a decent crowd in any county seat, which would give me an opportunity to communicate with them. We had only one such appearance, and it proved my point. This occurred in Franklin County, situated on the Alabama border. In 1968, it had given Wallace a larger percentage of its vote than any other county in the state, or 66 per cent of it. (Nixon and Humphrey divided the remainder about evenly.) Our joint rally there attracted about 1000 people. I spoke with all the wile, wit, and power at my command, addressing the issues and how I and my opponent had voted on them. After that night, there was no more doubt about how Franklin County would vote. It went Democratic by more than 60 per cent.

But in parts of west Tennessee, where racial tension was high and where no unity prevailed, I was unable to get an audience. Though I had loyal friends, many people simply did not consider it respectable to be seen at a Gore affair. The Haynsworth-Carswell votes were constantly cited against me: their names became code words to brand me a "nigger-lover." As "Wink" C. W. Bond, my long-time personal friend and former mayor of Arlington, a village twenty-five miles east of

Memphis, said to Richard Harris of *The New Yorker* Magazine:

> People who feel strong against Gore can't tell you why. Mostly they say he's too liberal, or something like that. When you try to pin them down as to why, they just fly away. Maybe they say because he voted against Carswell. I told them I talked to Gore about that and he explained how Carswell lied to a Senate committee. I tell them he just plain lied, and ask, "Hellfire, you want a liar on the Supreme Court?" 'Course, some wouldn't mind that as long as he was a Southern liar. I try to explain how Gore knew it would hurt him bad politically but he had to do it because he knew it was right. I tell them any senator from down here who voted against Carswell has *got* to have guts. That convinces a few, but mostly they just don't like Albert Gore—they somehow don't feel close to him—and so they find a new reason to be against him. Arguments don't change their minds.

I commissioned no polls (no money for that), but those commissioned by Hooker (at least those we were given access to) showed that by October 1 my campaign had begun to pick up strength significantly. I needed no poll to tell me what I could sense. The candidate's sensitive antenna—the "feel" of a campaign, the reaction of the people the candidate meets—is important and tells him a lot. After the primary, I had been practically written off by the national press. By mid-October, however, word of my growing strength began to seep out and the national press came back for another look. The kinds of stories they wrote were important for financial reasons, as well as for the morale of my supporters and the psychological factors that are important in a campaign. Unless the press gave me a chance to win, the money would stop coming in.

Gene Graham, a former Tennessean reporter, who was taking a sabbatical from his position as professor of journalism at the University of Illinois, was another key-volunteer staff member at headquarters. He had signed on for the duration to help out with press relations. The word got out, not only in Tennessee, but across the land, that we had something going. Among other things, the second look by the national press helped us get through the campaign without a substantial deficit.

Obviously, I am not in the best position to make a wholly objective characterization of the kind of campaign my opponent ran. I can only report how it seemed to me and offer the observation that it seemed that way to a great many people. Over-all, his campaign was designed to take advantage of the emotional climate that existed in Tennessee and elsewhere in the South. More than a year before the election a careful survey had been made of Tennesseans' prejudices, their hates, and their fears. A massive propaganda campaign was then mounted to appeal to these baser instincts. The thrust of Brock's campaign was focused on the communications media —television, radio, billboards, printed literature, and newspaper ads—with much less emphasis on personal utterances by the candidate. He mostly walked around a little, seeking to project a boy-scoutlike concern while the Tereleavan organization perpetrated a massive attack. Though the strategy called for the candidate himself to say but little, the scenario included hired-gun types who would do the dirty work.

I would like to cite another interview with one such Tennessean, reported by Harris after spending a week in Tennessee. The subject mentioned, and the way it was handled, was typical of the Brock campaign.

Of all the television and radio political appeals I had heard in Tennessee, by far the most effective were those featuring a man named Alfred MacFarland, a lawyer from Lebanon, in middle Tennessee. Formerly a supporter and friend of Gore's, MacFarland had turned against him and was now head of a group called Democrats for Brock. Many observers felt that he had been having a devastating effect on Gore's chances. One of MacFarland's 30-second radio spots, delivered in a resonant and inexplicably convincing voice, went, " 'No child ever got an education riding on a bus.' Bill Brock said that the other day when he was talking about a subject that concerns every parent of school-age children—busing. I'm Alfred MacFarland, of Lebanon, I'm a lawyer. And I agree with Bill Brock that busing is un-Constitutional, that it's wrong, and that our elected representatives ought to be doing everything they can to stop forced busing. However, Senator Albert Gore has failed to do that. In fact, he recently opposed an amendment which would remove from the federal courts' jurisdiction the administration of our local schools. That kind of misrepresentation is one of the reasons I'm backing Bill Brock for the Senate seat now occupied by Albert Gore—even though I've been a Democrat all my life."

When it came to misrepresentation—not of constituents but of facts—MarFarland was a match for his candidate. From the start, Senator Gore has steadfastly opposed the busing of children to achieve racial balance in public schools, because he believed that the value of community schools was greater than the value of racial balance. And the amendment that MacFarland referred to—submitted by Senator Sam J. Ervin, Jr., Democrat of North Carolina, earlier that year and withdrawn for lack of support—had been aimed not at busing but at wiping out altogether the Supreme Court's desegregation order in the landmark case *Brown* v. *Board of Education*. . . .

An extravagant propaganda blitz against me started nine days before election day. We expected this kind of tactic because Treleavan had handled the campaign against Senator Ralph Yarborough in Texas, where a smear campaign had been waged. Moreover, my junior colleague in the Senate, Howard Baker, had let the cat out of the bag by introducing in the Senate a proposed amendment of the Constitution about prayer in schools. After it passed the Senate, we learned about a telephone call from Baker's office to my opponent's headquarters in Nashville to the effect: "The ball is yours now."

The subject of prayer in schools came into the campaign by a question from the audience during a joint appearance by my opponent and me on October 21 before a largely Jewish audience in Memphis. I replied that I favored voluntary prayer by anyone, anywhere, but that I was opposed to any proposal to grant authority to any government official to prescribe or to require a particular prayer by public-school pupils or anyone else. The audience cheered my statement. Brock agreed. The *Memphis Press-Scimitar* of October 22 reported: "Brock said he had supported the free expression of faith on the part of school children but said he could not support state-prescribed prayers by teachers." Yet less than a week later thousands of prayer ads—by television, radio, full-page newspaper ads, and handbills—began to flood the state and to saturate all media until the polls closed on election day. They proclaimed:

Albert Gore has taken a position against school prayer three times. . . .

BILL BROCK BELIEVES that children should be allowed to pray

in schools. His Constitutional amendment to permit school prayer has passed the Senate.

The truth was that I had not at any time "taken a position against prayer." I had opposed the Dirksen amendment which would authorize government to provide a prayer—precisely what Brock had told the audience in Memphis he "could not support."

With these prayer ads blaring every few minutes all over the state, this became a chief topic of conversation. Many people were confused and disturbed. Others, especially some religious leaders, rejected the proposed amendment and supported my record. For instance, Reverend Foy Valentine, executive secretary of the Southern Baptist Convention Christian Life Commission, issued the following statement:

> We deeply regret that an emotional appeal is being made for Tennessee voters to support or oppose candidates on the basis of their voting records on so called "prayer amendments" to the Constitution. We would remind the members of our denominations that those congressmen who voted against such amendments were concurring with the actions taken by official church bodies.

Religious leaders themselves paid for full-page ads with this message. Among the organizations listed as supporters of this statement were: The Southern Baptist Convention, The United Methodist Church, The Lutheran Church in America, The Union of American Hebrew Congregations, The International Convention of Christian Churches, The United Church of Christ, The United Presbyterian Church, U.S.A., the Legal Department of the National Catholic Welfare Conference, American Baptist Convention, Central Conference of American Rabbis, The Lutheran Church-Missouri Synod, and others.

This issue reinforced the support of many Tennesseans to whose reason I had appealed during the campaign. Many thoughtful conservatives and some stanch Republicans who had been counted among Brock supporters so resented the prayer issue as invalid and false that they switched to me. One voter who called himself a "former Brock Believer" noted that "this issue has marred the integrity of Brock's image," and further hoped that "it would cost him the election."

The issue threatened to backfire. So Brock abandoned his boy-scout pose, and on October 29 said, "Prayer is the real issue in this campaign. . . . Our religious heritage is part of the thing that makes America what it is. My opponent has three times voted against voluntary prayers in our schools."

I fought hard, calling this charge false and saying that Brock's campaign "is directed by an out-of-state propaganda firm that pictures me as anti-Tennessean, anti-Southern, anti-American, and now anti-God." More church leaders rallied to my support, and it appeared that we had blunted this cynical smear, but the TV and radio blared the prayer ads every few minutes, as did full-page newspaper ads and hundreds of thousands of handbills distributed house-to-house. Eventually, all our telephones were jammed with calls from simple, uneducated people who wanted to know, "Why is Senator Gore against prayer?"

The barrage included "busing," gun-control, and racism, and the saturation was complete.

We had specific forewarning of the blitz. Gene Graham reported to me the very day that MacFarland and others had gone to a certain television studio to make spots on "busing,"

"Carswell and Haynsworth," "prayer in schools," and "guns," and that television and radio time had been purchased to run the spots "7000 times" during the last days before election. The alienation splurge was at the saturation level on all media for nine days:

> On Gun Registration
> Tennesseans said No,
> but Albert Gore said Yes.
>
> On Busing of School Children
> Tennesseans said No,
> but Albert Gore said Yes.
>
> On School Prayer
> Tennesseans voted Yes,
> but Albert Gore voted No.
>
> On Carswell and Haynsworth
> Tennesseans said Yes,
> but Albert Gore voted No.
>
> Isn't it about time that Tennesseans
> said No to Albert Gore?

We did the best we could with what little we had by then to offset monstrous assault, but there is no way to offset this kind of mass attack except by an equally massive communication. Tennessee has a population of 4 million people, who live from Memphis on the Mississippi to Mountain City, 650 miles to the east. Even if we had had the money—$1 million was the estimate—the choice television and radio time had already been tied up. And even if we had had the money and the time, making and editing effective spot advertisements requires time. That's why smear campaigns start nine days before an election. They cannot then be effectively answered. Those are the witching hours.

And that is one more reason why money in politics is such a great threat to our system of government. The most vital single action of a self-governing society is the election of public officials, and the election period ought to be a time of serious discussion, a time when political philosophies and programs are analyzed and debated—not for the sound they make but for their meaning, not for their marketability but their merit, not for their packaging but their content. Unless the will of the people can be determined and maintained through the electoral system, there is no such thing as popular self-government.

Public confidence in government, and in the integrity of the people's representatives who constitute that government, is the bedrock upon which the foundation of our social order rests. Self-government is only as secure as the public faith in it.

We are supposed to be a government of, by, and for the people. It is time we began to live up to Lincoln's definition.

In the closing days of the campaign the national press and media were giving it much coverage. One of the nation's best journalists, David Halberstam, spent a week in the state. Here are some brief excerpts from his article in *Harper's Magazine:*

Campaigning in Memphis, flying down here with the Senator. . . . He had debated Brock the night before and had eaten him alive. Brock is a weak speaker, and though his campaign is filled with charges against Gore, he does not make them in person. "Subliminal smut" is what young Al Gore calls it. A month ago the Gore campaign had been going very poorly, but in the past few weeks it has begun to catch on and is moving; indeed, there are reports that Brock's polls show Albert ahead now. The staff (the staff today is his son and a twenty-three year old press aide, for there is not even an advanceman on this trip) is trying to keep the news away from him. They think he is cocky enough without it.

The schedule is like this: jet rides into the four great media sections of Tennessee, trying to hit at least two a day, make news, get on the night news show, and then move out. . . . It is all plastic now. There is a good deal of apathy about the election in the state—and I suspect that one reason is that television has made it all less personal, less direct in one sense, standing between the voter and the electorate; and yet it has made the campaign too long in another sense; bringing the candidates into everyone's home every night for five months. . . .

Bill Brock is sincere. (His billboards and television clips say: Bill Brock believes. Believes is the code word for Nigger. Against busing, for the war, for Carswell and Haynsworth and someone worse if they nominate him, I'm sure. They expanded the billboards later in the campaign to say, Bill Brock Believes in the Things We Believe In.) Bill Brock is young and up-and-coming. An achiever. Gets into clubs and becomes the President. He has the look of the President of the local Jaycees who has just led the other young Turks in the club against the old order on the issue of serving better luncheon meals. For good government and against muscular dystrophy. A success in business, rising to the head of his company (the Brock Candy Company). Runs for Congress, wins, and the real Bill Brock emerges; the Democratic party had deserted him all right, he votes a straight Goldwater economic line. A great record for Albert to run against, and he is running very hard indeed against him. It has made Brock vulnerable and has helped turn the campaign around; Gore now has a chance. . . .

Though in debates and in personal confrontation and in his own speeches he stays away from the issues he has raised, this is in fact the most disreputable and scurrilous race I have ever covered in Tennessee. It is made all the more shabby by the fact that he injects this stuff into the atmosphere at one level and then acts the nice young man. His newspaper ads and television ads are hitting away daily at the most emotional issues they can touch. His media firm came down here a year and a half ago and found that the five most emotional issues were race, gun control, the war, busing, and prayer, and they are making this the campaign. Keep Gore answering false charges. It is not the old, sweaty, gallus-snapping racism that was once used against Claude Pepper; rather is cool and modern. And while I have covered shabby racist campaigns in the past, there is something about this one which is distinctive. This is the first time that a campaign like this has been tied to the President, the Vice-President, and the Attorney General of the United States. . . .

As election day approached, I knew the race would be close, but I expected to be the winner. I had won back a substantial majority of former Wallace voters by my persistent appeals to their interests and reason. I had overcome much of the rejection of me as a liberal by talking about the contents of the package instead of the labels. I contemplated the "three states" in Tennessee—Appalachian east Tennessee, Democratic middle Tennessee, and Mississippi-oriented west Tennessee. I hoped to hold my opponent's margin in east Tennessee to 60,000 votes, where I had made inroads among normally Republican voters. I counted on a modest margin in Memphis, which I had always carried, to give me an even break in west Tennessee. I was confident of a solid majority in middle Tennessee, my home. Much still depended on getting out a big Democratic vote, particularly that of working people and blacks, who account for about 15 per cent of the state-wide vote. And this was no easy task. While black leaders almost unanimously supported me, some of them were not all that enthusiastic, for they never felt that I was quite *their* man. While I had supported civil-rights legislation generally, I was not the kind of person to "clear" things in advance with black leaders—or any other kind of leader.

A principal worry in the closing days was the race for governor. My running mate's campaign had virtually collapsed, and there were disturbing signs that a band-wagon vote— worth no less than 50,000–100,000 votes in a Tennessee gubernatorial race—would go to his unexpectedly strong Republican opponent, Winfield Dunn. In a speech at a big party rally in Nashville in the last week before election, I placed my greatest emphasis on the governor's race, trying to stem this band-wagon roll.

Up until now, I have avoided post mortems of my campaign, but I hope it is possible now to offer some brief analytical comment. I can say with conviction that, given the available resources, I can think of no major changes in strategy or tactics that would have changed the outcome—except having a unified campaign, but this lack was not my mistake. This is not to say that I ran a perfect campaign, or that I had the funds to do what I knew should be done. There are always mistakes in a campaign, and I have never been in one when there was enough money. I mean only that I can think of no major decision I made that was fatal, nothing that I did that I now think should have been done in a different way. I am proud of the campaign we waged and I think it was effective.

To what, then, do I attribute my defeat? As in most elections, there were many factors, some of which were beyond my control, but from the standpoint of the campaign itself, a very important factor was the nomination for governor of Winfield Dunn by the Republicans. He was an appealing candidate from our largest city which had not had a governor for forty years. Coupled with the faltering campaign of my running mate, John J. Hooker, Jr., this was a terrific handicap, especially in Memphis.

The backlash on racial problems was especially acute in Tennessee in 1970 due to the severe racial polarization in Memphis and west Tennessee following Martin Luther King's assassination, my votes against confirmation of Haynsworth and Carswell, and the falsely raised school-busing controversy.

Then, my opponent's perfectly enormous outlay of money for campaign workers, for "hired guns," for computer letter-writing, for his advertising smear-blitz on prayer, busing, and gun-control, and his willingness to resort to such tactics.

Finally, there was the political climate, for in Tennessee in 1970 many citizens were uneasy and frustrated. My real battle here was for the allegiance of whites in the middle economic group: workingmen and women often not affiliated with organized labor, small shopowners, clerks, people who may or may not identify themselves with any particular group. An independent myself, these were the people I had tried hard to represent, though many of them may not have recognized or appreciated how I had represented their interests (because they had no pressure group presenting their interests to Congress or to interpret my action to them). In absolute terms, they were better off than had been their fathers and mothers. They made more money, lived in better homes, ate better, had a better car (perhaps two). But from a relative standpoint, many felt that they had not climbed many rungs up the ladder of the American dream. Inflation seemed to keep them from getting ahead financially. They were disturbed about crime and all too quick to point a finger at the Supreme Court and Democrats as being responsible for it. The country was in a tragic war that seemed endless and without purpose, but it was their country and my opposition to the war seemed to many of them to be opposition to the country itself. Many who had not attended college (and some who had) resented what they considered outrageous conduct by students. They were vaguely frightened by the threat to their position in the pecking order of society which was posed by what they considered unjustified government-induced progress for black Americans. And Democrats had started that! In many cases such citizens have not defined, even in their own minds, the specific ills of society that troubled them, much less analyzed the real causes or settled on the proper remedies. On Vietnam, for example, there was the latent, nagging feeling that, right or wrong, we ought to have won the war—and would have if everybody had been red-blooded about it.

Though appeals to emotion tended to overwhelm logic on such matters, it was encouraging to note that these tactics failed to influence many. I estimated that I had the support of 60 per cent of the 1968 Wallace voters, and some Republicans were so outraged at the tactics against me that they voted for me too. (In Memphis, for instance, I received 6000 more votes than my running mate, Hooker, in Nashville almost 20,000 more, but fell behind him in rural west Tennessee.)

Had my votes in the Senate brought about the real or imagined troubles that plagued and frightened people? I doubt it. Only on the broad question of racial equality under the law and Vietnam policy do I plead guilty, and if an election analyst some day should attribute my defeat to my position on these questions, so be it.

But whether responsible or not, I had been there—"there" being Washington—for a long time, so I must be responsible. This was the opposition's theme, and I was not surprised at the tactics. For two years, Agnew had been spouting the same line as he sought to polarize American society by an appeal to the emotional prejudices of those to whom he and Nixon referred as the silent majority. This was the heart of the Southern Strategy in 1970, which was designed to persuade the Wallace voter of 1968 to become a Republican voter in 1970. But I had talked sense to them and I had been pleased that a substantial majority had come back to me, for they had long been my friends and I theirs.

Very few Americans have had the opportunity to serve in the Congress for thirty-two years. It was a glorious experience, and my gratitude to the people of Tennessee for this honor was and always will be deep. We had done the best we could, and, without benefit of genuine party leadership support, we had restored liberal democracy to a point of sharp contention in a border state. From the dark days of August we had come a long way—almost, but not quite far enough.

There was a kind of satisfaction in the last moments of my political career. After a battle in which I had fought with every ounce of my being for what I sincerely believed to be right, I stood before loyal supporters filling the Hermitage Hotel Ballroom and on television before the people of my beloved state and nation, to acknowledge defeat. I was proud of the fight we had made, and I expressed gratitude for the honor I had enjoyed, the consideration and support I had received. I closed by saying, "The causes for which we fought are not dead. The truth shall rise again.''

A tremendous cheer came from the people, as if we had won. Perhaps we *had* won a moral victory, at least within ourselves. For the fight had been made on principle, and my political career had ended with my family and many friends gathered near, all full of conviction and fight. I left the stage feeling that "defeat may serve as well as victory to shake the soul and let the glory out.''

CHAPTER VII

A New Day

AFTER MY DEFEAT, I was tempted to do what the South has so often done in its defeats—turn to glorification of a past that is gone. For many years I enjoyed much personal popularity, which Victor Hugo called "glory's small change." And this heady wine is hard to give up, even in memory. Fortunately, several universities invited me to lecture and teach classes in the various and variegated arts of politics. At first my puzzlement almost exceeded my gratitude. Why did this opportunity come right after my winning techniques showed the likely need of marginal improvement? Were the invitations based on Alben W. Barkley's definition that a *statesman* is a *dead politician?* I wondered. It is no news that politicians die hard, but I rather doubted that defeat had made me wiser.

My friends were saying, "You are more popular in defeat

than you might have been in victory." For me that was cold comfort. I not only had wanted those next six years, but had felt that the country needed my Senate votes and accrued experience. But my son had the correct attitude about that situation. When I asked him how he would feel if after thirty-two years in Congress—good record, very clean nose, etc., etc. (much pouring on of balm!)—he lost to an opponent who had no accomplishments except to have been consistently wrong for eight years, his calm reply was, "Dad, I would *take* the thirty-two years." Which shows, I think, that the youth of today *is* realistic, as well as more accommodating and aware of the nuances of human events than I had realized.

The colleges that so generously invited me to their halls must have wanted someone who could relate from experience in both winning and losing. Not only at Vanderbilt University, where I accepted an invitation to lecture, before turning to mend my financial fences through the practice of law and to help elect good candidates for the U.S. Senate by leading the Council for a Livable World, but out in the State of Washington, down in Texas, up in Ohio, at Harvard, at Yale, and in other places—I sampled the students' questions and their learning, and I was exhilarated by both. I gave assurance that in my classwork I would be as objective and nonpartisan as it was possible for me to be under the circumstances. I assured them that my attitude about Washington would be that "everything is wonderful and if something isn't done quickly, it'll get worse."

Invariably, curious adult friends would ask about students, "How did you find them?" "Are they really alienated?" "Do they care about the future of the country?" The answers were that I found them wonderful, and that they felt *themselves to have been alienated*—that is, they felt unwanted in the political sector and smarted under the idea that the length of their hair and skirts was considered more important than their ideas. Perhaps they worry about the alienation gap even more than their parents do, although I think the *rapprochement* between the generations is closer than has been advertised. As for caring about their country, I doubt that any generation has ever cared more or been more eager to serve it. Their enthusiasm and energy are boundless, their questions endless, and their vivid idealism a joy. They believe in freedom and equality, in *actuality*. Democracy is something that should work and they are impatient with delays.

There should be a rule that would require politicians, at certain stages in their careers, to have close communication with the young people of the day and to instruct them in their arts. It is leaven to the spirit of the mature, whetstone to the curiosity of the young.

At first I wondered whether someone of my independent and liberal persuasions could be nonpartisan enough to present the other side clearly enough as a teacher, but I learned that philosophically they already knew the other side. The whys and wherefores of my having been both a winner and a loser was intriguing to them, and they seemed to appreciate my small ironies. I found them basically gay and hopeful; most of all, they were curious as to how they might get into politics themselves to change things for the better. (Most of them seemed to think of "politics" as elective office only.)

The youthful voters, if I can judge from a widespread sampling, are very ready in 1972 to challenge any candidate who tries to appeal to them on the basis either of emotions or of short-term interest. They will reject narrow regionalism or anything less, really, than a comprehensive view of the public interest. That, I believe may be the key to McGovern's appeal to youth.

True, they are apt to be skeptical of authority and of politicians, but the politician who equates this with radicalism is in serious error. Perhaps they are more volatile than their parents, perhaps more impatient, and surely more demanding. But what is wrong with impatience with injustice and a demand for its correction? This is the very core of democratic politics. Any sentiment less lofty is phony. And they dislike nothing so much as phoniness.

What the young in particular are questioning, or so it has seemed to me, is our own view of ourselves. They are scrutinizing those parts of our legal and social system which do in fact lend credence to class division among us. Given their passion and their intelligence, their idealism and their patriotism, national leaders should respond to them with trust and appreciation.

The young want rational solutions, but solutions that are humanly rational—not the kind of mechanical nationalism which views the unemployed as only a percentage point on a graph, not the chilly rationalism that computes the maimed, dead casualties of war in terms of "body count." In brief, they want to act with honest intelligence and to see honest intelligence in action.

Unfortunately, all too many of our leaders have resented them and have tried to stifle dissent without analyzing the causes of violence. This is to sell our country short. It displays a lack of faith in America's moral and spiritual reserves, and in its ability to withstand political and social stress. If the fabric of our society is strong enough, anchored deeply enough in its basic precepts, it can take this assault and battery—and come out stronger and healthier.

In earlier periods of our history it may have been easier to appraise the causes of discontent. Many were economic—the lack of economic justice. Some of them still are and may always be, because in a free society based upon equality of opportunity, there will always be elements seeking to monopolize opportunities and resources. But youth's discontent today is much more broadly based. In the army of dissidents today march the rich and the poor, the old and the young, white and black, the cynics and the idealists, militants and pacifists; bound together only by a common disillusionment over the gulf between the promise and the reality of American society. They have both right and reason to despair, but their despair vests in them no new rights. It is incumbent upon everyone, whatever one's generation, to ponder the causes of current disillusionment and move to correct as many of them as possible. But youth must realize that violence is the antithesis of reason, whether used to coerce or to destroy, and that they must conform to the legal disciplines of society even while seeking change.

Partisanship, the kind of intense loyalty I early felt for the Democratic Party, seems to have but scant appeal to our young today. This may be a great gain for our body politic, but it makes the two- (or three- or four-) party system extremely volatile. In fact, the most complimentary thing one can say about any generation is that its primary interest is in issues and causes.

The politics of elective office is exciting to our young people, but they are turned off when a strife of interests masquerades as a contest of issues, and when, as with an iceberg, two thirds of the motives are concealed. Yet despite the faults of our electoral system, they should be encouraged to participate in elections, particularly federal ones. For in no other arena, with the possible exception of the judiciary, do so few people shape human and political events as the 537 popularly elected officials of our national government. It is upon the integrity of this small group that the nation depends for the efficacy of the federal system. (And I am more convinced than ever that the government must itself regulate *and* fund all election campaigns for federal office, forbidding any private subsidy by either the candidate or his supporters.)

At the root of all incentives to run for public office must be human ego: a desire for the approval of others, a yearning for self-expression and self-assertion; love of power and attention; zeal for success, for contest and contention; concern for issues and the public interest. To describe these motivations is not to deride them. Without them neither our country nor our economy nor our culture nor anything else of value would be possible. Politicians are blessed and plagued with an abundance of human vanities, but they share these qualities with the actor, the musician, the athlete, the student, the professor. So politicians are of the warp and woof of our society, usually highly and commendably motivated, I believe. (There are, of course, other less commendable motives: factional or personal hate, private interest, glamor, and the love of money questionably gained.)

There are genuine rewards from an honorable campaign for public office. The intimate contact with the people and the competitive challenges of a political campaign are extraordinary emotional and intellectual experiences. One gets an insight into the workings of the American system and comes to respect the grandeur of a moral and well-motivated citizenship. A high-level campaign on issues will draw one's family and circle of friends closer—an added joy. Even though unsuccessful, then, a campaign can be rewarding, provided one does not wish too badly to win.

Victory, too, has its dangers and opportunities: performance in office is the measuring rod. "You cannot please everybody"; but one had better try, even though it is impossible to do so on controversial issues. Argument with a constituent about an issue with which one is in disagreement is, I found, particularly unrewarding. I recall a session about oleomargarine with a group of Tennessee dairymen a few years ago. They wished it outlawed. I expressed the view that industry had developed a nutritious product that should be available to the public who might prefer it to butter. One Davidson County dairyman expressed his moderate reaction: "I hope you drop dead."

It is the deep emotional issues concerning war, race, and religion that stir and move people massively. On these there is little if any room for compromise. Here one must, I think, take one's position on principle and stand. This adds zest, even joy, to the struggle.

American politics will be changed vastly, I believe enriched, by the millions of young people who will be voting for the first time in 1972. The change will likely be greater in the South than in any other region, because, I believe, the differences between youth and age on the social issues are greatest there.

Youth is only one of the reasons, however, why the South that Richard Nixon and George Wallace and Hubert Humphrey battled over in 1968 is a vastly different battlefield in 1972. Progressive Democrats have regained leadership in most of the South. Virtually shut out in the 1968 Presidential sweepstakes, progressive or moderate Democrats scored resounding victories from Florida and South Carolina to Arkansas in 1970, with the sole exception of Tennessee. Armed with its Southern Strategy and Spiro Agnew, the GOP had then hoped to gain three senators and at least two more governors in the South. They lost two incumbent GOP governors (in Florida and Arkansas), and managed to capture only one statehouse and one U.S. Senate seat—both in Tennessee. In addition, several incumbent Republican state legislators were defeated in Texas, Florida, and Tennessee. In the Congressional voting, the number of voters casting GOP ballots decreased seven percentage points from 1968.

But the election of 1970 showed more than just a Republican setback. For it was not the old-line reactionary officeholders, tinged with backlash, who led the Democrats to victory. Reubin Askew of Florida, Jimmy Carter of Georgia, Dale Bumpers of Arkansas, John C. West of South Carolina are of a different breed from the Faubuses, Bilbos, Talmadges, and Wallaces of the past. As the styles of the new Democrats were moderate, so were their politics, except with an occasional overtone of populism. Unlike most of their predecessors, they avoided or minimized the race issue. Not one promised to stand at the schoolhouse door or proclaimed himself an old-fashioned segregationist. They stressed economic, social, or political reform in varying degrees. In doing so, they built a coalition in their states that not only was the key to their elections but may also suggest the future of politics in the South for years to come.

Ever since 1968, when Nixon made a deal with Thurmond and captured 58 of the South's 128 electoral votes, Republicans have expected to make the Old Confederacy a GOP stronghold. Indeed, the South is a cornerstone of the vaunted new conservative majority, so hopefully and frequently predicted in the White House and in the Justice Department. But Nixon and his strategists reckon without more recent Southern developments. They have neglected to mark the social progress and the sharpening of the conscience of the white South during the 1960s. They have failed to take note of the pull toward national norms exerted on the South by the churches, labor unions, and colleges, by television, by the national corporations that have moved southward, and by the young.

The Southern Strategy of 1968 was based on the premise that conservative Republican candidates could win in the South by adding the assumed conservative Wallace supporter to the normal Republican base. After all, the combined vote received by both Wallace and Nixon in 1968 topped 60 per cent in every Southern state. Kevin Phillips assured readers of his *Emerging Republican Majority* that this coalition would provide the finishing touch to an emergent *national* Republican majority. So, Southern Republicans would shun the moderate examples of Linwood Holton of Virginia and Winthrop Rockefeller of Arkansas and basically write off the black vote while seeking the Wallace vote by every possible innuendo, code word, or other appeal to racial prejudice. Small wonder that 1970 found nearly every Republican state-wide Southern candidate staking out the extreme right of the political spectrum. The Democrats for the most part let them do this. (In some instances, such as South Carolina and Florida, the Democrats pushed the Republicans even further to the right.) They professed their purity on law and order and then picked up voters on other issues. These candidates brought back to the Democratic Party many voters who had earlier been casting Republican ballots.

What do these elections in the South mean for Nixon and

for the Democrats in 1972? Perhaps the meaning is mixed. They show, for one thing, that Republicans and Wallaceites are different kinds of people, and that the Southern Strategy appeals only to some of them. A basic error of the Southern Strategists is their inability to comprehend that people who voted for Wallace were not motivated entirely by racial prejudice, nor were they entirely conservative. The Wallace voters of 1968 appear to have cast a majority of their votes in 1970 for Democratic candidates (ranging from around 60 per cent in Tennessee to 80 per cent in Arkansas).

Wallace voters divide into Black Belt and upcountry types. In the Black Belt, where race is made more important by the majority or large minority black populations, the basic motivation for voting for Wallace was predominantly racism. These areas had also cast racial-protest votes for Dixiecrats and for Barry Goldwater. In the upcountry areas, such as mid-Tennessee, panhandle Florida, upcountry South Carolina, and parts of other states, George Wallace's populism was more important. His attacks on "interests," intellectuals, big government, and high taxes—the big boys who bossed around the little man—were a major draw. Many of these areas had held for Johnson in 1964, and in 1970 it was in these areas where the largest percentages of former Wallace voters returned to the Democratic Party, attracted by the neo-Populist appeals of Lawton Chiles, Carter, Bumpers, and me. Even in Black Belt areas there was some degree of return to the Democratic Party.

When we try to look more closely at the Wallace voter there emerges a pattern of interconnected motivations for his behavior. Several surveys have shown that Wallace voters are far more opposed than other groups to school integration and neighborhood integration; but they are also more willing than many other groups to agree that the govennment ought to help blacks. This is an interesting divergence from many Northern patterns, where whites complain about blacks being helped or "given a free ride." The white Southerner may hold racist views, but he also recognizes and understands more clearly the sources of black problems, especially economic problems, and is more sympathetic toward them.

Wallace voters are also surprisingly nonideological. They feel themselves tremendously alienated from the American political process, but they do not see this as a problem of liberal versus conservative, as many Nixon strategists do. They are disturbed by many developments of modern society but, like most people, cannot work out a coherent framework for analyzing their troubles. They feel that government doesn't care, that it is too complex, that it cannot be influenced. Wallace offered them a way of expressing their feelings. He pretended to speak for the "average citizen" and many accepted the pretension.

Surveys conducted by Independent Research Associates show that Wallace voters in the South were not generally conservative on economic propositions. They favored federal aid to education, health-care programs, social security, public housing. Many of the Wallace voters are poor and they know that the country needs these programs. When they overcome their racism, they support governments that try to meet their needs.

The architects of the Southern Strategy misunderstand the true aspirations of most Southerners, but its provincial and racial appeal to large segments of Southern people is undeniable. Nor is its appeal limited to the South. Beyond the former confederate states, Senator Joseph Tydings in Maryland fell victim in 1970 to a localized brand of the Southern

Strategy, and Senator Vance Hartke barely survived it in Indiana. Wallace outran everybody in Michigan's 1972 Democratic primary. To call the appeal to bigotry, hate, and fear a "Southern" Strategy is a libel to many Southerners. The strategy is, in fact, less Southern than attitudinal, being based on the assumption that people have deep-seated prejudices that in times of social unrest can be counted upon to outweigh their sober judgment. Aiming, as its authors do, for a general purge of Congress, they use the South as the opening wedge simply because that area—so often chosen as the guinea pig for "corrective" ideas—has been in the throes of decades-long integration and public-school crises, and because it is the base of Wallace's American Party: an apparatus which Messrs. Nixon and Agnew seek to mold to their own purposes.

It should, therefore, come as no surprise that the Southern Strategy for 1972 has been modified so that it now pivots not just around the anti-Negro red-neck but around the economic and social conservatives of the South, the West, and the "hard-hat" suburbs of the North and East. This is very nearly the same linkup that was made after Reconstruction, and it is one on which the Republican Party has usually relied in pursuit of its minority politics. The difference is that now the social issue is sharpest in the suburbs, and the GOP is aiming for a majority coalition. Kevin Phillips explained (in a June 22, 1971, column) the Republican tactic on social issues in 1972:

> The major ingredient of President Nixon's new suburban housing policy appears to be political fakery.
>
> Mr. Nixon is following the same pattern he has followed in his "defense" of the neighborhood school—*a heavy opening barrage of conservative rhetoric followed by a subsequent activity in the other direction.* His repetitive statements opposing "forced integration of the suburbs" are designed to create

a strong enough initial impression to stick in people's minds. Thereafter, Nixon strategists hope, events to the contrary will not be identified with the President.

Actually, Nixon officials know they will be moving in liberal directions—with a zig-zag or two—from the moment they complete their calculated conservative public relations buildup. Thus, they tell civil-rights groups to *"watch what we do, not what we say"* [my italics].

A similar tactic of double direction and confusion has been applied to the emotion-packed question of school busing. In perhaps a new high, or low, for inscrutable statements, Nixon said on August 3, 1971, "I am opposed to the busing of children simply for the sake of busing." What could this mean? Though the language defies definitive interpretation, it conveys a message. To add to the confusion, he said he would "continue to enforce the orders of the Court, including busing," but instructed his aides to "work with individual school districts to hold busing to the minimum required by law." On the same day, Elliot Richardson, Secretary of Health, Education, and Welfare and administrator of the program, "left for a month-long vacation" and was unavailable for comment.

A close examination of the South, state by state, will reveal both the resurgence of a progressive, Populist-oriented Democratic Party and a more enduring Republican Party with strongest roots in suburbia, in cotton-land communities, and in the traditional upland Republican strongholds. These conditions are pertinent to the 1972 political contests.

Florida, the nation's ninth largest state, is a key state for the Republican Party. In 1968, Richard Nixon carried the state with 40.5 per cent, while Humphrey had around 30 per cent, and Wallace trailed with 28.5 per cent. The Nixon plurality was assembled in the technically oriented east-central area around Orlando and Cape Kennedy; the retirement centers in west central Florida, Sarasota, and St. Petersburg; and the Gold Coast, Fort Lauderdale and Palm Beach. Wallace swept north Florida and the central ridge section. Humphrey carried only the Miami area and the university city of Gainesville. It was the first Southern state to have a Republican governor *and* senator at the same time (Claude R. Kirk, Jr., governor in 1966 and Ed Gurney, senator in 1968). And in 1970, the GOP had high hopes of retaining the governorship and of picking up the Senate seat of the retiring Spessard Holland. But Kirk's well-noted antics as governor and the party-splitting primaries weakened both Kirk and the Republican's senatorial candidate, Bill C. Cramer.

Meanwhile, the Democrats nominated two moderate-liberals, Reubin Askew for governor and Lawton Chiles for senator, and they ran a well-meshed, unified campaign. Askew, campaigning on tax reform and against Kirk's irresponsibilities and "backlash" politics, trounced him with 57 per cent of the vote; Chiles captured 54 per cent of the vote against Cramer, who conducted a Southern Strategy campaign of "law and order" and antibusing. The Askew-Chiles ticket amassed over 90 per cent of the black vote, yet the thirty-four counties of panhandle Florida, where in 1968 Wallace had received a large percentage of the vote and which provided the margin of victory for both Kirk and Gurney, also gave Askew and Chiles an overwhelming majority. Chiles and Askew carried all forty-two counties that were carried by Wallace, and the usually Republican suburbs as well. In addition, the Democrats captured four Republican statehouse seats to give a Democratic margin of 81 to 39, and added another seat in the State Senate, giving them control of the upper house 33 to 15.

During the New Deal and Fair Deal, north Florida had been a haven of economic liberals, although on race matters the voters were extremely conservative. In south Florida, social liberalism was considered more acceptable, although businessmen there strongly favored economic conservatism. During recent years, it had been *thought* that north Florida had become conservative in economic as well as social matters, while south Florida had subordinated most traces of social liberalism to economic conservatism. In short, Florida was supposed to be conservative all around. But the results of the 1970 election indicated something rather different. They appeared to favor government spending for relief and farm assistance, social security, Medicare, progressive income taxes, and a favorable government attitude toward labor unions. In 1970, Florida Democrats took a progressive stance, managed to unite blacks and Wallace supporters in striking victories, and clearly progressed far along the path toward revitalization.

Yet Wallace received 42 per cent of the vote in the 1972 Presidential primary against ten opponents—more than the combined total of his nearest three rivals—Humphrey, Jackson, and Muskie. Most national observers attributed this sweep to Wallace's exploitation of the "busing" issue, but I think there was more to it than that. Another big factor in his greater appeal to Floridians was undoubtedly regional. In any event, the racist appeal inherent in Wallace's whole record underlay his success, and this refertilized the Florida field for another Nixon harvest in November 1972 over McGovern.

In South Carolina, birthplace of the Southern Strategy, the South—and the country—has the problem of Strom Thurmond, who bolted the Democratic Party and ran independently for President on the Dixiecrat ticket in 1948, and who defected to the Republicans when they looked strong. More recently, however, the GOP hasn't been faring too well in the state. In 1968, Nixon carried the state with 38 per cent of the vote, while Wallace had 32 per cent (primarily from the traditionally Democratic upcountry), and Humphrey 29 per cent. At the same time, Democratic Senator Ernest Hollings, who in 1966 barely carried the state for the Democratic Party with 51 per cent, beat the same opponent 62 per cent to 38 per cent, taking, it appears, both Wallace and Humphrey voters. In addition, the Democrats in the 1968 election reduced the number of Republican members in the state legislature from 25 to 8.

In 1972, State Senator Nick Beigler is making a strong race to retire the aging Thurmond. A coalition of moderates, traditional Democrat loyalists, upcountry Wallace voters, and blacks could produce a victory for the entire Democratic ticket.

In Arkansas, Wallace carried the state in 1968 with almost 39 per cent of the vote, while Nixon gained 31 per cent, and Humphrey had 30 per cent. Republican support was concentrated in traditionally moderate northwest Arkansas, where there are few blacks and the race issue is not very important—reflecting the moderate position of Rockefeller Republicans. A Southern Strategy today will probably alienate more of the base vote than it would gain in Wallace areas, and the Democratic candidate could count on picking up the support of some of the black and liberal voters who supported Rockefeller.

Governor Dale Bumpers, who drew nearly 90 per cent of the Wallace votes and 61 per cent of the total, will likely tip the scales to the Democratic nominee for President. Of all the

Southern states, Arkansas is most likely to give its electoral vote to McGovern.

North Carolina—basically divided into three sections: 1) the coastal plain, with both blacks and Wallace voters; 2) the Piedmont area, with growing cities and growing Republican strength in the suburbs; and 3) the mountain areas, which have been Republican since the Civil War—is one of those Southern states with a history of Republicanism. The 1968 results were: Nixon 39 per cent, Wallace 31 per cent, and Humphrey 29 per cent, (fractions omitted). Recent suburban and industrial growth has increased the Republican vote, though Democrats have managed to hold most offices. The defeat of conservative Senator B. Everett Jordan by the younger and more progressive Congressman Nick Galifianakis for the senatorial nomination and the nomination of Hargrove Bowles as the Democrat for governor in June 1972 brought a changed image and new blood. And here a revitalized Democratic Party is absolutely essential in the growing towns of the Piedmont, which hold the balance of power.

This vigorous new progressive leadership greatly improves the outlook for Democrats. Because of a greater degree of tolerance than exists in the deeper South, a Southern Strategy racism may even weaken the Republican base area in the mountains and the suburbs without making significant gains elsewhere. Odds favor a Democratic victory.

Tennessee, the only border state (and only one of seven in the nation) with a Republican governor and two Republican senators, tilts strongly to Nixon. An acute "busing" issue in both Nashville and Memphis adds to the burden of the Democratic Presidential nominee. Senator Howard Baker and Representative Roy Blanton, both stanchly conservative, are battling for the Senate seat.

Virginia has distinct areas of traditional Republican support, new suburban Republican growth, racist Democrats,
liberal Democrats, and various different types of Wallace
voters. The local Republican Party was hurt by the Administration's support of Harry Byrd in the 1970 Senate race, and
this may help the Democrats. But, the size of the Republican
base vote and the decidedly conservative record of Virginia
voters makes it seem likely that Nixon will again sweep the
state. Even so, Senator William Spand promises to hold the
Senate seat for the Democrats.

The coming of Goldwaterism to Georgia in 1964—the first
Republican victory in Georgia's history—was not without its
tragic aspects, for it destroyed the progressive work of many
good men. In running up 616,000 votes to Lyndon Johnson's
522,557, Goldwater turned the state's traditional voting patterns upside down. Black Belt south Georgia, home of the
strongest segregationist Democratic sentiment, went overwhelmingly for him, while in the north, where there had always been stubborn pockets of Republicanism, north Geor-
gians voted heavily Democratic. On the other hand, the Negro wards in Atlanta, once Republican territory, gave Johnson huge margins. But Republican fortunes have not looked
as well since.

In 1968, George Wallace carried Georgia with nearly 43
per cent of the vote, while Nixon had 30 per cent, and Humphrey had almost 27 per cent. Nixon can do much better than
he did in 1968 or Carter's Republican opponent did in 1970,
but Governor Jimmy Carter, elected in 1970, could swing the
state to McGovern by a hair, despite the coolness of Senator
Talmadge toward the Democratic standard-bearer. The Democratic seat in the U.S. Senate now held by Senator Gambrill
may depend upon party unity.

In Louisiana, the Democratic Party has a long way to go. The state consists of Populist, racist north Louisiana and the French Catholic south, more moderate and liberal. A liberal from Crowley, Edwin W. Edwards, was elected governor in early 1972, and he soon indicated a surprising degree of tolerance toward the National Democratic Party. No movement toward a genuine two-party system has begun; there are no Republican congressmen or legislators. If the Republicans want to win state offices, they must have new men preaching reform and renewal: this might begin a cycle of change that would lead to a new Democratic Party. The 1972 Presidential election could be close to a tossup, for the Republicans could win in the north and the Democrats in the south. With the Senate seat of the late Senator Allen Ellender at stake, Governor Edwards and Russell Long are likely to rally the party to a victory all the way.

Texas politics do not really fit into the traditional pattern of Southern politics. Texas is only partially a Southern state: east Texas is in many ways similar to the South, but the German and Mexican areas of Texas have differing political motivations and distinct histories. Republican strength is greatest in the panhandle, in a string of German counties across Texas, and in Dallas, Houston, and the suburbs. Democratic strength in recent years has been greatest in Mexican and black areas, among the working and middle class of the cities, and in some rural areas.

Texas politics in 1972 are further complicated by spirited contests for both governor and U.S. senator. Barefoot Saunders is leveling a serious challenge to Republican Senator John Tower. And then there is John Connally, Nixon's peripatetic former Secretary of the Treasury and a former Texas governor. Texas? A tossup either way for Senator, a sure

Democratic victory for governor, and a Nixon majority over McGovern.

Kentucky has escaped the political paroxysms of race that has seized her neighbors to the south and east. Like Tennessee, Kentucky's eastern mountains remain strongly Republican. It seems not to matter whether their nominee is a liberal or a conservative, a big Republican majority rolls from the east. But unlike Tennessee, Kentucky's western flatlands areas have remained Democratic. Wendell H. Ford, a Democrat, was elected governor in 1971 in a campaign in which he made the Nixon Administration his principal target. The Governor's good friend George Huddeston is the Democratic nominee for U.S. Senator, facing former Governor Louis Nunn, the Republican nominee. The odds favor Huddeston so decidedly that McGovern has an outside chance to carry the state too, particularly if Governor Ford really goes to bat for the whole ticket.

Mississippi, for the first time in many years, has a new Democratic governor, William Waller, who tried to cooperate with his party's national leadership and to keep his home base. His path is a troubled one. (Goldwater's majority over Johnson in 1964 was 7 to 1.) To gain acceptance of his leadership by the national leadership, his delegation had to conform to the new reform rules which required a delegation generally and proportionately representative of the rank-and-file party membership. This was impossible, even for a popular new governor. Moreover, the national political symbolism of Mississippi—its history and its imagery—compounded the problem.

A Nixon victory in Mississippi is as sure as Jim Eastland's re-election to the U.S. Senate. If the polls open on election day, both will win.

Alabama will be almost as strong for Nixon as Mississippi. The U.S. Senate race, however, will be closer, with odds favoring veteran John Sparkman over former Postmaster General William Blount.

The general movement back toward the Democratic Party that has been under way throughout the South has been slowed, if not derailed, by the emotion-packed issue of busing public-school students to achieve racial integration. Of course, much school transportation is customary and necessary, but "busing" purely for the purpose of achieving "racial balance" is highly unpopular. Though racism may motivate much of this opposition, there is certainly more to it than that. Inconvenience and possible dangers to children being taken to another or distant school, the interference with the community aspects of schools, including athletic and social events, serve to generate opposition and fear to out-of-neighborhood transportation. Solutions are extremely difficult and complex. Some have even supported an amendment to the Constitution that would once again permit "separate but equal" segregation of races in public schools. Separatist sentiment is being increasingly voiced by blacks, too.

The South, then, is still wrestling with its ancient and peculiar social problem, except that it has now become national in character. It has surely slowed, but I do not believe it has stopped, the popular movement back to the Democrats in the South. It survived the 1970 campaign, which was one of the shabbiest political episodes in American history. Despite the refusal of the people of most states to be tricked by its base appeals, Nixon described the 1970 election results as a "moral victory." I can hardly think of two less appropriate words.

If it can be said, as I have illustrated, that the South elected Richard Nixon in 1968, it may also be said that the conditions that culminated in his election, and events that have since transpired, resulted in a startling defeat for his philosophic bedfellows only two years later, and set the stage for a rebirth of progressive politics in the South. This is the real hope for a permanent two-party system in the South. As long as conservatives who call themselves Democrats controlled the state governments in the South, there was no place for a separate conservative party led by Republicans. For the most part, Republican leaders, satisfied with Democratic control on the state level and primarily interested in convention politics and patronage from Washington, have not especially cared about state elections at home. State politics in the South, then, was long left without the benefits of a genuine two-party system, and few people in history have been so miserably served in this respect as the people of the South. But now it is different. The South is moving through a period of transformation. Each state is at a different stage, with different aspects of the transformation predominating in the political character of each. Indeed, they have *always* been at different phases, with different proportions of urban dwellers, varied economies, different pockets of Republican resistance dating from the Civil War, and varying proportions of blacks. Some, therefore, have been more vulnerable to the siren call of the Southern Strategy than others but its baseness is now recognized everywhere. There is little doubt that the future will bring a South essentially different than that foreseen by the prophets of doom or by the hate-filled prognosticators of an "emerging Republican majority."

In each state of the South, I find similar phenomena. First of all, there have been splurges of Republican voting. In South Carolina in 1966, Florida in 1966 and 1968, Tennessee in 1966 and 1970, Georgia in 1966, and Arkansas in 1966 and

1968, the Republicans enjoyed surprising and often comfortable victories. But we have seen the emergence of new men with progressive programs in the Democratic Party of the South and a new day dawns.

Behind all of this is a general resolution of racial tensions, as an increasing number of people come to accept the fact that massive resistance to equality is over. As the people increasingly come to acknowledge this, the Republicans of the Southern Strategy will be left holding an empty bag.

When we look closely at the future of the race issue, we see a variety of new factors. In some areas, there seems to have been great progress; in others, such as Alabama, Mississippi, and portions of other states, there has been little progress. But blacks have been steadily entering the political process, adding new strengths to the Democratic Party, and racial problems may be nearer to solution there than elsewhere. Increasingly, young white Southerners are unwilling to maintain the old attitudes of their parents. The backlash and bitterness that we have suffered for so long will in time subside.

As blacks form an increasingly important part of the political process, Southern whites will not be able to ignore them. White politics must and will adjust. First of all, any white politician can appeal for black support—as their number grows in the electorate whites will be unable to resist. Furthermore, where the blacks hold majorities, any attempt that whites make to flee to the Republican Party will simply result in their being shut out of local politics, while gaining no advantage from a government which cannot roll back to the 1960s.

The Southern Republican Party also has been evolving. It has its traditional base in anti-Secessionist areas in the mountains, centers of northern immigration, high-income voters, and suburbanites. But with the Southern Strategy, we find the party that was making gains throughout the 1950s and 1960s as it presented new and progressive faces to the voters now rejecting those men and their views and once again offering conservatives. And, of course, this new ideological party is financed by those wealthy and elitist elements that profit from its growth.

The Southern Republican Party has pinned its hopes firmly on Presidential politics and its Presidential politics firmly on the race issue. It does not yet have the material to create a broad-based majority coalition to conquer the South. Any lessening of the race issue will erode its support, not strengthen it, but the race issue is losing support with each succeeding generation.

Reinvigorated state Democratic Parties in the South threaten to shatter Nixon's re-election dreams—in the very region where he has clearly expected to reap victory. McGovern is far from a popular candidate in the South. But there was a growing enthusiasm for him after his nomination, and the number of volunteer workers for him exceeds anything I have ever seen. Shortly after his nomination, a well-to-do scion of a Tennessee family who was helped out of poverty by the New Deal asked me, carefully articulating for his buddies to hear, "What do you think McGovern is going to do for the Democratic Party?" "Probably the same thing," I said, "as Andrew Jackson did when the great unwashed elected him to the White House, or maybe what Roosevelt did when so many people in rags voted for a change."

Southerners, like most other Americans, look to their President to satisfy at least three needs. First is the need for reassurance. They want to believe the President is a good man, and they turn to him for a sense that things will be all right. He is a refuge. Harding made this appeal with his "normalcy"; Roosevelt with his New Deal; Eisenhower with his father image; Kennedy with gallantry, grace and wit. People want to have pride in their President, feel protected in their jobs, in their personal rights, and in their future. They somehow place reliance on the President in these regards.

People usually want also a sense of progress and action. What the people appreciated most about Franklin Roosevelt was the feeling that he was taking effective action, moving forward with some kind of program when the nation was in trouble. I think people like to feel that the President of their country has political competence and drive. This creates a general aura of respect and affection. He is supposed to be a take-charge man, a doer, a turner of the wheels, a producer of progress and well being—even if that means some sacrifice of serenity. In a time of general well-being they may react well to a bland President, but in a time of stress they react against "do-nothing" government, especially if the President seems merely to be holding the office instead of actively performing his role.

Then, too, people want a sense of legitimacy in the Presidency. They expect him to be a master politician who yet remains above politics. A contradiction? Yes, but that is the way the people are or want to be, about their President. He should have a rightful claim to his place and a rightful way of acting in it. The President is expected to personify our better qualities, to express a moral idealism in what he does and in what he says. This may appear the very opposite of "politics," but it is normal and traditional Presidential politics in America. A sense of security or confidence, of action, and of legitimacy is what Americans want to feel about their President, and they want to have these feelings about the man for whom they vote.

The political climate in America is now fraught with doubt and antagonism: a lack of faith and confidence. There has long been a sense of continuing doom without a discernible program of action either to alter a calamitous war policy or to pursue the existing policy to success. Racial rancor has deepened the chasm.

Our country, more especially the South, has been passing through a turbulent period of social rebellion and unrest, of war and of technological change, with consequent paradoxes which baffle the minds and trouble the spirits of the noblest and best of our people. The revolutionary new means to store and retrieve information, as well as the new kinds of rapid transportation and instant communication, have enormous implications for the kind of world we will live in tomorrow. Perhaps we should pause and reassess our social order, and then contemplate the role of moral values in our future; think about the extent to which the "credibility gap" is real or a myth; and ponder the manner and style by which tomorrow's politician will justify or destroy public confidence in government—and thus sustain or subvert self-government.

Our voices are amplified, our strengths multiplied, our powers of achievement unexampled—but peace and understanding defy our grasp. The marvels of our time excel those of all the ages, but man's inhumanity to man has never been baser nor as destructive. Never have the spirits of man soared so high nor had such glorious opportunities for perfectibility of living, yet our hates and our fears threaten to consume us.

Everywhere, but especially in the South, the need and the

hope is for education and equal opportunity, and for leaders of vision, courage, and action. The people of the South, with all their uniqueness—which I have tried frankly to analyze and portray—are warm, proud, faithful, industrious, and aspiring. With these attributes, with their fierce regional loyalties, and given leadership worthy of them, they will become a powerful force for progress. United in hope and in trust instead of divided in prejudice and fear, they will help the nation lift the shades of the past from the new day.